The Write to Happiness

THE WRITE TO HAPPINESS

How to Write Stories That Change Your Brain and Your Life

Samantha Shad

NEW YORK

LONDON • NASHVILLE • MELBOURNE • VANCOUVER

The Write to Happiness

How to Write Stories that Change Your Brain and Your Life

Published in New York, New York, by Morgan James Publishing. Morgan James is a trademark of Morgan James, LLC. www.MorganJamesPublishing.com

ISBN 9781642798098 paperback
ISBN 9781642798104 eBook
Library of Congress Control Number: 2019950040

Cover and Interior Design by:
Chris Treccani
www.3dogcreative.net

Morgan James is a proud partner of Habitat for Humanity Peninsula and Greater Williamsburg. Partners in building since 2006.

Get involved today! Visit
MorganJamesPublishing.com/giving-back

Dedicated to all the writers. Hope it helps.

CONTENTS

INTRODUCTION   xi

   BACKSTORY   xi

   WHO CAN WRITE THEIR WAY TO HAPPINESS?   xii

   WHERE TO START   xii

PART ONE: HOW TO WRITE TO HAPPINESS   1

   FINDING THE STORY   3

   THE RULES   4

   WHAT IS A STORY?   4

   OPENING NOTES   5

   THE NUB   6

   THE IDEA   7

   HOW TO FIND YOUR STORY   7

      GO OUT AND SEARCH FOR YOUR IDEA   8

      SIT BACK AND TELL YOUR IDEA TO COME FIND YOU   9

   TECHNIQUES FOR OPENING THE DOOR   10

   FINDING YOUR IDEA: A HYPOTHETICAL   12

YOUR TEMPORARY MAIN CHARACTER   13

THE GOAL   14

THE BUT   16

BREAK THE GLASS SOLUTIONS   19

CHARACTER   25

    HOW TO DEVELOP CHARACTERS   26

    MAIN CHARACTERS   27

    HOW TO DEVELOP YOUR PROTAGONIST   28

    THE PERFECT FIT   30

    THE ANTAGONIST   32

CONFLICT   35

    THE OBSTACLES   36

    PLOTTING   37

    BETTER OBSTACLES   38

STRUCTURE   41

    SCENE ORDER   44

    TENTPOLES   45

    THE BEAT SHEET   47

    THE LAYING OF THE CARDS   50

    THE REDUCTION SAUCE   55

WRITING   57

    GO WRITE   57

    THE REWRITE   57

    ALL IS NOT LOST   59

    ALL IS TOO LOST   59

    AND IN THE END . . .   62

AFTERWORD: HOW IT WORKED   63

PART TWO: WHY IT WORKS   **67**

STORY   69

     WHAT IS A STORY?   69

     WHERE IS STORYOPOLIS?   72

     WHAT'S IN IT?   76

     HOW DID STORY HAPPEN?   80

     SOCIAL BEINGS   88

THE SOCIAL SCIENCES   91

     EXPRESSIVE WRITING   91

     PENNEBAKER'S FINDINGS   96

     UNDERSTANDING YOUR OWN WRITING RESULTS   99

     WHAT YOUR WRITING CAN TELL YOU   99

     THEORIES AND EXPLANATIONS   102

     WHY DOES EXPRESSIVE WRITING WORK?   105

     SONS OF PENNEBAKER   106

     HAPPINESS, INCORPORATED   108

     OPTIMISM   112

     ATTITUDE IS MORE THAN A POSTURE   113

     MEANING   115

     PURPOSE   117

     TOOLS OF THE HAPPINESS TRADE   119

     GRATITUDE JOURNALS   119

     BACK TO THE FUTURE   120

     WRITE YOURSELF SOME LETTERS   120

     READ A BOOK   122

     WRITE A STORY   125

     GO BIG   126

     JOSEPH CAMPBELL   128

THE HARD SCIENCES   135
   SAVE THE CAT   135
   MEET YOUR BRAIN   139
   TRIPLEX BRAIN   145
   TECHNOLOGY   149
   MAKING MEMORIES   152
   THE MYTH OF MEMORY   159
   THE GRACE OF THE FORGETFUL BRAIN   163
   NEUROPLASTICITY   166
   THEORY OF MIND   173
   DEFAULT MODE NETWORK   181
   MIRROR NEURONS   187
   VULCAN MIND MELD   194
   PATTERNICITY   199
   THE INTERPRETER   205
   READ A BOOK, THE SEQUEL   208
   WRITE A STORY REVISITED   211

WHY WRITING STORIES WORKS   219

FURTHER MATERIALS FOR WRITERS   223
   STORYBONES: WORKSHEETS FOR BUILDING YOUR STORY 225
   FURTHER READING FOR WRITERS   229

REFERENCES   233

BIBLIOGRAPHY   245

ABOUT THE AUTHOR   271

INTRODUCTION

BACKSTORY

I was a screenwriter for 22 years. At the beginning, I was as neurotic and miserable as the top one percent of crazy in the Writers Guild of America, West. At the end, I left because I was happy and there were better places for me to enjoy my life.

Yup. I left because I was happy.

I knew that writing had transformed my life. Every script I wrote seemed to pose an interesting question that had been smoldering below my consciousness, and a few months later that particular problem was gone. The burdens of life lightened because I sat down and wrote about imaginary people doing fantastic things in fictional places.

There's magic in writing creatively.

There's also neuroscience.

If we diagrammed the template for good storytelling and then diagrammed the template for changing our minds for the better and laid them on top of each other . . . they would be exactly the same.

Part One of this book is a how-to guide to writing to a better life.

Part Two explores the social and hard sciences of changing your brain and your mind for the better. It explains why it works.

Maybe there are better ways to change your life. Maybe the decades of therapy or the immersion tanks or the peyote actually do work. But I know of no better, more efficient, or more enjoyable way to find happiness than to write your way to it.

WHO CAN WRITE THEIR WAY TO HAPPINESS?

Anyone who uses words to tell a story can write their way to happiness. If we put those words on pages or screens and agree to look at them again to improve them, we are writers.

If you journal, you're a writer. If you tweet or send memos or mark papers or jot down notes or thoughts or post to Instagram, you're a writer. No matter your size, shape, age, politics, passions, or professions, if you use words to tell a story, you can write your way to happiness.

WHERE TO START

How much do you need to know before you start your journey of writing to happiness?

If you are impatient and just want to get to the writing, please do. A beautiful fact about writing to happiness is that it works whether or not you understand the mechanism.

If you've bought one too many pep talk books and want to be sure this isn't just some digital hokum, no problem. You can start by reading Part Two of this book, which provides the social and hard science evidence for the effectiveness of the program.

If you don't want to read the hard stuff but need to feel that you did your due diligence before jumping in, a commonsense explanation helps. Here goes.

We humans know the template for writing good stories. We also know the template for changing our brains for the better. For writers, the templates are identical.

A story that has endured over time has a protagonist who has a goal but is blocked by an obstacle that seems insurmountable. The protagonist faces all the difficulties imaginable, but in the end, overcomes these hurdles through a new synthesis of information (or, in the tragedy, faces the consequences of failing to grow).

Each lasting story is a journey from innocence through a road of trials to an integration of lessons that results in a victory and resolution. Storytelling developed this structure over the millennia because it proved to be the most efficient way of communicating important lessons. We paid attention because the format was entertaining. We slipped all the important messages into the exciting fictions we created. As a species, we humans found that storytelling was the best way to spread the crucial knowledge of how to be a better or happier or more successful human being. We follow the general rules of good storytelling because they are successful in meeting those needs.

Our universal love of good stories comes from their ability to absorb us on a journey in which we safely experience serial attempts at solving problems until, in the end, the character solves the problem by learning something. We the audience identify with the main character, experience the many attempts at solving the problem, and enjoy the ultimate resolution, thereby learning more about how to be a successful person. Stories teach us how to thrive at being human.

People who read stories are happier, healthier, and live longer.
Wonder why reading makes us happier?
Check out *Read A Book* in Part Two of *The Write to Happiness*.

> **Wonder what reading does to your brain?**
> **Check out *Read a Book: The Sequel* in Part Two.**

What happens when, instead of being a passive member of the audience, we create the story? What happens to the writer?

When we write a story, the benefits of reading a story are increased exponentially. Writing a story is everything that reading a story is, times a thousand.

In order to write a good story, we need to pay close, serious, highly engaged attention and continually challenge ourselves. Writing a good story is hard work. It never gets easier. Period. But if you stick with it, you will receive benefits beyond your imagination.

How do we choose what to write?

Some part of us, our non-conscious mind, lobs up a character that is a piece of us. Because stories are problem-solving machines, that piece of us will have a problem that is also a piece of us. Little ideas or ruminations or questions roll around in our sub-conscious all the time. When we sit down to write, a few of those little darlings from the deep lagoon will bubble up. The problems we face on the page are the problems we are afraid to face in real life. When we make a list of the obstacles our hero must face, we are listing challenges we fear we will confront in our real life for which we have no solutions. We have consciously lost hope of ever finding a way out. In our writing, the moment when all our previously known solutions have failed is the bottom of the second act. We are working on the page instead of in reality, and we have the incredibly good fortune of fictionally seeing problems from different angles and from within different characters. We aren't limited to the individual perspective of one person, our main character, but rather can see the challenge from within each other character, from an overview position, through time, through space. Our options are increased, our empathy expanded, our problem-solving capacity enlarged. To get into the third act, the main character finds new combinations of actions and wisdom gained on the journey of the story to create a new solution. The audience gets to experience the satisfaction and knowledge gained by the character. Stories are problem-solving machines for the audience.

Real life is too acute, too harsh and too unremitting for us, but fantasy has a way of transforming those nasty difficulties into gorgeous quandaries. We will follow them because they absorb our attention in their new fictional costumes. Stories are problem-solving machines *for the writers*.

When we write, we have an increased facility at problem solving because a great deal of our creative output comes from a unique part of our brain (the default mode network) which focuses on our view of ourselves in relation to other people. Our solutions come from a deeply social, interpersonal consciousness. It is the place in the brain most adept at figuring out personal motivations and successful interactions. What could possibly make that network even better at story writing? It just so happens that that part of our brain disengages from reality when we are creating. That nasty *internal editor* who keeps telling you that your writing sucks? That editor that any good writing instructor would tell you to shut down? Guess what? That same part of your brain that is so adept at understanding other people will automatically shut down your reality-testing, nitpicky internal editor. When you write, that part of you that keeps saying "don't do that" is undone and your ability to see new possibilities rises up, a new superpower.

Of course, you and your character will make mistakes . . . plenty of them. But you'll sit down again, write and rewrite more thoughts and solutions, and the one thought that will use the information that you already know in a way you didn't previously conceive will bubble up. Your character will see or do something you didn't expect and put ideas together in an entirely new construction, and you will have created exactly the resolution you or your character wanted all along.

"But it's all just fiction, just a fantasy," you say. "It's just made up, a bunch of cheerful lies."

Yup. And that's great. Another part of your brain, called *the interpreter*, doesn't care whether it's true or just fantasy. It takes the new information from your fictional experience, wraps it up all neat and tidy, remembers the lesson of it, and packs it away in your brain for use later when you need it. Just like your imaginary character, you've learned the lesson without suffering a single scratch, and your brain remembers everything that mattered. You've learned the most potent lesson you can (because you came up with it) on how to be better at thriving as you, the very specific human being you already are.

Writing a good story requires that we focus intently and repeatedly on material which we have chosen specifically because it is challenging. Why does that matter? Why did we say that paying deep attention mattered? Because that level of concentration is inherent in writing. It matters because, as Michael Merzenich, a granddaddy of the study of brain change and neuroplasticity, says, "The key to brain change is the close, serious, highly attentive engagement at a level on which you are continuously challenging yourself."[1]

Writing a story is an intense, lengthy, impactful neuroplastic exercise in learning the solution to the problem that was bothering you in such a way that you change your brain around the solution.

That's why you can write your way to happiness.

PART ONE

HOW TO WRITE
TO HAPPINESS

FINDING THE STORY

How do we start down the road of writing to happiness? First, let's accept that we are writers. We're not talking about publishing deals and bestseller lists. For us, writers are people who are comfortable putting words down on a page and who are willing to look back at it to make it better if necessary. It requires a bit of thought. It requires something more than typing.

We'll pretend to find order in the chaotic mess of writing a creative story by picking out the essential elements and building on them in sequence. We start by finding the *nub* of the story, which is the arena in which the story takes place. We choose a temporary main character and a goal that expresses what we're thinking about. Then we figure out what stands in the way of our main character achieving the goal. After that, we can define our characters. When we have the nub and the main character, there will be certain challenges that the hero simply must face. We'll make a list of those challenges, and that will be the outline of the whole story. It looks simple and orderly. It is neither.

THE RULES

These are the rules to writing to happiness:

1. Follow the rules of good storytelling. It took thousands of years to refine what readers and audiences like in stories. Don't fight it.

2. Stay focused. There are no awards for having the most characters, subplots, and storylines. Aim to go deep, not wide. Keep it simple. Stay focused.

3. Make friends with your sub-conscious mind. If it wants to show you something, take a look. Your best material is floating in there. You'll know when to tamp it down. It's pretty safe to let it run around when you're sitting in your office and the only available weapon is your keyboard.

4. You must finish the story with a real ending. No third-act Hail Marys.

5. Your first draft is a car that can only go forward. No fixing, no editing, no going backward.

6. Typing isn't writing. Typing is throwing a lot of words on a page. Writing is crafting a story so that a real or imagined reader will be engaged in it. You will have to rewrite. It takes time, but you will get it right.

WHAT IS A STORY?

The basic unit of writing to happiness is the fictional story.

A *story* is a specific unit. It has a beginning, middle, and end. It has a protagonist and an antagonist. It has a theme, though usually you can wait it out and the theme will sneak up on you. It has obstacles, helpers, and conventions of dialogue.

A *universal story* is a journey through which a character faces a challenge, overcomes obstacles, and reaches a conclusion. A universal story has a particular shape.

If you have had a specific experience and you've written it down from beginning to end, you've written something, but it isn't a story. A story isn't an accurate representation or catalogue of events. It's the presentation of a *journey by characters through the selection of elements presented to the audience for their enjoyment and edification*. In other words, it isn't necessarily *the truth*. As David Mamet, the preeminent dramatist of our time, said, "In a drama, as in any other dream, the fact that something is 'true' is irrelevant—we care only if that something is germane to the hero-quest . . . *as it has been stated to us.*"[2]

A story is the reworking of real or imaginary events for the effect it has on others.

Aiming a story at others is the mechanism that makes us follow the rules for resolving the problem our work presents. The rules make for good drama, but for our purposes, they also force us to explore the issues in front of us and find both our own and the universally applicable answers. We're all poor, clueless authors. We go on this journey and, unbeknown to us, we discover exactly the solution we needed all along. Voila!

OPENING NOTES

What do we need in order to start writing? We need the nub or arena in which our story takes place. The nub is the irreducible smallest unit of your story. When we writers have the nub, we can build the *story idea*, which is the skeleton of the story.

We have a story idea when we have a *character* who has a *goal* but faces an *obstacle*. That's it. This is the place where what the character wants and what stands in her way coexist. After that, we can define our characters. When we have the nub and the characters, there will be certain challenges that the hero just has to, unavoidably, face. We'll make a list of those, and that will be the outline of the whole story.

There are two known species of writers. *Plotters* sit down and figure out every twist and turn in a long outline before they write a word of prose. Later, they will struggle to bring vitality and life to the story.

Pantsers are the second species of writers. Pantsers sit down and write by the seat of their pants without an organized plan and stop writing when they get to the end. Later, they will struggle to bring focus to their stories.

We are all both types of writers, at different times. Pantsers are better at finding and following creative ideas. Plotters are good at cleaning up a creative mess and making it comprehensible to the audience. It isn't a straight line. We alternate without all that much logic. Here, we will try to adhere to a plotter's approach to how to write to happiness. At times, you will want to veer off because you've had a great thought or a transfixing idea. Great! That's your pantser having a moment. Follow it. *But you must come back to your story*. Remember Rule #4: *You must finish the story with a real ending.*

THE NUB

"I want to write a story about _____." The blank is the nub of your story. The sentence might be "I want to write a story about . . ." death row, snowboarding, pumpkin festivals, sex in space, Tomorrowland.

The nub of a story is something that is bothering you, the writer. It is the arena in which your actual story will take place. Perhaps it's something you've read online or been dreaming about. Squibs of thoughts and printed articles pinned on your wall are nubs of a story. A lot of writers have a file tucked away of little tidbits that are so unformed that you can't even call them ideas. Those are nubs. I want to write a story that's about family dysfunction. In a hospital where everyone gets sick(er). About that guy on death row. Each of those is a nub. It's not yet a story or an idea or even much of a thought. It's an area or zone you want to explore.

When you can say "I want to write a story about _____," you have your nub of a story.

THE IDEA

Every story starts with an *idea*. How do you find your idea? When do you know you have it?

This is the formula for an idea: A CHARACTER has a GOAL, but there is an OBSTACLE.

When we can fill in the blanks in this sentence, we have an idea. Can you fill in these blanks?

_____ wants _____, but _____.

The usual order for finding your idea is to find the nub of it, put in a placeholder for the hero, determine the goal, and figure out what is standing in the way.

HOW TO FIND YOUR STORY

The most important truth to carry with you as you journey forth to find your next story is this: ***It doesn't matter how you find your next story***. Writing a story that can change your life means allowing material that is bubbling in your non-conscious mind to come to consciousness in some form that isn't too frightening. The beauty of this truth is that no matter what you are writing, the material will float into your consciousness and your writing as long as you let it.

Rule #3 is *Make friends with your sub-conscious mind*. We've been trained to control that nasty reservoir of lusts—our-sub-conscious—but it's also where your best material floats around to marinate. Give your sub-conscious a hug. It's part of you, and there's plenty of good stuff down there. Maybe if you give it a little respect, it will send you some great ideas.

In terms of your writing, your non-conscious mind holds voluminous material. When a non-conscious idea bubbles up, through a dream or in meditation or daydreaming, respect it. Understand that you are receiving your best material. Your non-conscious mind is your friend, and it will send you what you need. When your idea veers off in a strange direction, follow it. The key, again, lies in not getting in the way of the idea that is ready to tap you on the shoulder.

So how do you find your next story? There are two ways:

1. Go out and search for it.
2. Sit back and tell it to find you.

Both approaches work. I personally prefer to tell it to find me, because while I'm waiting, I can get a lot of gardening done.

GO OUT AND SEARCH FOR YOUR IDEA

Searching for an idea means researching until something captivates your interest. Swim in the news media. Read websites, blogs, newspapers, news feeds, gossip sites. Read all kinds of stuff, and pay great attention to what nags at you. If it nags for more than 10 minutes, print it and tape it to the wall. It must be physically in front of you, somewhere you might see it when you aren't looking for it. You can't get this done by putting it in electronic form. You're just cleaning off your desk and you keep checking out this one sheet you have about the guy on death row? Great. The fluff piece about a Silicon Valley exec who you just know can't be as good as his press? Good. Your sub-conscious will turn your attention to a page or two hung on your wall. As always, trust your sub-conscious.

If you have a few nubs, go back to the library and research them for real. Physically going to the library is like setting an intention: It brings focus to your search. It tells the universe that you mean it and that it should show up to help you. Decide you are looking for hard-core information, and try to stick to that purpose. The point of flowing in the river of information is to see what piques your interest. Even though it may look quite goal-oriented, this search will give you a sense of freedom. It is *not* the search for the perfect hook or pitch or concept. We writers hold on to the fantasy that there is a perfect idea that will be the key to the kingdom, the million-dollar script, the bestseller. But if you want your writing to be a tool for your biggest heart and greatest internal dreams, the great seven-word hook won't work, ever. As the master himself, Steven King, cautions, "Let's get one thing clear right now, shall we? There is no Idea Dump, no Story Central, no Island of the Buried Bestsellers; good story ideas seem to come quite literally from nowhere, sailing at you right out of the empty sky: Two previously unrelated ideas come together and make something new under the sun. Your job isn't to find these ideas but to recognize them when they show up."[3]

Looking for the perfect story idea is like sending out engraved invitations to the judges, editors, superegos, and all the forces of your internal universe that can say "no"—and inviting them to party in your brain. This approach manufactures procrastination and frustration. We are looking for the story that will help you write to happiness, and external success won't get you there. Neither will stories intended to please others instead of yourself.

SIT BACK AND TELL YOUR IDEA TO COME FIND YOU

My favorite way to find an idea is to do nothing. Stare at the ceiling. Go for a run. Take a long, aimless drive. Walk with music blasting through your head. Keeping your mind relatively empty of ideas and external focus will free up your brain to float around and make associations and connections you wouldn't otherwise entertain. In turn, this allows those pesky little issues that you keep repressed in your sub-conscious to swim about in your most creative brain space. Doing nothing is very fruitful for creative production, and there's a ton of science to back up the great benefit of doing nothing.

> **Wonder why doing nothing is so productive?**
> **Check out *The Default Mode Network* in Part Two.**

TECHNIQUES FOR OPENING THE DOOR

The purpose of concentrating on doing nothing is to let your non-conscious mind come through with ideas and to try to catch them before your conscious mind slaps them back down. The right idea for you will be something that you don't want to face head on. You open the door to that idea by giving your conscious brain the day off. There are a lot of ways to accomplish doing nothing.

Dreams are a glorious source for your idea. When you are going to sleep, make the conscious decision to dream for an idea. Do it for several nights in a row. When you get up, make notes about your dreams. Ask yourself what the dream felt like and which problem it seemed to be looking at. After a few days, lay the dreams out in some order and look for the common elements in them. What's popped up several times? Whatever it is, there's your story idea.

Journaling is another favorite way to open the door. The rules are simple: Set your alarm for 20 minutes, put pen to paper, and keep it moving until the alarm sounds. Then underline the most important things in the pages. Put down the pen. Journaling is best done at the same time every day, and mornings are great. Handwriting is more effective than typing, so even if you are a speed typist, use the pen. If you don't know what to write, just write, "I don't know what to write" over and over again until something else sneaks up on you.

> **Wonder why journaling works?**
> **Check out *Expressive Writing* in Part Two.**

Meditation works, although it throws some curveballs at creative types. If you are comfortable meditating without further explanation, then pursue it. Most of the creative people I know can't meditate worth a damn. They try to clear their heads of ideas, but the things just insist on shooting into their minds. Or it clears for just the shortest wisp of a second and then, wham! That itch of a thought comes flying in. Those writers spend their energy chasing ideas away. Here's the good news for writers: Forget about the directive to rid your mind of your thoughts. If you are a writer and, while meditating, an idea comes in that just won't go away, *follow it*. If ideas are coming to you while you meditate, open the door. Follow where the lightning bolts lead you. Line them up, see what the common nub is, and write it down. Your idea is in there, trying to come out.

There are a few other methods that can allow your bubbling idea to come out when you aren't looking. Doodling while you are doing something else (usually a boring conference call) can lead to useful thoughts. Painting works. Long showers work. So does taking a long drive.

All of these activities work because they keep you occupied. This frees your non-conscious mind. Material you would ordinarily smack down can now bubble up and reach the surface. *The material that has to sneak up on you because you really don't want to deal with it right now is exactly the material you need to deal with right now.*

Let it come up in fictionalized form. It's easier on everyone that way.

FINDING YOUR IDEA: A HYPOTHETICAL

Here's an example of how I look for an idea:

My conscious thoughts had been revolving around the information in this book. But I just couldn't think of a fictional idea to use as my example of a story in this book. I wanted it to be useful to you, the reader, interesting enough so that you didn't throw the book across the room or shut it down—and universal or impersonal enough so that you wouldn't know too much about me.

It was a difficult series of needles to thread, with a typical series of requirements: Don't be boring; don't show the writer's personal wounds; don't, don't, don't. Then for two of three nights, I had dreams about a credit I gave up on for a film that later surprised everyone with accolades. Why hadn't I fought for that credit? It either got lost in my divorce or wasn't worth the fight, but now, decades later, my sleepy-smart brain was still irked. Of course, the dream also included space ships, Angola State Prison in Louisiana, and my usual lost cellphone, but the center was that crazy old credit I never got. Two nights later, there was a dream about my father's old record collection. When he was a kid, he bought two copies of each of the great jazz performances of his day. He played one of each, but saved a pristine copy of each of these performances, unplayed and in its original sleeve. In the dream, I couldn't get to them, couldn't find them, and maybe even didn't search for them very hard. They were taken by someone. The taking was a betrayal.

In real life, I hadn't thought about that record collection for a long time, and it had been literally five decades since anyone had played or paid attention to the collection. I can't say that the record collection mattered in any concrete way. I didn't know if the records had any value, though I had always expected to donate the unplayed 78s to my alma mater's music school. Someone would want them, I thought; someone might listen.

These two dreams were about the same thing: In the dreams, someone took something from me that I felt was deservedly mine. That is the core of what is bothering me now, in my life. My dreams were telling me what my conscious mind would never allow to come to thought: that I felt betrayed and that it really bothered me. That's what the story has to be about, because that's what's trying to break through at my vulnerable time, when I am asleep: stories of betrayals and loss.

In this arena, I wonder what kind of loss—right now, a loss of a thing, a record collection and a credit. What do they have in common? Well, they are physical manifestations of creative work. Hmmmm. . . . That could be the theme, but that's running ahead of myself. Right now, I know only one thing: to write about a betrayal, a loss of something valuable and ephemeral.

That's a nub.

YOUR TEMPORARY MAIN CHARACTER

Your temporary main character is a distant version of you or an unrepresentative slice of you. Bigger or smarter or stupider or younger or whatever. A different person who happens to have shared a partial Vulcan mind meld with you. Give the character a name that sounds completely different from your own.

Choosing a name that doesn't sound at all like your own helps create distance between yourself and the character. Give the main character the freedom of having a distinctive name and the interesting peculiarities that will come with that.

For this one moment, a temporary name for the protagonist is perfectly fine. We'll come back to the main character later, when we need her input on the story.

I usually use Maxine, Grace, or JoAnne for my temporary character names, because I don't know a soul with those names. Grace sounds soft, even graceful. Gracie is even better. I'll use that. Because we will follow the development of this story and because the main character is female, let's refer to our hero as "she." It's appropriate for our hypothetical story, and the world could well use more female heroes.

How much of a story idea do we have? Let's fill in the blanks.

Gracie wants an ephemeral item.

Okay, it's a beginning. Let's put some story meat on those bones.

THE GOAL

If you have a main character operating within an arena, you're ready for the next step. Ask your character what she wants.

Every good story has a character who wants something. Having a goal is essential. At the beginning of the story, the goal is often general. In a lawyer story, the lawyer usually wants to win the big case or make partner. In a medical story, the doctor wants to cure a disease. In both of these arenas, the goal may be to find success, whether it is making partner or getting a key position in a prestigious institution or a remunerative specialty. In the movie *Black Panther*, the new ruler wants to be a good king. In *Mandela*, Nelson Mandela wants to establish racial justice.

The goal has to be reasonably specific and succinctly stated. If you need to explain the goal, it's not ready. If it takes a paragraph to describe it, it's not ready. If your main character is a writer, she must want something we can hold on to: perhaps winning a Pulitzer. Or writing a bestseller. Or she has a condition or disability, and the writing is only a collateral issue. Choose one, *but only one*.

Defining the goal may require a bit of psychological excavation. I had a student who had a story about a young doctor who wanted to be a dermatologist. The writer was absolutely certain about that specialty. It took a long time until she could go deep enough to realize that the character wanted to be a dermatologist because it was an easy specialty that made a lot of money and thus she would have a cushy life with a big house. It's important to know *why* your character wants that particular goal. In the medical story, dermatology was code for, "I want to look like a specialist, but I don't care much for curing people; it's all about me the doctor." In defining the goal of the character, these material aspects were crucial not only to the character, but also to everything that followed. If the core of the character was essentially a physician who didn't want to work hard, everything about the story will be different from the medical story about the doctor who wants to cure cancer because her mother died from it, or the poor kid who got into medical school because the income is good and his family needed money.

Here's the fill-in-the-blank for your character:

My character wants or wants to be a(n) _____ because/ for _____. In our hypothetical, what's Gracie's goal? Here's a way to work it out: What was taken from her? I take out a piece of paper and list a bunch of things that could be stolen from her:

- an heirloom
- a byline
- a diamond
- a necklace
- a piece of gold
- a record collection
- a car

Whew, those are all over the place. But what interested me at the beginning was the odd value in my dreams, the ephemeral value of a screen credit, the historical but not financial value of a record collection. Somehow, it's not about overt, objective value. In the dreams, the value was emotional or interpretative. I don't want to use the record collection in the story: It's too personal to me, and I will feel too vulnerable to dig deep into the emotions I would feel if I use it. I need something like the record collection or creative credit—but more comprehensible to the audience.

- A fictional McGuffin, like an award given to an ancestor would work. "Yes, that's Grampa's Oscar."
- Mom's wedding dress?
- How about paintings?

Mom's wedding dress is very sentimental. Grampa's Oscar tells the audience that it's a story about the movie business, but that's not what I want to write. But a painting? That could work. Some art that hung in the character's home and which she always expected to inherit. Yes, the art might have an objective value, but it has the emotional pull; it was in Dad's study when the character was growing up. Dad even promised it to her. Okay, the thing is a painting that had been promised to her. I imagine the painting as pretty big and well-framed but not on a hook. It's leaning against the wall, propped up on a table with books holding it in place.

Gracie wants the leaning painting.

All we need now is to find *the BUT*.

THE BUT

In all good stories, we have a protagonist who wants something but is stymied by the BUT, the thing that stands in the way of the character and achievement of the goal. Within the idea, there must be conflict. If it's just a thought—"I want to be a doctor"—there is no story. There is a subject, medical studies, but nothing happening within it. A story always has a BUT. "I want to be a doctor, BUT I don't have the money for med school."

Here are a few examples of the BUT:

- "I want to experience the dinosaurs, BUT they could turn on me." (*Jurassic Park*)

- Mandela wants to lead a revolution, BUT he's in jail for 27 years. (*Mandela*)
- All love stories start out as "I'm in love with somebody, BUT somebody is far away, married, from the other side, dead, or otherwise unavailable."
- "I want to be a best-selling writer, BUT I can't hold a pencil." (*My Left Foot*)
- "I want to be a successful lawyer, BUT I just screwed up the only case I have." (*The Verdict*)
- "I want to change the world, BUT I'm being sued by the moneybags for stealing the idea." (*The Social Network*)

Your idea is the arena or question you want to look at. The BUT makes it into a storyline. Once the BUT is added, it's a story because you have added a direction to the narrative.

For example, if Mandela wants to lead a revolution but he's in jail, how can he accomplish his goal from solitary confinement? The BUT leads to a series of questions your story must answer. How can he communicate to the outside world? What does he want to communicate? If he can't go outside, that is, effectively lead the free people of his country, can he go inside, that is inside himself for a different vision?

If "I want to be a doctor" is the idea, then what is stopping your character from becoming a doctor? If it's because the character doesn't have the money, a world has opened up. The question you will pursue is this: How do I find the money to become a doctor?

The BUT is the thing that stops your main character. The BUT is the reason your idea isn't just a topic, but an issue with direction and energy.

The BUT is the obstacle that will define your hero's journey. Can you fill in these blanks with very few words?

My   character   _____   wants   _____   BUT
_____.

In our hypothetical, what is the main character's BUT? Why can't Gracie get the painting? I make a list of reasons Gracie can't get the painting:

- It's been destroyed by a fire? By an act of vandalism?
- It's still in the study, but the lock has been changed? By whom? Can she get a key? Does her demented mother have it? Another member of the family for safekeeping? Another member of the family as a theft?
- Has it been stolen? By a robber? By friendly fire, that is, someone Gracie knows?
- By someone with legal rights of some sort? A creditor? An executor of the will?
- By the will because her father gave it to his mistress? To his illegitimate son, the brother Gracie never knew she had?

It's been stolen. I like it.

OK then, how did the painting get stolen? Did someone sneak into her father's home and steal it? Maybe. Maybe the house was lost in foreclosure. Or the painting was sold at the estate sale when the house was liquidated. Or the executor of the estate sold it off. Any of these will do. If it was sold at the estate sale, then we have a story of tracking down the painting from a possibly innocent party. What obstacle poses the greatest challenge to Gracie? A thief makes the story a mystery. The demented mother makes it a family drama, which is likely to deal with the problems of the mother and other family members, not Gracie's sense of being betrayed. In a fire? What does that do to Gracie's goal? Does she give up? Does she fight for insurance money? Are either of those satisfying? I like the executor-of-the-will idea. It's a soft theft, not an at-gunpoint event, but a dramatic conflict. It opens up a lot of juicy questions: Who is the executor? In whose interest is the executor acting? Another family member's? His or her own? Some faceless, impersonal authority that can't recognize the emotional value of the painting? Yup, I like the executor idea; it gives a lot of juicy possibilities. The executor won't give Gracie the painting.

If the executor sold it, then we aren't going to be that interested in the painting, but we are going to want to know what is going on with the executor. Did he or she lie to Dad about the estate? Did the executor take advantage of Mom, who is suffering from dementia? I like the executor line better because it gives the story a real antagonist. It gives the story more emotion: conniving in the past, betrayal of trust, what kind of person steals from an estate they are serving? That's it. Here's our story idea:

Gracie wants the painting that hung in Dad's study, but it was stolen by the executor.

Can you fill in the blanks for your idea?

_____ wants _____ BUT _____.

> **For more help on developing your story,**
> check out *Storybones: Worksheets for Building Your Story* in **Part Two.**

BREAK THE GLASS SOLUTIONS

If you've tried everything but are still devoid of an idea, rejoice!

Your brain doesn't care whether your story ideas are true or not, real or not, or even original or not. Your brain just wants some story to work with. If you're ready to break the glass, do what the professionals have done since time immemorial: Lift someone else's material.

For writing to happiness, it doesn't matter if you lift your story idea because no matter the source, your sub-conscious is going to add the material you need to process. You can't hide from your non-conscious mind. So, lift from Shakespeare or Grimms' Fairy Tales or the Bible. If you have any dream of publishing—and you should carry that dream— then please lift only from public domain sources. With that very small caveat, lift away. Stories that have lasted throughout time present a smorgasbord of good material that will help with the selection and cultivation of internal themes.

Try a fairy tale. Check Google and Wikipedia and make a long list of all the elements of a fairy tale that all the various versions contain. At a recent seminar which only allowed for 20 minutes for finding the idea, I asked students who had no current project to look at my list of story elements from "Little Red Riding Hood" to pick out the five elements they liked the most, and to build a quick story on those, and only those, elements. Here are the elements I found in some of the many versions of "Little Red Riding Hood":

> Little girl
> Walks through creepy place
> Has orders from her mother not to get sidetracked
> Carrying goodies for older relative
> Mean wolf
> He wants her and the food
> Girl naively tells him where she is going
> He diverts her by telling her, "Go get some flowers"
> Wolf goes to relative's house
> Gains entry
> He locks relative in closet
> He kills relative
> Girl arrives
> Grandma looks strange

Relative says, "What a deep voice, the better to greet you with," cat and mouse game

Wolf destroys/consumes girl

Wolf sleeps

Guy with tool arrives for other reasons

Guy with tool uses tool to destroy wolf, free girl

Girl and relative are rescued and are unharmed

They fill wolf's body with rocks/concrete

Wolf tries to escape

Wolf collapses

Relative hides in closet

Girl escapes with help of guy with tool before being consumed by wolf

Wolf forces girl to take off her clothes

Clothes thrown in fire

Girl escapes into the woods

Wolf ties a string on her

Girl does or doesn't slip the string off

Wolf chases after her

Girl escapes with help of another woman, e.g., laundress who puts taut sheet over river, girl climbs over it

Wolf follows and is consumed by the river

Girl listens to wolf's advice on the road, thinking him wise

Girl passes through woods filled with lumberjacks

Wolf consumes her; the end

Stranger with tool is a lumberjack she passed along the way

Lumberjack is a stalker

Stranger with tool is a huntsman wanting the wolf's skin

Relative and girl set physical traps for wolves for their skins

Girl is in love with unsuitable guy, a lumberjack

Girl is betrothed to attractive (rich) suitor

Girl's sister is betrothed to rich suitor

Girl's sister is murdered

Girl's sister is murdered by fiancé

Girl's sister is murdered by wolf

. . . and a priest comes to town

IT TAKES PLACE:

In the 9th century

14th century

17th century

20th century

21st century

THE BEAST IS A:

Wolf

Tiger

Ogre

Werewolf

RELATIVE'S BODY IS:

Unharmed inside the beast

Left in parts (and girl eats the meat, cannibalizing grandma)

THE RELATIVE IS:

Grandma

Mom, unbeknownst to Girl

Girl's evil sister who deserves to die

Each student picked five elements and strung them into a single sentence. One student told the tale of rape in a Western town in the 1840s. Another told the story of a bitter feud between a mother and daughter during World War II. A third wrote a steamy forbidden love story about Red and a Baptist preacher in the South during the civil rights movement. Each of us will choose the elements of the story that speak not just to us, but to the part of us that is simmering just below our consciousness. The woman who wrote about rape in a Western town was struggling with sexual abuse. Expressing the real trauma in her life was too difficult for her. But writing a story about someone who was definitely not her, just an imaginary person in a place and time she had never visited, gave her enough room to allow the emotions and problems of a sexual abuse trauma to rise to the surface. This was her story idea, and the longer she followed it, within the strict confines of a fictional character in a specific time and place, the easier it was for her to access the very real emotional issues that the rape elicited and to resolve them.

If you're stumped trying to find a story idea, choose a fairy tale. Pick five elements you like, change the time and location, and write your story. Write it as if it is your own, because it will become your own as you write.

If you're a pantser and you've been wanting to follow your ideas and write, write, write, then this is the time to do it. Go write for a while. Ask your characters who they are. What they are afraid of. What they want. What they hate. And what the heck they are doing. But remember, you have to come back.

CHARACTER

What is character?

Character has two relevant definitions. First, a character can be a role in a fictional piece, the *dramatic persona,* for example, the father or the boss. Such characters tend to have specific ages and particular physical features. Often, these are the people you wind up with when you use software or questionnaires to define your characters.

Second is the question of *character*: the ethical or moral standards at the heart of the matter, or the internal landscape that affects the external behavior. Simply, *the heart of the person.* As writers, when we speak of character, we speak of this internal landscape brought out by behavior. While there may be many roles in any piece, this heart and soul is the character of your hero and also your villain. It always means the sum of the spirit and emotional history of the person and the behavior that we can see as a result. It is deeper and more significant than a role, and it is what you want your main character to have. If we want to touch the soul of our readers, we must share our own. Character is the map of the nooks and crannies of the heart.

For our purposes, character *always* means this internal map or psychological picture of the person. It is *never* the physical description of a person in your story, though if physical descriptors of any sort help guide you to their internal material, that's certainly useful.

What about all the other roles in your story? Your two main characters need to be well-developed and nuanced because the character of the protagonist and antagonist determines a lot of your story. The characters of the other roles don't serve the story; they serve the main characters. In other words, they can be important, but they are ancillary to the core of your story. When you have a story idea and maybe a few other scenes or elements of your finished product, you need only two roles: Your protagonist, the person we will root for, and the antagonist, the bad guy or person who stands in opposition to the protagonist. These two people will embody the conflicts, both internal and external, that form the core of your writing.

All the other characters, romantic interests, threshold guardians, comic relief, ghosts, mentors, the whole bagful of people you will need later on to tell your story are just distractions now. Put them back on the shelf. Tell them you'll get to them when you need them, and not a moment earlier than that. We can add the love interest and the mean boss later. Don't get sidetracked.

HOW TO DEVELOP CHARACTERS

Like so much of the creative process, it doesn't matter *how* you do it; it matters *what* you wind up with. Many writing teachers will tell students to fill out biographies for their characters: where they live, what schools they go to, what color hair they have. There are plenty of ways to generate characters, including software that will ask you what it believes are the important specific elements of a character. If software helps you find your character, great.

Any process that helps you discover the heart of your character is a good tool. However, please remember that all the externals—like the schools they attend and the color of their hair—can never be the heart of your characters. Those externals are the tools for navigating to the heart of the character, not the character itself. For example, let's say you have a character who went to Harvard. What does that tell us? Smart, probably, but not much else. The follow-up questions might help. Why Harvard? Was she a legacy? That tells you something about how she was brought up and therefore could lead to her assumptions about her life. She went to Harvard but waited tables and ate spaghetti for four years to get by? That's a different character. Wait, she went to City Junior College? Why did she go to a local junior college? If it's because her mother is ill and she has to be around to care for her, that's one character. If it's because she almost failed out of high school because she was dating the local bad boy who is in prison now and she can't get into any other school, then that's a very different character. In each of these examples, the exterior characteristics are useful only to the extent that they lead you to the character's heart.

Disregard people who think a character and a role are the same thing. Your reader is wiser. Your audience doesn't care about the externals, and there is a pile of science to explain why.

Wonder why?
Check out *Theory of Mind* and also *Mirror Neurons* in Part Two.

MAIN CHARACTERS

Your story needs a *protagonist* and an *antagonist*.

The protagonist is your lead character, the hero that the audience will follow on the journey that is your story. Your audience needs to root for the protagonist, so that character must be sympathetic, relatable, and active. Is there one word that encapsulates all these flying adjectives? Yup. Your main character must be *bondable*. Your protagonist must be so relatable to your audience member that they will automatically, non-consciously, identify with the protagonist. That does *not* mean the character has to be nice and sweet. It means the audience member can see a behavior and think, "Wow, I know what that feels like." This explains why a character with perfect taste and manners may not "get to us," but a character whom we meet when she is puking from being too drunk last night grabs our heart.

The antagonist is the person or force that stands in constant opposition to the protagonist. She is the bad guy, the evil one, the black hat.

These definitions appear simplistic and wooden. The characters will become more interesting and nuanced as you develop their internal lives and put them into active situations so their behavior expresses dilemmas within your story. In short, they are stiff right now.

They will develop into interesting characters because you will bring them to life. Be patient.

HOW TO DEVELOP YOUR PROTAGONIST

Ask your main character to join you for tea. Really. Or for a chat. Or a walk. When looking for the outlines of the character of our character, we want to know why this particular person wants that particular goal. In our painting hypothetical, does Gracie want the painting because she thinks it's actually worth a bundle of money? Or does she miss her dead father and it reminds her of how much he loved her? Or did her mother always lust for that painting and if Gracie winds up with it, it is a well-deserved victory for the long-suffering daughter? Obviously, the possibilities are endless, but the choice you make is important. Each one of these choices tells you something different about Gracie's heart, and therefore much more about the journey she's beginning.

How do you find your character?

We want to have heart-to-heart talks with our characters, just as you would with a friend. We want to know what's the best thing that happened to her today. What's the worst? Does she have a big laugh? Does she have a bunch of pals or just one or two buddies? What do *they* talk about? What's bothering her today? What's just annoying? Is her house neat or a wreck or just a room she rents with some people she doesn't actually like? What's she afraid of today?

Idea maps are a great way to open the door and allow the character bubbles to get to the surface. It's free play, and that is absolutely the right way to approach it. Giant sheets of paper are a good start. So are colorful pens and markers and dancing music. Put your character's name smack in the middle of an oversized piece of paper and ask her what she loves. And what she hates. Why she wants her painting. What it means to her. Keep going.

Once you get moving on an idea map, some of the spokes will have more energy. Follow that energy, because it's also your enthusiasm.

Another way to find your main character is to talk with her. At the keyboard, write the dialogue you want to have. And let your character answer. It might feel awkward for a few minutes, but if you can withhold judgment, characters often get chatty and will lead you right to the juice. If you have software or macros for writing scripts, use them. Call yourself the writer, and call your character by whatever name she's using.

WRITER
Hey, Gracie. What are you up to?

GRACIE
I'm hanging out waiting for you to ask a good question.
You got one?

WRITER
Wow. Hostile.

GRACIE
. . . .!

What does the character say in response? Whatever it is, it tells you something. "Hey, sorry about coming on strong" reveals a different person from "I've just been waiting to get the painting; what's the holdup?" and "I'm not some friggin' rose on the vine, y'know!" Whatever the comeback is, you'll know your character a lot better. Keep at it.

If nothing else works, fill out the dreaded biography, remembering that where someone goes to school or lives or what they drive doesn't matter. Why they made those choices matters a lot.

THE PERFECT FIT

You now have your hero, an imperfect person with emotions. And you have a *problem*, which is the gnarled center of your idea. Why is this particular character the exactly perfect person to face this specific problem? When you can answer this question, you have the skeleton that will be your entire story. It's simple, but it ain't easy, as many a wise man has said.

Your protagonist will be someone who is broken in exactly the place where your story will challenge him or her. In a love story, the happy bachelor meets the perfect woman but is unable to commit. Why is he unable to commit? A broken heart from a first love? A mom who loved him so much she will never be equaled? Or a mom who loved him so little that he's become programmed to reject love?

In *Black Panther*, T'Challa wants to be a good king for his isolated country, but the outside world (in the person of Killmonger) wants to blow it open. What is the perfect fit for T'Challa? He adores his father and seeks to follow him, but his father's isolation for the country produced the evil that T'Challa now faces. His dedication to his father is in direct conflict with the needs of his people.

In *Spotlight*, the story of the journalists who broke the sexual abuse scandal in the Catholic Church, Robby, the hard-charging journalist, is determined to publicize all the Church's horrible offenses. What is Robby's wound that makes the fit perfect? Robby is a Catholic with a history of giving the Church a pass on its misdeeds. The closer Robby gets to the criminal priests, the closer he gets to the wound of his own subtle complicity. His wound, the complicity, is a perfect fit with a story line of righteous exposure of wrongdoing.

The perfect fit often pits the external goal of the character in direct conflict with a pre-existing emotional or moral wound that is expressed in the *backstory* of your protagonist. Backstory, when used well, is not "what happened before the story begins." Backstory expresses your protagonist's pre-existing emotional condition or the wounds which caused her to be hurtled into this specific story to begin with. Backstory is useful when it reveals what is in the character's heart.

As you write the full story, you will have to decide when to show the reader the backstory or wound. In *Black Panther,* T'Challa's particular wound is disclosed over the first two acts of the film. In *Chinatown,* Faye Dunaway's character finally tells us that "she's my sister *and* my daughter!" late in the film. In *Spotlight*, we discover in the very last scene that Robby has been giving the Church a pass on previous abuse. The choice of when to tell the reader why the obstacle and the character fit each other perfectly is determined by when you as the writer believe that the revelation will have the deepest resonance.

However, you, the writer, must know why your main character and the main obstacle form such a profound challenge before you write a single page. You may not be telling your audience, but you will know it and write with that shadow, so that when it is fully revealed, the audience will feel the full depth of the dilemma. What you know about the character and what you tell the reader about the character are two separate things.

THE ANTAGONIST

Your *protagonist* needs opposition that personifies the reason why your hero hasn't already achieved her goal. The opposition can be a person, force, institution, even The Empire. This is a force or a person who opposes your hero and will do everything he/she/it can to prevent your hero from achieving the goal.

The *antagonist*, whether a person or a force of nature or whatever else, is what or who your hero is up against. Your antagonist deserves real time and development. He or she must have the resources and the will to be overwhelming. What tools does the antagonist have? Let's consider some examples:

In *Mandela*, the antagonist is the South African government and the laws of apartheid.

In *E.T. the Extra-Terrestrial*, the antagonist is the whole humanoid world, including scientists and our so-called modern technology.

In *The Fugitive*, Gerard, the Tommy Lee Jones character, personifies the relentless determination of US law enforcement.

In *The Untouchables*, the antagonist is the mercilessly violent mob boss, Al Capone.

The smarter/better/more brilliant your antagonist, the better your hero will be forced to be. That is exactly what you want. So, to find your antagonist, the map is pretty straightforward. Given the obstacle you've chosen for your story, who is the one person you can conjure up who can impede the hero in the strongest way? Really? Make the villain stronger! Smarter! More powerful!

Who is the perfect villain in our painting hypothetical? The role of the executor already has a lot of power because in an estate situation, the law is on the executor's side. Who would be the most challenging executor for Gracie? We could consider the relationship the executor has to Gracie. Is he the trust department guy from the bank? A relative who is a lawyer, maybe Uncle Alan? How about a rich relative, like Cousin Jack? Each one gives the story different angles.

The trust guy from the bank would have a lot of authority and the bureaucracy of the bank and the courts on his side, but the role doesn't inherently bring much personal juice. Uncle Alan, the lawyer, will have specialized knowledge of the law, and, to me, a righteous attitude that will grate against Gracie's emotional reason for achieving her goal. What about a relative, a rich aunt or uncle, or a Brother/Cousin/Nephew Jack? A relative brings more raw emotions and attitudes. A brother makes it a sibling rivalry story, and that isn't quite right, I think. A cousin, though, a cousin could work. What could make a cousin more formidable? A guy, I think, because maybe Dad thought Gracie would benefit from a strong, male figure? How about a rich cousin, someone Dad thought would look after Gracie but who is full of himself and out to grab more than just the painting?

What if Dad thought that Cousin Jack would be perfect to help Gracie, so Dad gave him extraordinary powers expecting him to use them for Gracie's benefit, but Jack just wants to take over everything? He's got money and he's got apparent authority from Dad. That's a worthy opponent. I'd use him. Why does Gracie want the painting? Is it because it is valuable? Or because it represents her relationship with her father and she is jealous of sharing him, in whatever manifestation, with anyone? If that's why she wants the painting, then Jack is the perfect antagonist because he covets not just the painting, but its underlying emotional value, the connection with Dad. Jack's an antagonist with an emotional investment, the powers of the will as executor and the power of plenty of money. He's a great antagonist because he has all the power. Gracie has all the determination. This will be a good fight.

CONFLICT

"**C**onflict is the basis of drama."[4]

"Conflict must be at the very hub of your story, because it is the core of strong action and strong character."[5]

So sayeth the gods of screenwriting.

The job of the writer is to keep the reader interested right through to the very last page. Keeping it interesting is a way of keeping our focus on the things that are important. We keep it interesting by keeping our characters in conflicts.

What, then, is *conflict*? It isn't chasing someone around in a car, nor is it punching someone's lights out. It isn't yelling, running, or shooting.

Conflict occurs when two parties hold deeply held opposing positions at cross-purposes with each other. If one character believes in the right to an abortion and the second character believes life begins at conception in a story about football, or cars, or life on Mars, these characters aren't in conflict because their opposing positions aren't relevant to the story line. If the same two characters are in a domestic drama and one character is a pregnant teenager and the other is her mother, that's a conflict. Two people or forces with inalterably opposing positions confronting each other is a conflict. That conflict drives the drama of your story.

In the film *E.T.*, E.T. just wants to go home. The adult scientists want to keep him here to study him. There is no middle ground. He's either on his home planet or not, and there is no in-between.

In the movie *The Untouchables*, Al Capone wants to have a liquor business. Elliot Ness wants to enforce Prohibition laws.

In the film *Mandela*, the protagonist wants equality for all people. The South African government wants apartheid.

Expert writers use direct, strong conflicts. Newbies pull their punches. Be forewarned: The less the drama, the less the interest. Don't commit the boring.

Your protagonist and antagonist must embody direct conflict in every story point.

Without direct and intense conflict, your story will fail. And so will your efforts to forge a newer, better, happier you. Make sure your protagonist and antagonist have a true, deep difference of positions.

THE OBSTACLES

> *The basis of drama is . . . the struggle of the hero towards a specific goal at the end of which he realizes that what kept him from it was, in the lesser drama, civilization and, in the great drama, the discovery of something that he did not set out to discover but which can be seen retrospectively as inevitable.*
>
> –David Mamet

What is preventing your hero from obtaining her goal?

The answer is the center line of your story. Your audience wants to see its hero face a series of ascending obstacles. What are the most challenging obstacles? Write them down. Think you've come up with enough challenges? Write down more and more and more.

As Kurt Vonnegut advises, "Be a sadist. No matter how sweet and innocent your leading characters, make awful things happen to them, in order that the reader may see what they are made of."[6]

Write down at least 25 things that can go horribly wrong in your story, and make sure to include the worst things that could happen. Be a sadist.

What can the all-powerful antagonist do to harm our protagonist, slow her down, impede her path? Write down at least 25 more things that he can to harm her, block her, and steal her goal again and again.

What happens when she loses everything?

Be merciless.

Welcome to the second act of your story, the road of trials.

We know what the protagonist and antagonist want, and we know some of the particular strengths they each bring to the conflict. So, what's the *plot*?

The plot is the ordering of the obstacles our protagonist must face on her journey to attaining her goal. Now is the time to make a long, long list of all the obstacles that could possibly stand between her and her goal. Are the obstacles severe enough?

PLOTTING

Take out your list of obstacles. This is the fun part.

We want to present our protagonist with the deepest, most juicy obstacles. Pick out the five to ten absolutely harshest obstacles for your protagonist. These are your character's *terribles*. Now put these in order, the least terrible of the terribles to the absolutely worst terrible. This is the *spine* of your story, the second act.

Each obstacle is increasingly difficult for your protagonist. By the end of the second act, everything has gone wrong. Every possible terrible thing has happened. And then, indeed, *all is lost*.

The most common thing new writers get wrong is failing to put the protagonist through hell. They take it easy on her. They pull punches. We all fail in this way because we care about our characters and frankly want to protect them from our own worst instincts. But when we are protective of our protagonist, we cheat our audience members of any satisfaction because they want to learn from our protagonist. They, too, want to experience the joy of finding new strengths and wisdom. When you go easy on your protagonist, you deny your audience the opportunity to grow and learn . . . and you deny it to yourself.

The end of the second act *must present a challenge to which you don't know the answer*.

We writers avoid our deepest challenges in real life because we doubt we can overcome them. But our protagonist is fictional, unblocked, free of our own traumas. This is the very point where you must trust your protagonist beyond the extent to which you trust yourself. Trust her. She's fictional and free from all the other baggage. Trust her to take a leap or see a piece of wisdom or find a special tool that her creator, you, didn't know she had.

This is the meat of writing to happiness. This is the very moment of transformation. All you need to do is to trust that your character will figure it out, though you may spend a week or two stomping around waiting.

BETTER OBSTACLES

Do you have a fantastic list of obstacles to frustrate and test your main character to her core?

Probably not. More likely, you have a list of obstacles that you think are pretty tough but can be overcome. Ornery but doable. We need more. Make a list of the most heartbreaking setbacks you can imagine for your hero. Betrayal? Yes. Abandonment? Yes. Death of a beloved? Yes. Complete and absolute failure? Yes. Her own death? Yes.

Your list of obstacles must be the things that are *the most difficult* you can imagine for *your specific protagonist*. If right now, as you are writing, you can imagine a way out of the problem, then it isn't a big enough problem. What is it that—when your character faces it—*all is lost*? If you can get out of it, all is not lost.

If _____, _____, and then _____ happens, all is lost.

Find what "all is lost" means to your hero. No shortcuts, no pulled punches. This moment is essential.

STRUCTURE

S*tructure* has plenty of names, theories, and ridiculous diagrams. There are structuralists, anti-structuralists, and structural gurus. There's plenty to say about it; almost all of it has been said—and said way too often. We'll stick to what matters.

A popular song has verses and choruses. Rarely does the listener pay any attention to either, but the pattern is set in our non-conscious expectations. If a song doesn't present those elements in the accepted manner, our sense of contentedness is shaken. We know something is wrong—but not quite what. I invited some friends over for dinner one night and had some classic Dave Brubeck playing in the background. My friend Erica was just plain irritable, not her usual state. Finally, she complained about the music, which had set her on edge. "Take Five" was playing, and Erica wasn't used to hearing music in 5/4 time. The unexpected meter in the music made her pay attention to the dissonance instead of the dinner conversation. The break in her pattern expectation took her focus and annoyed her.

Story structure is the same. When story is experienced in the expected pattern, we pay attention to the story and not its structure.

When it breaks that shape or melody, we suddenly focus on the dissonance instead of the story itself. Which element is dissonant? When we come out of the story and focus on the structural anomaly, it breaks the effectiveness of the storytelling. We adhere to structure because our audience wants it and we want them. Our brains are wired to be receptive to that pattern

A story has a beginning, middle, and end. That is the container of the audience member's expectations for the order of a story.

> **Wonder why readers love structure in their stories?**
> **Check out *Patternicity* in Part Two.**

One way of presenting structure is:
- Act I—Once upon a time, there was a character who lived in a place . . .
- Act II—Then one day, something happens . . . and eventually . . .
- Act III—The situation is resolved.

Another version is this:
- Once upon a time . . .
- And then one day . . .
- And just when everything was going so well . . .
- When just at the last minute . . .
- And they all lived happily ever after.

Movies adhere fairly strictly to three-act structure. In Act One, we meet our main character and the world in which she lives. We identify the theme and major elements and have everything we need to send our hero on her journey. Then *something big* happens to throw the protagonist into Act Two.

Act Two spins the character into action, generally with some upward movement until things fall apart into a complete crisis, a pseudo death. In Act Two, the protagonist makes plans for reaching the goal and is progressively challenged until all is lost.

In Act Three, from the ashes of all is lost, the hero faces the ultimate confrontation and resolves it. She is changed by the experience.

Act One is usually one quarter of your total number of pages, words, or scenes, whichever applies. Act Two is half the story, often with a dramatic moment at the midpoint, smack in the middle at the 50% mark. Act Three is, again, a quarter of the length.

Each act has a job. Act One introduces us to the milieu of the story and to our hero, who, regardless of age or experience, is an innocent as to the material in this particular story. For example, in *As Good as It Gets*, Jack Nicholson is an older, world-weary man of a certain age, but he is childlike in his knowledge of mature relationships and meaningful communication. He is an innocent at the art of life. He's about to be challenged and learn a whole lot, and we get to learn along with him.

Something happens at the end of Act One that throws our story into high speed, and our character must react and plan the journey.

Act Two is the meat of the story. Our hero has plans, but is challenged. The plot becomes more complicated, often with subplots, and eventually the situation gets the better of our hero, until there is a moment when the character and the audience feel that all is lost. In *E.T.*, a movie with perfect structure, E.T. is dead on the operating table. It is the moment in the story when all is lost. In *Black Panther*, King T'Challa lies dead and Killmonger has taken the throne.

Act Three is a form of return, when everything our hero has learned comes into play. Tactics and weapons become skills and wisdom, and the ultimate threat is overcome. The Hero's Journey is complete, and the hero can rejoin her world as a sage figure with wisdom to share in her community. We the audience have shared the journey and gained the wisdom of it.

SCENE ORDER

Scenes proceed in an order of *cause-and-effect*. Once again, this looks easy but is hard.

Cause-and-effect means that the events in the preceding scene (scene A) must trigger the events in scene B. The events in A *require* that we go to scene B *next*. Scene A doesn't just precede scene B, but propels us into scene B necessarily.

Cause-and-effect is how we humans make sense of the world. Cause-and-effect means that A causes B causes C causes D, ever onward. Without it, it could be A-D-B-A or D-B-Q-X. The world could be entirely random, with nothing connected to anything else except by random time. Life would be random and complicated. Cause-and-effect allows us to believe (however falsely) that events are related and that we have some control over them. It allows us to predict what comes next and prepare for it. It allows us to feel a sense of efficacy in our own lives.

This consideration of the signal importance of cause-and-effect prepares the ground for understanding its importance to your story. If events just happen, your readers will put down your writing. They will hate the sense of randomness and so will you, the writer. It may present a lot of pretty words and impulses, but it isn't a story and, for us, it has no utility. That's how important cause-and-effect is.

When we write a story, we are required to present the events in a cause-and-effect order. This sequence helps all of us make sense of our world, and, importantly, allows the reader to confidently surrender to the story.

We order the scenes in a sequence which we believe will best keep the reader's interest. How do we do that? Each scene requires the protagonist to go to the next scene in order to achieve her goal. As David Mamet explains, "Dramatic structure consists of the creation and deferment of hope. That's basically all it is. The reversals, the surprises, and the ultimate conclusion of the hero's quest please [the audience] in direct proportion to the plausibility of the opponent forces."[7]

We lay down the order of our scenes and thus the story as if they are train tracks because story is indeed a freight train going at full speed without ever jumping the guardrails. Include every scene required to move your story forward. If a scene isn't necessary, its only function will be to divert the reader's attention. The train will jump the tracks.

We writers also look at each scene and ask whether the story could continue on its tracks without that one scene. If the answer is yes, then cut the scene. Cut it mercilessly. If you aren't exactly sure what the scene adds to the story, cut the scene. If it doesn't either tell us something important about the character or move the action forward in a required manner, cut the scene. Your reader won't want to follow you off the tracks and into the scenery—pun intended. And, yes, again, there's good science to demonstrate why.

> **Wonder why scene sequence is crucial to your audience?**
> **Check out *Patternicity* in Part Two.**

TENTPOLES

How do we structure our stories? How do we shape them? We determine what the important events in the story are. We put them in the best order we can come up with, and we call them *tentpoles*. They are the scenes that will support the rest of the structure.

What are the important events or scenes in your story?

To build a story, you need a list of the elements to be included.

Build the list.

These are the moments in the beginning of the story: How do we meet the protagonist? The antagonist? What does the world of the protagonist look like at the beginning? Who are the important characters in your hero's world? What matters to the hero? What does the hero want?

These are the moments in the middle of your story: What is your protagonist's plan to achieve the goal? What event hurls her forward into action? Who are the friends, helpers, mentors, and other characters she needs along the way? What goes wrong? What else goes wrong? What *else* goes wrong? What is the "all" in all is lost?

These are the moments of the resolution of your story: What does your hero do when faced with the ultimate challenge? What strength, change, or piece of wisdom does the hero use to face the challenge? Who wins the challenge . . . and how? What does your hero do with the new wisdom in order to bring it back to her ordinary world?

This isn't a checklist. Only you know what events you need to tell your story. Answering those questions will help you see your material and identify the most important moments in your story.

Make a list of the moments in your story. What looks like a good Act I break? Is there a scene that throws the hero into the main action of the story? That's the end of Act I. If not, why not?

I try to find these specific scenes and use them as eleven tentpoles:

Act I:

- the opening
- a real complication
- a turn into the action

Act II:

- a scene that sets out the proposed journey's plan

- a moment when things are going right, and we are hopeful
- a scene where things turn decidedly bad for the hero
- the moment when all is lost

Act III:

- the moment of recommitting to achieve the goal or moment of learning
- the ultimate conflict with the antagonist
- resolution (victory!)
- return to the ordinary world with the wisdom gained by the journey

Those are the 11 scenes that are pivotal to any story. When we feel we have the correct 11 scenes on which the whole story will hang, we'll have our tentpoles. We will have defined the structure and rhythm of the story.

It's time to fill out the story with a *beat sheet*. A what?

THE BEAT SHEET

Now figure out everything that happens in your story and make a list of every important event. Yes, you are ready. Yes, it's a lot. And yes, you are the only one who can figure out what your story needs. It's time to shape the story.

Novelists write outlines. Everyone writes bullet points. And PowerPoints. Screenwriters write beat sheets. A beat sheet is a list of all the beats in your story. A *beat* is a necessary thing that happens in your story. It can be emotional (a character realizes her lover has been cheating) or a specific incident (the car crashes into the tree). Realizations and emotional moments can be very important to the development of the story, and if they require a major character to behave in a changed manner, they are beats. Most beats are incidents, which require the character to change behavior, impelling the story forward.

A beat is something that must change the course of the story or your principal character. If it doesn't change things, it's not a beat; it's fluff. If you can take it out of the story and the story doesn't change, it's not a beat and it needs to be cut. Conversely, if deleting the beat makes the story fall apart, like pulling at a thread and the whole sweater goes with it, then it's a beat.

The beat sheet for the first pages of *The Godfather* might start like this:

1. Meet the Godfather. How he does business with a supplicant.
2. Connie's wedding. Meet the family.
3. FBI watching. It's the mob.
4. Godfather and Tom dole out favors.
5. Meet Luca Brasi. Meet Michael and Kay.
6. Meet Johnny Fontaine, singing heartthrob.
7. Michael tells Kay the story of helping Johnny. Luca Brasi holds a gun to someone's head. Makes an offer he can't refuse.

The beat sheet is for your own use, so don't put in explanations or descriptions. You know who each of the characters is, so you don't have to put down anything general about them. You do need to say "meet the family" because bringing in your cast of characters is essential and if you cut the scene, we wouldn't know who the characters are or how they are related to each other. The FBI presence tells us we are on the wrong side of the law. We need to see Luca Brasi to understand that he's an assassin and that he's afraid of the Godfather. Johnny Fontaine will be an important character, so meeting him also matters. And right there at page 11, we are introduced to the Godfather's methods of enforcement and the classic line that sets the tone for the rest of the movie: "My father made him an offer he couldn't refuse." Every one of these beats is essential to the story. There is nothing extra.

Here's another example, the opening ten pages of *Spotlight*:

1. At a police station. An abusive priest.
2. Bishop schmoozes victim's mother.
3. Bishop shepherds priest away. Police do nothing.
4. At *Boston Globe*. Meet Robby.
5. Meet other members of the Spotlight team.
6. New editor about to be installed.
7. Robby and Marty, the new editor. Will there be staff cuts?
8. Marty's first editors' meeting. Marty asks about an old article about an abusive priest. Robby hears the order to investigate.

Again, the first ten pages, like the opening in any story you or I would write, has to introduce us to our hero's ordinary world and the characters we will need in our story. But, at around page ten in a screenplay, you'll throw some gas on the fire.

A beat sheet is a list of your proposed story points in the proposed order. "Proposed" appears twice in that sentence to underscore that nothing, yet, is written in stone. The sheer number of beats, the order, the significance—they are all up for grabs at this stage.

I prefer beat sheets to outlines because an outline feels more rigid and, much more importantly, allows for sentences or even whole paragraphs of explanation. It allows for fudging on focus. A true beat only takes a few words to communicate. "Darth is Luke's father." E.T. says "phone home." Using a beat sheet is an exercise in focusing each scene in your story on its most important element. If it takes you a paragraph to describe, you probably don't know what that single moment is.

I'm not quite sure why novelists write outlines. It could be to practice some of the language, or to get a feel for each scene, or to get an agent. Some novelists I've worked with go on and on in their outlines, describing the weather, the clothing, the song coming from the speakers. All of that is surplus. The elements of the story are all we want to know on a beat sheet. It's for your own use only. It's how you organize your story without character, scenery, or diversions.

Anything that can be cut must be cut. If you are working on a beat sheet, excess means failure. If what happens in that beat doesn't propel the story to the next scene, then the one you are writing can be cut, and must be cut, because it is somehow a diversion from the fast-moving freight train that is your story.

The beat sheet, in the end, is the train track. Every place that your story must go is on it. Everything else is cut.

Why is the beat sheet so important? Because it's your road map. If it's on there, it's essential. If it's not essential, it's off the map. Perfect. There is no smelling of roses in a well-written story. No slowing down of the freight train. When the writer slows down, the audience falls asleep or leaves. When you and I as writers slow down in the story process, we're diverting our own attention, probably because the very next real beat is too challenging to face today.

Don't get diverted.

If your pantser instincts are kicking in and you just *have to* go write, then go write. But come back for the *Laying of the Cards*.

THE LAYING OF THE CARDS

In some ritual healing traditions, the healer lays hands on the sufferer and, miraculously, in the moment that the hands are upon the body, the subject is alchemically transformed into someone better and happier. *Laying out the cards* for your story can have the same impact. Let's try.

Get a pack of index cards and put each important beat from your beat sheet onto a card. You can leave out the scenes that are transitional or character-based. Lay out the important story points on the cards on a big table, in order.

Now, the big question: Are the scenes laid out in the best possible order? Or, if you reverse the sequence of a few scenes, can you heighten the drama?

Looking at the *Spotlight* beat sheet, we have the following scenes in this order:

1. Meet the protagonist.
2. Meet Robby's team.
3. Find out there is going to be a new editor.
4. Meet the new editor. Possible staff cuts.
5. Marty, the new editor, holds his first editorial meeting. Soft assignment of priest story to Robby's team.

Spotlight is a well-made finished product, so it's hard to imagine the scenes in any other order. But what if we put the #4 scene where we meet the new editor and possible staff cuts before the #2 scene where we meet Robby's team:

1. Meet the protagonist.
2. Marty's first editors meeting. Soft assignment of priest story to Robby's team.
3. Meet the new editor. Will there be staff cuts?
4. Meet the other members of the Spotlight team.

If we see that Robby is worried that there will be staff cuts, then when we meet the other members of the team, we the audience will be wondering who is going to get the ax and how Robby might make that decision. Robby's relationship with his team will be much more tense. There are stories in which that would be a good change, but is it a good change in *this* story?

What if we move the cards around so they look like this:

1. Robby gets the soft assignment to look into the abuse cases.

2. Robby and new editor Marty have their first meeting, over lunch. Will there be staff cuts?
3. Then we meet the team.

In this order, Marty's interest in the priest story will seem much more like a direct order from Robby's new boss. Robby is likely going to follow the order, no matter what. What's his attitude about that? Is he already pissed at the new editor, even before we meet his team? And the staff cuts? Well, even Robby is going to look at his team and wonder how to handle the assignment. Are any of them Catholic? Is that going to be a problem? Doesn't the team usually choose its own assignments, so getting ordered to do the priest abuse story might really annoy the reporters? Are the staff writers resentful? Is there tension now between the staff writers and the new editor?

In the film itself, we meet Robby and then his team members. Because we see them before the idea of cutting staff is presented, we see Spotlight as the team whose members are Robby and the writers. We give up some tension between Robby and his team members but gain more tension between the team as a whole and the editor. Which tensions are better for the story? Do we want to see tension between Robby and the journalists, or do we want to see tension between all the writers as a unit versus the editor or the priests?

Later in *Spotlight*, major scenes are presented in the following order:

1. The publisher tells Marty (the editor) to pursue a court order against the Church.
2. Montage of team doing research. Find out there is another abuser priest.
3. Ben (another editor) threatens to kill the story.
4. Team members dig in to push back against threat to story.
5. Marty meets with the Cardinal. They are adversaries.

6. Interview with victims. Learn much more about the abuse, sympathetic victims.

What would happen if we saw Marty and the Cardinal and the lines being drawn between them *before* the publisher authorizes the editor to pursue the court order? There would be *a lot* more drama in deciding to pursue the court order, because it would be a more frontal attack on the Church. More drama is good. But it might send us off into a legal drama, instead of a personal drama. Every decision accumulates in shaping your story. Where could we put the victim interviews? There's real emotion in the victim scenes. If they go before the publisher scene and the Cardinal scene, we will hate the Cardinal when we meet him. If we already know, through the victims, that the Cardinal is evil, have we changed the tone of the entire story? Will it be about getting the Cardinal? Will it draw attention away from the efforts of the Spotlight team? The victims? Which line of sympathy is the most important? The victims offer the greatest amount of pure emotional connection, but do you and I, as the rewriting authors of *Spotlight*, want the emotional through-line to be about the victims, which would be juicy, or about the reporters, who are less emotionally juicy but more heroic?

There are no right and no wrong answers to these questions. The point is that you and I as the writers have the power to order the scenes in the progression we believe will have the most impact *for whatever we choose to be the most important values in our story*. The sequence of our scenes is important. New writers approach a story as if the vision they have in their head at the beginning of the writing is the only order in which it can be told. But as new *authors* we have *authority* over the story, and the elements are ours to arrange and rearrange as we search for the greatest impact. There is no single correct way to tell a story. Lay out the cards. Lay them out differently. And differently again. See if you can improve the drama in your story.

You embrace the power you have over your story when you play with sequencing.

If changing the order of scenes makes the hero's road even more intense and difficult, then make the change. If it deepens the conflict, then it's a good change. Remember, we left the transition scenes out of the card pile, because when we reorder scenes, we will have to get from one scene to another in a new way. Don't worry about the transitions now. Just get the events in your story into the sequence that maximizes the tension for your characters.

Raising the stakes is a well-worn cliché that writing instructors use the world over. If you've heard it, you've probably been tempted to put a murder in your mystery, making it seem, you think, scarier. And if that hasn't made the road hard enough for your protagonist, you were told to raise the stakes again, so you put in a kidnapping plot. On the third verse of raising the stakes, you put in some guns and bullets. If you followed this advice, you changed your mystery into a thriller, without conforming the underlying structure. The stakes will be bigger but less effective. You will have pulled your readers out of one genre and into another one, and they'll focus on what's dissonant instead of what matters in the story. You've messed up a good thing.

Raising the stakes doesn't mean you should put bigger, more action-packed beats into the story. It means you should make the elements you already have in the piece more deeply emotional and affecting. Raising the stakes doesn't mean *go big*. It means *go deep*.

How do you go deep? This is the moment to remember the psychology of your main character. We non-consciously identify with the main character, so we care about the difficulties she suffers in her journey. To that end, the main character must be deeply emotionally affected by the order of your story. The story must present *obstacles to your main character's emotional wounds*.

Is a given obstacle a reminder of something terrible that happened in her past? Does it present exactly the problem she most feared at the beginning of the story? Has she failed to overcome similar obstacles and been shamed about her failure by someone she loves? These dilemmas deepen the obstacles for your hero and increase our identification with her. If she isn't hurt enough at the end of the second act, go back and, again, be the sadist. We raise the stakes by making the situation more psychologically affecting.

It's all about the emotion. Not the bullets.

Have you reordered your cards so you maximize the drama inherent in each scene? Great!

You need to get the transitions from one event to another back into some order. Figure out what new transitions will get your character to proceed in the most dramatic order and still make sense.

Have you finished the laying of the cards?

If you're a plotter, you probably have a pretty detailed outline now. If you must, go off and write. But come back for the *reduction sauce*.

THE REDUCTION SAUCE

Take out a single index card and your favorite writing instrument. Yes, this must be done by hand, slowly, in your most careful writing. It must be done with clarity of mind and purpose.

On one side of the index card, in handwriting no smaller than you can read without your glasses, write down, in order, your list of essential beats in your story, no more than eleven of them.

Read it back to yourself until you are sure these are the most important ones you have.

Now take the other cards, beat sheets, and working papers and affectionately place them in a drawer for a while.

Take the one index card, which is your road map to your story, and place it somewhere convenient. It is your reminder of the essential moments of your story, and it is now all you need.

If you have your tentpoles, you have your act structure. Everything else may change in your story, but if your structure is right and your act breaks are solid, the structure won't change. The foundation of your house has been built; the concrete has dried.

You are almost ready to write.

Remember Rule #5: *Your first draft is a car that has no reverse gear.* It only has a forward gear. No fixing, no editing, no going backward, no doubting.

There's plenty of time to fix everything endlessly in all your later drafts. For your first draft, your inner editor and inner critic are banned from the space in your head. Don't let them in. If they slip by, hurl them out remorselessly.

You are ready for the sweetest words in writing: *Go write*.

WRITING

GO WRITE

Build yourself your best environment, put on your special outfit, place the Do Not Disturb sign on the door, pour cups of your favorite beverage, prepare an infinite supply of sharp yellow pencils, fire up the printer, put on your favorite music, dance yourself into a frenzy, become your fullest pantser, and *go write*. Write with abandon. Write with frenzy. Write all id, no superego. Lose yourself. Go write.

Come back when you're finished with your first pass.

THE REWRITE

You've worked your butt off, you put everything you've got into it, and you have yourself a story. Most writers need a huge serving of praise at this point. Feel free to indulge by giving a draft to one or two of your best friends, or your partner, mother, sister, or any other entirely reliable other. Tell them their job is to praise you. And by all means, inhale all the praise.

Then get over it, and get back to work.

The job of the rewrite isn't to gain praise. The job of the rewrite is to make your piece better. Select a few different readers whom you trust for their ruthless honesty. Their job is to tell you what doesn't work. Listen carefully to their comments. Take in every one of them.

If you are fortunate enough to have more than one good reader, pay special attention to the bumps and comments that more than one person offers about a particular aspect of your story. If a few readers are uncomfortable in the same place in your story, you have a bump you must fix.

The key to taking comments is well explained by Neil Gaiman, who said, "Remember: when people tell you something's wrong or doesn't work for them, they are almost always right. When they tell you exactly what they think is wrong and how to fix it, they are almost always wrong."[8] My personal experience is that Gaiman's comment is entirely accurate. Your readers know when you fudged or flew over a problem or otherwise dropped the ball. And because we are writing for readers, their opinions of where bumps exist are always valuable. They are the jury. You can try to argue them out of it, but it's already too late. If the writing pulled them out of the story enough for them to feel uncomfortable, the bump needs to be addressed.

Their suggestions for how to fix the problem will always be wrong. Only you know your character well enough to go deeper to find the answer. Only you understand how to address your character's wound. You are the god of the kingdom you have created, and sometimes being all-powerful is a hard gig.

The most important potential problem in writing to happiness is the failure that's likely at the bottom of the second act. What happened when all was lost? The problems come in two flavors:

1. You took it easy on your character, and all is less than lost.
2. All is very lost, and you can't get them out of the Hell you built.

ALL IS NOT LOST

If the bottom of your Act II took it easy on your hero, don't worry. You can almost always make it worse. Did you throw all the worst of the worst at her? Or, the ultimate question, *is she dead yet*? How bad does it have to get at the bottom of the second act? It's usually a sort of death, including the sort where someone in fact dies. In *Black Panther,* T'Challa has been heaved over a waterfall and fallen to his death. In *E.T.,* E.T. is so dead that he's been pronounced dead by all the scientists. In *Field of Dreams,* the dream is dead.

Does your character suffer the actual death of a loved one? Of a goal? Of a dream? Does your character suffer a pseudo death—the death of the soul or spirit? Your hero doesn't have to be physically dead, but in the sense of the journey that you have made her travel, she must suffer at least a pseudo death or a death of all hope.

Go back and be even more sadistic. Enjoy it. How often do you have permission to be your most evil self? Seriously, go be your baddest. But do come back.

ALL IS TOO LOST

Ah, this is great. You dug your hero into such a deep hole that you can't get her out.

I know this feels like hell, and I've spent plenty of days stomping around my office, bereft of any thought of how to get my hero out of that hole. I know it feels terrible.

Here's the good news: You will find a way out, and it will transform your story.

At the bottom of the second act, your character—and that bit of your sub-conscious that was there for the creation of that very hole—has run out of known fixes, moves and rationalizations to try to get out of this hole. Your conscious and your sub-conscious have no answers. And this is *great.* We've crystallized a problem you've probably carried around with you, in real or fictional form, for a long time. And you have no old answers. This is the golden moment. You must create something new, something you have never thought of before, but which is well within your capacities and knowledge. You haven't put it together yet.

Creativity is the act of making something entirely new. It is that spark, that step into the unknown. It's time to be creative in the deepest sense of the word.

Use whatever techniques worked for you in opening the door to your story. Go meditate, dream, garden, sew, dance, golf. Turn your brain over to daydreaming. Allow your non-conscious mind to cook on it. Yes, it can take days. If you think the act of creation is quick, you are in the wrong business. It's hard, it takes a bit of time . . . and it is brilliant.

If you can't get the hero out of the hole, try some of these techniques:

1. Write the end of Act II from the perspective of the other characters who are present. When you change your perspective, you get new information to include.

> **Wonder why changing perspective changes the story?**
> **Check out *Expressive Writing* in Part Two.**

2. Go back to your statement of the goal your character had set. Now make it more spiritual or internal. What has your character learned about herself that now must become material? Can the doctor who wanted merely to live a cushy life realize that a good doctor has to do good for the patients? Did the lawyer learn that she didn't merely want to practice law and that she wanted to champion justice and truth? What are the deeper meanings of the original goal?

3. What has your hero discovered along the way?

You have just run your hero through all nine circles of Dante's Inferno for the entire second act. Simply put, what has she learned?

In the absolute worst-case scenario, it is possible that the thing your character has learned is that there is, in fact, no way out. Sound ridiculous? Take a look at the classic romance, *An Officer and a Gentleman*. The hero's goal was to make it as an aviator in the US Navy. He was scrubbing out. The script had exactly this problem: a hole the writers couldn't get the hero out of. Producers, studio executives, directors, writers, people on the street all came to the same conclusion: There's no way to get the Richard Gere character out of the hole. Finally, the team gave up. They gave Gere a single line: "I got nowhere else to go!" In effect, Gere throws in the towel. He can't get thrown out of the Navy because he has nowhere else to go. He suffers a spiritual or pseudo death. He is a complete failure. He has no choice but to go forward and grow. Amazingly, it works. We believe that he finds unbelievable strengths, values his romantic relationship, and honors his military superiors, because he has, in effect, made his goal even deeper: not just to be in the service, but to be the manifestation of the values that being in the service means.

If your character is still in the hole, ask yourself what greater understanding can she find? What deeper meaning is available? What truth hasn't yet been addressed? What is *more true*? Your hero must now make the leap from an ordinary character to a special person, a wiser one.

Allow your brilliant mind to show you where and how to make the great leap.

Remember, this is the richest moment in your writing to happiness. Almost everything you have done thus far has led you to this magnificent, unsettling point. Your victory, like that of your protagonist, comes in this moment of rising through the difficulties presented with greater understanding, depth, and wisdom.

The goal of the rewrite is to make that moment of near death into the beginning of the sequence of rebirth. How does your character change? What is the lesson that makes everything different? What is the wisdom gained?

Once you develop the sequence from near death to bigger life, go rewrite as much as you want. Let your inner editor go nuts. Invite your inner critic to the party. Be as persnickety as you can be.

Do you have that transformational moment? If so, great.

Go rewrite.

AND IN THE END . . .

Embrace the journey. Smooth out all the bumps. Revel in the victory over the antagonist in Act III. And remember: The duty of the hero is to bring the wisdom of the journey back to her community. Bring the boon to the world. In *Black Panther*, T'Challa opens up a youth center at the very location of the original sin: the abandonment of Killmonger. He ends the isolation of the Wakandans, not with armaments but with acts of deep kindness toward the outside world.

AFTERWORD: HOW IT WORKED

I wrote screenplays for 22 years. I faced all the real-life and fictional dilemmas that the job entailed. I was also very, very fortunate. Writing saved my life in many ways.

My first script was about a lawyer who wanted success but was on the wrong side of a case. I chose the topic because I had been a lawyer at a big-time law firm and believed I could write what I knew. I had no deeper purpose. Nevertheless, the character somehow kept finding questionable ethical issues, not the stuff of your typical screenplay. But there it was, little painful sellout after little painful sellout. The script was technically proficient but emotionally insufficient. It was unfulfilling, and I didn't know why. My main character was driven to succeed but faced a sympathetic, well-prepared opponent. I was cruising down the 405 one night, on my way to have dinner with a friend who had been a suite-mate at my old law firm. Music came blaring out of the speakers. The song was about Roxanne, a woman who didn't have to put on the red light, didn't have to sell her body to the night. It hit me like a lightning bolt. That was my character: a lawyer who had sold herself out to be a legal hired gun. A legal whore.

That was my BUT. She wanted to be a big-time lawyer, but she was paying a high cost when she represented well-heeled corporate clients who were causing harm. She had to choose between her desire to be a successful lawyer and her love of justice. When I finished that script, I felt lighter about my experiences as a lawyer. I didn't understand why, but the salutary effect on my psyche was real. Lawyering was a skill at which I thought I had failed—until I wrote that script and digested its lessons. Representing rich corporate clients had hollowed out my soul. I came to understand the importance of doing morally right in the world. I was at peace with an experience that had tortured me prior to writing the script. I hadn't set out to learn anything, but the writing had changed my life anyway.

I wrote a script for a prince of Hollywood who had chosen me to do the writing because of my reputation for writing strong and complex women. The story was about sexual harassment in the era before #MeToo. The hero was in a deep hole at the end of the second act: She was on probation at the police force, had no allies, and her partner, who had caused the evil harassment she was investigating, was in the hospital with broken arms and legs. Really, everyone wondered, what could she do now? We were all desperate for a way out of the hole, and I had tried everything anyone had suggested. Then one night, in my jammies, I went to the keyboard and asked my hero what she really wanted to do. I watched as the character seemed to take over the keyboard. She wrote the next sequence by herself. She walked into the intensive care room, looked at her critically injured partner, and punched the crap out of him. When I handed in that sequence, the producer, director, and execs looked like I had kicked the crap out of *them*. But then there was a group deep breath. And everyone broke out into back-slapping happiness. Yeah, it was a shockingly unexpected way to respond to an injured partner. But it was also emotionally correct: My hero had to express her rage at the harassment, and it was bigger and truer than her partner's merely physical injuries. And over the course of the next month or two, I dealt with all the emotions I felt about a rape I had suffered and suppressed long before. I was so much better off for having let my character do what she needed to do.

And finally, I wrote a long fictional manuscript about a woman with no emotional baggage and a man with way too much emotional baggage who were thrown together by circumstance. They had to learn the joys and limits of love in the real world. It was really hard. I put in a lot of car chases and bullets—until I could find the real means of achieving a genuine relationship. I took most of a year off from screenwriting to do it. Finally, my big-time literary agent told me what the next rewrite had to be. She was right. It needed the changes she suggested. But I was anxious to go back to my real job, screenwriting, and I was satisfied with the story as it was. It still had bullets and car chases, but it also had the emotional resolutions that I had sought. My characters had learned what they needed to learn about falling into and keeping love, and I had learned it, too. The piece was a complete success for me, though an absolute failure in the writing world. I had learned everything I needed from it. I had spent 22 years screenwriting and proving how very strong and independent I was. But when I finished that manuscript, I somehow non-consciously knew what mattered in life and love.

A few years later, I married the love of my life, and we have lived happily ever after.

That's what writing to happiness means.

And how you do it.

PART TWO:

WHY IT WORKS

STORY

Writing stories can change your brain and your life. What is it that makes them a force for change in our lives? Of all the magnificent abilities we humans have developed in our long evolution, what is it about making up tales that gives story the singular power it can have?

On a journey to understand the place of story in our lives, we'll look at a few elements. What is a story? How widespread are stories? What is their shared content? How did they develop over time? Finally, what larger purpose do they fulfill?

WHAT IS A STORY?

We use the word "story" in many a colloquial way, particularly when we are referring to psychology and personality. What's your story? Tell your story. Live your story. Change your story. Change your story, change yourself. That's my story, and I'm stickin' to it. "Your story" can mean your thing, your view of your life, the basics of who you are, your shtick. Let's call this the vernacular use of "story," a shorthand that just doesn't help much here.

As writers, on whatever level, the word "story" has a specific definition. Ever since my 11th-grade teacher started a full year of English Literature with a discussion of the definition of "literature" and the class went comatose for the next 10 months, I've been leery of starting anything with a discussion of "the definition," but let's get a handle on it.

A story is the product of a writer/creator/author/storyteller who *selects* a series of events and *presents* them in an *order* intended to appeal to us. In the craft of writing, it is the *presentation* of a character who *wants something* but faces an *obstacle*. In everyday language, it is the presentation of events for the purpose of entertaining the audience. We will spend plenty of time sculpting detail and nuance into these definitions later. For now, the important thing is to notice that a story is *not* a rote recitation of facts or events as they happened. A Story requires that the teller selects the events for their impact. There is an action on the part of the teller, the selection, and an intended audience to which it is directed. Two elements—the *selection* of the events in the story and the consideration of the *audience's reaction*—are essential to our understanding of Story.

A Story is not a list of things that happened. *I drove my car. It was raining. My car was clean. The light was green. I'm at my office.* This isn't a story; it's a string of events. These events weren't chosen and placed in a particular order. What would the audience think of those five sentences? They would be bored.

I drove my car through the rain and skidded at the light when I had to make the right turn. Thank God no one was at the intersection. But my hands were shaking and when I finally parked at the office, I sat in the car for 20 minutes trying to calm down. Then Joe came by and sat on his horn, and I guess I was in his parking space. He was really pissed. I started shaking again and moved the car. Man, I'm glad to get here in the office, even though I'm still dripping rain on the good carpet in the reception area.

That is a story. Not necessarily a good one, but one where the elements in it have a logic to why they were selected, and one that is intended to get and keep your attention. It also has a beginning and an ending.

Story is not what happened. Story is how we choose to tell what happened.

As Alfred Hitchcock said, story is "life with the dull bits left out."

Like it or not, authors have *authority* over their work. They have the power and the obligation to select and rework each event so the whole expresses more than the totality of the list of events. Fact or fiction, a story requires a shaping activity to mold the incidents into a package that transcends the list.

"But it really happened that way!" Students and new writers always think this is the killer defense to criticism, as if reality is somehow persuasive. Reality, or the truth, is not all that interesting. The brain doesn't particularly favor factual accuracy, as we will explore in the section on *the interpreter*.

"I walked the dog this morning" isn't interesting to you. It's not even interesting to me, and I was the one doing it. It is the truth, though. The truth is a list of events that includes the dead space of normal life and the memorable events, which read as if they are unmemorable if they are slotted into the laundry list. If we knew the full list of what happened on, say, the moon landing, we would have hour after hour of guys snoring on their way to the moon. Making freeze-dried food in baggies would take up a lot more room than Neil Armstrong's step on the lunar surface. We would have an hour of interesting stuff spread across several days. We would sleep right through it, and rightfully so.

There is a reason why reality television shows have writers. Reality straight up doesn't interest us. By us, I mean everyone—man, woman and child, all 7.75 billion *Homo sapiens* on earth. We need the connective tissue that gives meaning to the events and thereby captures our attention. We need the events, which may or may not be true, to be ordered in a cause-and-effect pattern, with all the improbable and irrelevant material removed so that the center line of cause and effect fills the entire space.

We all live in a place entirely constructed of events selected and placed in an order intended to get or keep our interest. It's called "Storyopolis." Let's go visit.

WHERE IS STORYOPOLIS?

Storyopolis is a place defined by stories. All of its citizens spend almost all their time immersed in stories. They communicate to their loved ones and strangers via stories. Their dreams and goals, their wants and hates, their accomplishments and fears are all stories, and when they seek change, they change their stories.

The place is held together by the themes of stories, and when things go wrong, they move more deeply into story because that is where solutions are found. Story holds the place together consciously, unconsciously, socially, progressively, even environmentally. Story is the tool for getting along with everyone else in Storyopolis. All of this occurs because the people of Storyopolis know, consciously or unconsciously, that Story is the way we grow to love each other and ourselves.

Story is that powerful.

I live in a place defined by stories. I live in Storyopolis, where the sports are made out of stories and the news is made up of stories. The music tells stories. Children go to school to learn old stories and live in houses that have stories. During the day, dads and moms work in places that make things which have stories or are stories themselves. Moms and dads drive cars with stories to pick up the kids and bring them home from story school to have dinner and family story time. At night, everyone goes to story-sleep.

In Storyopolis, Story is king. Story is religion. Story is a necessary element to sustain life. Oxygen, check. Story . . . check?

Perhaps I overstate it. Story can't be that important, can it? Hmmm . . .

My phone alarm rings in the morning. Half-awake, half-asleep, I slam the snooze button because I am dreaming. No, wait, I'm awake, I'm daydreaming. *"What if I just quit this crappy job? That's it. I'll just walk in and tell my boss I'm outta here, and I'll get in my car and drive. No wait, how many payments do I have left on the car? Oh, crap; I can't just quit."*

We daydream vignettes that are *stories*. I daydream a lot—first thing in the morning, last thing at night, a zillion times during the day. It's never a laundry list. It's always *a story* of me going somewhere and finding out something, or of my kid, or of the world, or of anyone I know, *doing something*. Usually *something happens*. And then, *I evaluate it*. Daydreaming is time spent in Storyopolis.

Am I a slug, fantasizing all the time? Are you? The average daydream is about 14 seconds long. We have 2,000 daydreams *a day*.[9] Wait, that's 14 seconds times 2,000 daydreams a day = 28,000 seconds a day or 466.67 minutes or 7.78 hours a day daydreaming. What's that a year? It's 2,840.84 hours a year, or 118.37 days a year. Life expectancy is 78.69 years, so 78.69 times 118.37 days is a grand total lifetime daydreaming of—ta-da!—9,314.38 days or. . . . We spend 25.5 years of our lives doing nothing but daydreaming![10] We spend one-third of our lifetimes writing stories in our head!

Daydreaming is story time.

But I pull myself out of it. Gotta get to the office.

I get in the car and turn on music. Songs are stories, usually about love and loss, and sometimes about what has or should happen in the world in which we live. I love music, so I probably listen to it more than the average American. That means I listen to it more than five hours a day—or 1,900 hours a year.

Okay, I get tired of all the heartbreak songs; thankfully there's news. News stories, to be exact. All events broadcasted as "news" have been repackaged into stories.

Sometimes I listen to the radio. I don't like it all that much because it has so much advertising. I feel like all I do is hear and see advertising. Is it just me? Nope, each of us is exposed to 5,000, yes five thousand, advertising messages *per day*. That's 1,825,000 messages a year. Roughly 140,000,000 advertisements in our lifetimes.[11] Every ad is a story in some format: a story of a family that loves its safe car and feels great about giving it to their teenager. A Clydesdale saving a lost puppy from loneliness. A place for mom. A drug that will keep you healthy; just call your doctor. I swim in a sea of commercial messages sent in the form of short or very short stories. And so do you.

Ah! I can finally escape Storyopolis in the office. I see my girlfriend pouring coffee, and we chat. Chatting with friends? "Personal stories and gossip make up 65% of our conversations."[12]

Finally, I can get to work. I spend five non-story minutes in a meeting. It's boring as hell, and I start daydreaming again. But the manager up at the front can see he's losing his audience, so he starts telling stories to loop us back in. The whole day goes like this: from daydreams to personal stories to anecdotes to radio advertising to music—almost all of it nonstop storyland.

I spend some time every day focusing on a specific task, and the rest of the day I spend walking, driving, gardening and cooking . . . and daydreaming all the while. We spend a majority of our waking hours in the default-mode network of our brain, daydreaming stories.

Meanwhile, the kids are in daycare. What's going on there? You guessed it. When kids aren't watching a screen, they're playing Princess or Cowboy or Ninja. Children "make believe" they are other characters and act out imaginative stories. Children tell and dramatize stories all day long. By the age of two, children play "make believe" by choosing characters and situations; changing their voices, clothes, and postures; and acting out imagined scenarios of Princess, Superman, Bad Guys, Cowboys and Indians, I'm the teacher, you're the student, and I'm the waitress, you're the customer. Childhood is spent entirely enmeshed in stories.

The day is finally over, and I drive home listening to musical stories and daydreaming at the same time. I try to corral everyone for dinner, but the kids are glued to their screens. My kids, your kids, everyone's kids are glued to their screens. What are they watching? Oh, you know by now. Stories. By the time they're adults, children in the United States have spent more time watching television than doing any other activity, including time spent going to school. The average American adult spends 590 minutes a day absorbing media, all of it composed of stories. Yes, roughly 10 hours a day—all media, all stories.

Thank goodness we can all finally go to sleep. Perhaps to dream. And you already know what dreams are made of. We used to think that you had to be in REM sleep to dream, limiting the dream time to two hours a night. Now we know that we also dream out of REM, and some scientists believe we dream all night. Story all night.

If it's the weekend, we get time for organized religion, all of which is based on important founding stories. Or we can go the "non-organized" spiritual route and meditate, wherein we will spend 20 minutes trying to not think in stories.

My husband spends the weekend watching sports. He watches epic rivalries with come-from-behind endings filled with characters overcoming challenges with amazing stories of courage. It's not just a series of plays in a game, but rather a series of stories.

We all live in this Storyopolis because we all live surrounded by and are consumed with stories. But stories aren't just all around us like bad streaming music in the hallways. Stories are how we organize experience. We understand through story. We pass on information with stories. Through stories, we find meaning and causation, the explanations that get us through life as individuals and as societies. It's hard to see storytelling as a minor entertainment when it is the infrastructure of daily life for an entire species and planet.

The more Netflix, game playing, screen time, novel reading, comedy club attending, and movie watching time we spend, the less "real-life" experience we have. Either we are so evolved that we now enjoy the luxury of expansive leisure time, or story time is in some way *more important and valuable than real life itself.*

This human immersion in story is universal: from the beginning of time through tomorrow, everywhere on the planet. Everywhere, all the time. How did telling stories become the technology of our lives? And why?

WHAT'S IN IT?

Our understanding of the world is overwhelmingly constructed of purely fabricated tales that we can accurately call "stories" or "untrue tales" or "lies." We used those fictions to build worldwide communications and sophisticated cultures and to dominate an entire planet. We didn't get wiped out by drastic climates nor clearly superior physical species. We beat all of the obstacles with well-told anecdotes. Take a moment to consider how profoundly amazing that is. A species tames and controls a planet through its ability to tell good stories.

What is it about stories that makes them overwhelmingly important to all people through all of time? How did we evolve to be so story-sensitive, and what do stories do to deserve all the attention we give them? What do they contain that render them universal and omnipresent?

One explanation is that stories are entertaining. We are drawn to them because they are fun. I'm all for fun, but as an explanation, it's pretty fatuous. The notion that we are drawn to stories because we enjoy them can be reduced down to "We like them because we like them." That logic is circular. If that's all there is to it, some other species would be off somewhere using all the time they don't waste on stories to develop tools and systems to conquer the planet. But that didn't happen.

If we are spending our time swapping stories and engrossed in gossip, we're paying attention to our friends and not the threats to our survival that surround us. Story must provide some evolutionary benefit more profound than a good laugh.

Another explanation for the prominence of story is the decidedly Freudian theory that stories represent wish fulfillment. Given that most stories are about horrible things happening to people, I wonder what Freud was wishing for. More trouble? Monsters in his dreams? Stories aren't so much about wishes fulfilled as horrors realized.

Yet another theory is that storytelling is a good way to spread important information. I find this an appealing approach until I think about it. Making stuff up is how you spread important information? Wouldn't telling *the truth* be more effective than inventing tall tales?

Attempts at rational explanation for our love of story just don't throw much light on the question. Maybe the way to understand the prominence of story is to look at what is in them, instead of what external justification applies.

What is in those stories that we find so compelling?

Stories that last through the ages have two-and-half things in common. We are pretty sure of the first two, and the third one gets only half credit because, well, it's from me and I'm not sure who will agree with me. The two agreed-upon things in common are 1) that they present universal problems, and 2) that they are organized in a common structure.

Stories are always about problems. Who did it? Who is behind the door? What will happen to Indiana Jones now that he has been captured? All trouble, all the time. An event that rolls along without any obstacles or challenges is simply boring and we won't pay attention to it.

Here's an example: "I went to the Walmart and bought new tires. They were fine." Not interesting, and you won't pay attention or remember it. But "I went to the Walmart and bought new tires, but the service guy said my front tire had been slashed by a 10-inch butcher's knife and he wondered who was out to get me." That's the beginning of a story because it poses problems.

You go to school to pick up your child, who had a nice day at school and jumps in the back seat. No story. You pick up your kid at school and he's got blood pouring out of his face. Do you say, "Put your seatbelt on?" No. You say, "What the heck happened?!?!" A problem. A story. It grabs your attention.

We go to the movies to see heroes fight dragons, journalists search for pedophile priests, wizards confront evil. People or their animal representations *fight* for or against *something big and scary*. Stories are always about obstacles to overcome and problems to solve.

Stories also have universal themes.[13] Love and loss. The world coming to an end. Good conquering evil. At a certain age, when your life is well-organized and you enjoy a comfortable relationship, you notice that 75% of the songs you hear are love songs. At least 75%. You kinda wait for the ones about political suffering or technological burnout, because you've settled the love thing, at least for now. Songs are mostly about finding and keeping love.

The vast majority of the books we buy each year are about finding out who the bad guy is. Many movies are about saving the world from a great threat. All these stories are about big problems that we all face in some form. Finding love. Protecting loved ones. Facing overwhelming fears. Identifying the dangerous person in our community. Universal themes.

Stories have a common structure. Stories that have survived over time have a particular structure and architecture. All stories are about someone who wants something, but faces obstacles, until he/she/it either gets it because she learned something or doesn't get it because she failed to learn something. The structure of story is:

> *THIS CHARACTER* wants *SOMETHING but*
> *SOMETHING* else *STANDS IN HER WAY.*

That's it.

Every new writer I have ever known complains that this formulation is too simplistic. Every veteran writer knows that it is The Truth. It's boiled down to the very core with no bells or whistles, but it is also the irreducible structure for every story that endures.

There are plenty of academics and writers who have come up with a menu of basic plots. Christopher Booker came up with *Seven Basic Plots*, Ronald Tobias came up with 20, and William Foster-Harris has three. Georges Polti developed 36, and on and on it goes.

There are a variety of ways to describe this common structure. Joseph Campbell called it the "monomyth." Jonathan Gottschall studied folktales from 48 different cultures and referred to that structure as universal folktales,[14] and there are other descriptions. The bottom line is the same: Somebody wants something, but an obstacle stands in the way. The story, once it gets going, is always about how the character handles the obstacle(s). Every story asks, *Who wants what?* and *What is standing in the way?* This is the universal content of a story.

I can't claim universality for it, but I believe that every story that lasts through time has one other element: It has "the tell." Every story is a delivery system for a message or bit of information that is useful to the audience. Film producer Sam Goldwyn famously rejected morals to the story when he said, "If you want to send a message, call Western Union," and many a sophisticated storyteller never give a single thought to the tell. Nevertheless, at the end of every movie and novel that I know of, if you ask the question, "What did you tell the audience?" there is an answer. In the movie *Rainman*, the money-driven brother played by Tom Cruise eventually gives up his attempt at controlling his brother's trust fund. It's an act of love toward his brother. The movie tells you that love is more important than money. In *Chinatown*, Faye Dunaway's character is killed. It looks like her horrific father has gotten away with it again. The movie tells you that only the rich get away with murder. In *Spotlight*, journalistic determination wins out, but the film also tells us that each of us can make the mistake of ignoring painful truths, so be careful. Every movie has a tell. So does every novel and most definitely every folktale and religious origination story.

We know that all stories are about a small number of issues and that they are all told in a particular structure. I believe all good stories have a tell. But what crucial function does story fulfill to give it a preeminent place in human development?

HOW DID STORY HAPPEN?

Which came first: language or story?

The answer is: the mime.

You know mimes, those annoying people in white face and gloves taunting innocent passers-by in Central Park and other urban greenways. Is there any way we sane people could consider this behavior significant to the species?

A while ago I was lucky enough to be walking to the Louvre in Paris with a good friend. A mime in full Marcel Marceau drag was working the area, and pedestrians formed a loose circle around him. We tried our best to avoid the mime, but he was persistent and, with great, exaggerated steps, followed us as we tried to get away. He got a few small laughs from the crowd, and he persisted. It was a little annoying, and my friend John was good-natured about it for about 20 steps. Then he gave me a knowing look and raised an eyebrow.

Did I mention that John was a comedian on network television with a spectacular gift for physical comedy? Yeah, that's him. The mime kept following us. John turned around and took a few small, fearful steps. The mime kept stalking us. My friend took in a dramatic breath and then transformed into a voracious monster from the frightened character he had embodied a moment before. With high kicking steps, he gave chase to the mime. The mime was surprised and stopped in his tracks. Then, realizing he faced not a mild-mannered tourist but Godzilla in human form, the mime turned tail and ran away as fast as he could. The crowd loved it and gave John a huge round of applause.

What had just happened? We could look at this as a complete story in three acts without words. Act One—the mime seeks out and finds the meek man, who is unaware of the risk the mime presents. Act Two—the meek man realizes the risk, makes a plan, and faces the mime. The mime doesn't change his behavior. Act Three—the meek man reaches deep into his character and transforms into a monster, confronts the mime and, victorious, chases the mime away. The mime is defeated, the man is a hero, and the crowd, filling the role of the community, rewards the man with praise.

My friend and the mime acted out a perfectly comprehensible story with no symbols and no words. The ability to communicate without words came before language and storytelling. Miming, language, and story are tools for communication that developed over time, just as other tools for survival developed over time. A glimpse into the development of those tools affords us an understanding of how profoundly powerful storytelling can be to each of us and all of us.

Imagine distant ancestors looking for food. One day the fishermen of the tribe are standing in the river, trying to grab some fish. One guy—we'll call him Fred—tries a few different ways to attract the fish, such as shaking leaves under water, kicking around to create bubbles, and throwing in berries. No luck. Frustrated, he hurls a stick into the water. Sooner or later, the stick is going to hit a fish in the head, the fish will get knocked out, and Fred will grab the fish and jump up and down with the thrill of victory. Dinner!

More tribesmen over more time advance the throw-the-stick-at-the-fish technique. Someone aims the stick at the fish. Then someone aims the stick into the fish. Generations later, another Fred tries sharpening the stick and increases the accuracy of the spear. A rock shaped like an arrow affixed to the spear is an even better tool. Rocks get sharpened and attached to ever-increasingly lethal spears and can bring down ever larger and more protein-rich food.

It's easy with our 20-20 hindsight to understand how the physical tools for the hunt were invented. What happens after you develop the first spear? A few of your fellow tribesmen copy the tool because they've seen you make it and use it. What happens next? Simply put, nothing happens. This vital information of how to make a tool to gain food and increase your survival can be shared with those few people who are living directly within your eyesight and can see the invention and utilization of the tool. That incredibly small group is subject to all the vicissitudes of life in the wild: animals, disease, environmental disaster, and more.

The odds of the design of a tool surviving the death of the first person to use it is remote. Knowledge couldn't travel to different places or different people. The tribe needs a different kind of tool. It needs communication.

Imagine that our early human ancestor, Fred, sees plentiful fish in the river. He needs to communicate this important information to his kin and fellow hunters. Does he stand there and wait a few thousand millennia for language to be developed? No. He jumps up and down for attention, mimics a fish swimming, points to the water, and runs down to the river. His fellow tribesmen follow, and they have a successful hunting adventure.

At first, the crucial information that there are fish down at the river is communicated through mimesis: mechanically reproducing the action of fish swimming in the river. Fred learns to grunt, jump, throw things, and whatever else works to get the tribe to pay attention. If the tribe is then successful, he becomes more important because he is the source of valuable information.

The more often this happens, the more successful the tribe is. Greed has already been invented, of course, so the communicator learns to elaborate by incorporating the successful return of the tribe and the resultant celebration into his act at the front of the tribe. He will be rewarded with the goodies the tribe has in the form of praise, food, and possibly mates. He has told a story without words, that story has benefited the tribe, and he, in effect, gets paid for it. This is the beginning of the development of communication. And of storytelling.

When sharpened rocks and lethal spears are available, protein-rich large mammals become the subject of the hunt. A few tribesmen try to bring down these behemoths and fail. The tribe learns that they need to coordinate their efforts in order to be successful. Communicating that one group will attack from the left side and the other group will attack from the right requires many layers of more advanced communication. They need abstraction like a future tense so they can attack in the future. They need directions like north and south. And they need trust in the group that the fruits of their efforts will be shared by all. They need more than a mime.

Our predecessor bipeds developed a repertoire of tools for communication: gestures, postures, facial expressions, and sounds.

First there was mimicry, essentially a mirroring of the exact thing or behavior. Later we developed mimesis, a set of physical gestures to communicate directly or *symbolically*. The leader at the front of the group added grunting and vocalization. Signing augmented miming, which then added another dimension: abstraction and symbolism. Grunts and vocalizations became words. Words became language. Then the leader at the front could speak, and a tribe member could *speak back*.

When language becomes interactive, communication is transformed. Words are open sourced. Interaction sharpens meaning and impact. Communication changes from a passive experience for everyone except the leader and into an active experience for everyone.

The ability to communicate in hunting parties and tool-making created more successful groups. The more sophisticated groups ate better, had more offspring, and in general, prospered. The value of communication as a means of planning and passing on essential information—like tool-making—rewarded each successive group. The more successful the groups that shared information became, the more valuable social sharing itself became.

Our tools for communication evolved. We used mimicry, then pictures, then words—each one less effortful, more successful, and requiring just a little bit more brain development and social skill. Language developed because the sharing of information became a highly successful means of survival. More language improves the sharing of information, which creates more progress, which creates more survival which, yes, creates more sharing, more progress, and more survival, and on and on.

Language and story each could thrive without each other through miming and other techniques, and it would be hard to prove that either is required for the development of the other. Some thinkers, like psychologist Glen McBride,[15] believe that narrative came before language, and that "storytelling," in the sense of an alpha standing in front of a group and directing activities through gaining attention and miming, preceded language. Maybe so. Maybe story came first and language came along as an improvement to storytelling.

What matters is that storytelling and language were created and developed together, and the benefits of each are inseparable from the benefits of the other. Language has taken the largest share of the glory, but remember that events without story are just laundry lists of words without connective tissue. We forget laundry lists. Story is the connective tissue that brings forth all the benefits.

Together, *story* and *language* created *narrative*. Narrative transformed not just the hunt, but knowledge itself. With narrative, we can *communicate knowledge and experience*. Instead of the costly system of having to learn each skill by individual trial and error, narrative and story spread this knowledge by telling and listening. Information can thus pass through networks of families, cultures, and generations. The storehouse of vital information expands exponentially. Knowledge passes through time by passing from one generation to another—and from one group to another.

Narrative, by its nature, is a series of events presented in a cause-and-effect pattern. A narrative proceeds in the order selected by the teller for its impact on the audience. Each cause becomes an effect, which in turn becomes a cause for the next effect. It is fundamental to the nature of narrative that there is an order and that it is based on causation.

At first, we could mime a state of facts that existed in the present and communicate it in the present to others. "There are fish in the stream now; bring a spear." Using words, "Hey, fish down there" becomes "I see fish down there today"; it's almost a story.

The communicator learned a crucial lesson: He needed to get and keep the attention of his audience. He could do that by doing a better impression of a fish, or by wearing outlandish outfits, or by extending the presentation with his imagination. Not just "I saw a fish down there today," but using his imagination to symbolically create the idea of fish, of how to draw his audience to a place where they aren't right now, to learn the skills of the great fishermen even when there are no fish immediately in sight but which may appear tomorrow or next week. With language, we could communicate the future: "Fish here later." Narrative allows us to plan into the future using our imaginations.

"Individuals began to learn to imagine events that happened to others and learned how to take them into account in their own decisions. We even began to look at the world not just to behave in it but also *'in order to tell about it.'"*[16] Each of these steps adds geometrically to our ability to communicate, which in turn increases our ability to plan, project, simplify, educate, coordinate, and march forth in progress.

When we could predict the future and describe the past, we could learn and share patterns of behavior. We could fly above the limits of the present moment. Because we could express the past, we could also analyze it and use it to plan the future.

Language provided an impressive list of inventions: narrative, story, the future, the past, pattern, planning, and analysis. But the greatest development that language has given us, to my mind, is that it allows us to have a place called "my mind" and also "your mind." One person can share an experience with another person who hadn't been present and who didn't have access directly to the experience. Think about how amazing a development it was to go from a world where your personal experience is the totality of your knowledge, to one where many people with many different experiences can share all of those experiences.

The melding of language and story gave us *access to the minds of others*. Experience is turned into a collective resource for the entire group. Surely groups who shared information were better prepared to face the environmental challenges and to meet the needs of their cohort. In this manner, individual experience turns into a cumulative bank of knowledge, to be shared by the whole group or tribe.

In turn, we become more social and more skilled at using all the information for the benefit of the group, fostering social agreement as well as tactics and skills useful to the entire group. Narratives can teach common values and skills, spreading information ever more widely. It "makes the social landscape more navigable, more expansive, more open with possibilities for all, changing the payoff of sociality for both individuals and groups. We therefore have a hunger for learning about striking personalities, situations, actions, and developments," scholar Brian Boyd explains.[17]

Our species went from experiencing the world ourselves directly to sharing experiences in time and space with others. The newly shared knowledge increased our success in developing our social world and gaining the resources from the natural world around us.

Knowledge is power, and our knowledge had just taken a giant step forward. And who appeared to provide that leap? The storytellers. The masters of the narrative.

The storytellers were tasked with spreading knowledge through time and geography. They provided the information and were rewarded for it. The competition for these plum jobs was fierce. The communicator at the front of the tribe had to wrest attention from everyone else and keep it long enough to communicate the information. The ability to use the words to get and keep the attention of the tribe was vital.

As competition for the role became more acute, storytellers got better at getting and keeping our attention. We, as a species, developed a hunger for the information the storytellers had—and for the storytellers themselves.

SOCIAL BEINGS

We were always a species without a spectacular range of physical attributes to further its development. We were strong, but not the strongest. We were fast, but not the fastest.[18] Gazelles were faster than us. Wildebeests were bigger and stronger than us. Still, our ancestors, as far back as two million years ago, could thrive in hunter-gatherer groups of 30 members or more because their brains were growing in size and complexity.

There are plenty of theories to explain why we humans were the one species to develop a complex brain. One approach, popular in the second half of the 20th century, held that we evolved ever bigger, more adept brains because we needed bigger, better tools for hunting. By the 1990s, the "social brain" theory came on the scene. It contends that our brains were bigger because our social networks were increasingly complex. This theory even goes so far as to correlate the size of the human brain with the complexity of monogamous human pairing. Like the riddle of which came first, the story or the language, there is a riddle in determining why the human brain grew in complexity while the brains of other species did not. Did we need to be smarter to use the tools to kill larger animals? Did we need to coordinate between larger groups of hunters? Did pair bonding demand larger brains?

There is no absolute answer. The net effect of the development of language, story, brain, hunting tools, and larger hunting groups is that we developed the capacity to cooperate with each other for common goals. We figured out that it was easier for a group of hunters to help each other by organizing an ambush of the wildebeest than to hunt and gather individually. We learned how to maintain kinship groups and tribes and to share our tools, our time, and the spoils of the hunt. We learned how to maintain cohesion. Other species stayed geographically limited to the area of the environment to which they adapted. We did not. Other species developed the few tools to assure that they were fed adequately and stopped progressing. Perhaps other species had found the right niche for their survival. We, however, kept developing tools of every sort.

We learned how to learn. And we learned how to change. We learned how to cooperate and gain the benefits of many minds working on common goals.

Our greatest strength was our ability to develop the ability to change. Natural selection could add high attention, story learning, and the ability to access and digest this experiential reservoir. "Stories contained more experiences than any youngster could expect to acquire personally in a lifetime. Telling whole stories was a single huge jump that potentially allowed youngsters to understand and prepare for experiences that could occur in their own future, the culmination of millions of years of natural selection to achieve experienced adults, cheaply, and effectively."[19]

Sitting around the campfire and hearing tales of obstacles faced and solutions found became the technology for progress. Storytelling increased our chances of survival.

How long do these developments require to spread through a species like *Homo sapiens*? An adaptation that increases our survival by one percent will spread throughout the species in 4,000 generations. Yes, it seems like a long time. But we've been using tools for at least two million years. It would take a relative blink of the eye, 100,000 years, for storytelling to develop and spread everywhere.[20]

I've often wondered how story itself could be so important to a species and to each member of it. But if storytelling was the most effective way to spread information, as it appears, then story is the premier technology of knowledge. It is the key to the whole system of information. It is both how we learn and what we learn. No wonder using story is such a powerful way to adapt and change. No wonder story became central to how we learn and interact with all the members of our species.

It's a powerful theory. Is there any hard evidence that we physically adapted to storytelling? Do we have an organ in our bodies designed to save us from extinction by spinning good stories?

Yes, there is.

Let's look at the sciences.

THE SOCIAL SCIENCES

Writing has been considered soulful for millennia, but in the 1990s it became something more serious. It became recognized as "therapeutic." How did writing move from the arts to the social psychology department?

EXPRESSIVE WRITING

All roads lead to the granddaddy of expressive writing, James Pennebaker, a psychologist at the University of Texas. His initial approach to writing was simple: Sit down and write about something emotional or traumatic for 20 minutes a day, four days in a row, and see what happens.

What happened was the birth of "expressive writing" and scientific research into the impact of writing on our well-being. How important is he? Check Google Scholar. As of this writing, he's been cited in academic research 65,664 times (and he doesn't get any residuals for that!).

Pennebaker was exactly the right man to start a global reconsideration of writing as a means of improving your life because he wasn't looking at writing at all. Two events in his life history opened the door for his research.

Pennebaker suffered from asthma as a kid. When he went off to college, he noticed that he was asthma-free. Then he went home to visit his parents and again suffered asthma attacks. Coincidence? Pennebaker knew better and developed an interest, both personal and professional, in the relationship between emotions and health issues such as asthma.

A few years later, Pennebaker and his wife were having a rough time in their marriage. He was depressed and searched for some way to improve the situation. Pennebaker sat and wrote . . . and wrote . . . and wrote. Turns out Pennebaker was a natural journaler and had a natural writer's instincts.

During the late 1970s, a new PhD in hand, he had studied the health effects of traumatic experiences. He looked at the full menu of horribles: physical abuse, sexual abuse, the Holocaust. He also worked with the FBI on polygraphs. The "lie detector" monitors physiological measures such as blood pressure and heart rate while a person is being interrogated. The theory is that lying is stressful, so a machine that measures stress also measures lying.

An interesting thing happens to guilty people strapped to a lie detector. As the stress increases on the subject, the polygraph operator hones in on the areas of questioning that result in the highest "stress" indicators. The operator uses the machine as a way of guiding the questions to increase the subject's stress levels with the goal of creating so much discomfort that the subject "spontaneously" confesses. The lie detector wasn't used to just detect lies. It was used as a GPS to find the exact location of the subject's greatest stress and hit it so that he felt compelled to spontaneously confess to his crimes.

The cops were satisfied, but Pennebaker pushed on. What happened to the subjects after they confessed? The subjects knew that the price they paid for telling the truth was years or decades incarcerated in a penitentiary . . . *and they felt good about that*. Their blood pressure went down. Their heartbeats went down. Their palms stopped sweating. The act of confessing to felonies *relieved* stress. Confession in the criminal sense was like confession in the Catholic sense: Speaking our terrible secrets out loud relieves us of stress, even if we know at the same time that we were subjecting ourselves to years of incarceration. Sharing, it turns out, is self-caring.

At the time, other social scientists studied how people react to traumas and, like Pennebaker, found that trauma victims who kept quiet about their sad secrets tended to suffer more than others. But it was Pennebaker alone who took the next, magical step in the research. Pennebaker had personally experienced a benefit from writing and wondered whether writing could be as effective as talking about our problems. It took a natural writer to take that step.

In his very first study, he gathered fewer than 50 students and asked them to write for 15 minutes a day for four days.[21] By a flip of the coin, the students chose whether their assignment would be to write about a traumatic topic or a superficial, non-emotional topic. A typical expressive writing exercise asks the subject to write for 15 or 20 minutes continually, four days in a row.

Exercise: Day 1

➢ Please write about an event in your past which you remember as traumatic or upsetting.

➢ Please write without stopping. Do not be concerned about spelling or grammar.

➢ Write from your deepest emotions, knowing no one will see this writing except you.

Try it. Yes, you reading this. Give this exercise a go.

If you tried this exercise, you've gotten through your first bit of expressive writing. If you are by nature a writer, the words probably flowed easily. If writing is not naturally your thing, this exercise is the beginning of loosening up that muscle. Now take the post-writing survey:

Post-Writing Survey

Please complete the following:

0	1	2	3	4	5	6	7	8	9	10

Not at All   Somewhat   A Great Deal

1. To what degree did you express your deepest thoughts and feelings? _____
2. To what degree do you currently feel sad or upset? _____
3. To what degree do you currently feel happy? _____
4. To what degree was today's writing valuable and meaningful for you? _____
5. On separate piece of paper, briefly describe how your writing went. You do not have to share the content of your writing. Rather, write about your experience of writing about your traumatic experience and your feelings about it then and now. Reflect on your experience of writing your story.

On the second day, do the following exercise:

Exercise: Day 2

➤ Today, please write about an event in your past which you remember as traumatic or upsetting.

➤ Please write without stopping. Do not be concerned about spelling or grammar.

➤ Write from your deepest emotions, knowing no one will see this writing except you.

Yes, Exercise 2 is the same as Exercise 1. Did anything new come up for you?

Follow each day's exercise with the post-writing survey.

Exercise: Day 3

➤ Now shift your writing so that you are considering the topic from a different perspective or different point of view.

➤ Write about how this event shaped your life and who you are.

➤ Explore, especially those deep issues about which you may be particularly vulnerable.

Exercise: Day 4

➤ Now stand back and think about the events, issues, thoughts, and feelings that you have disclosed.

➤ Really be honest with yourself about this upheaval and do your best to wrap up your writing about this topic in a meaningful story that you can take with you into the future.

Pennebaker's initial studies randomly divided his subjects into expressive and control groups. Twenty minutes, four days in a row. How important could 80 minutes be?

PENNEBAKER'S FINDINGS

Well, pretty important. Pennebaker wanted to quantify the health effects of expressive writing. He measured it by how many illness-related medical visits the subjects had before and after the experiment. In the six months after the first study, the "expressive" writers had *half* the number of visits to the health center compared with the control group. Immediately after writing, the subjects experienced increases in feelings of anxiety and sadness, but they also expressed a greater sense of meaning. Pennebaker repeated the experiment four times before he published his results.[22] The expressive writers cut their visits to doctors by 43% over both the non-expressive writers and non-writers three months after the experiment. If fewer doctor visits means you are healthier, then these results were a smashing success.[23]

The *anxiety or sadness after the writing exercises*? Intuitively, you can sense that writing about a troubling experience would bum you out. But months later, the subjects overwhelmingly described the process positively and expressed the impact in terms of gaining insight into their lives. The results were not an expression of momentary relief of stress, but rather something larger and deeper: insight.

Social scientists need money for research, and they need measurable results to demonstrate the potential benefits of their studies in order to keep those research funds flowing. Pennebaker's results turned on the spigots of research and hundreds of studies of expressive writing ensued. All those experiments produced voluminous information on the health effects that were the initial focus of all the studies.

Early analysis of how writing affects the body showed that the immune system is enhanced. Chronic illnesses like asthma and rheumatoid arthritis show improvement. AIDS patients show increased white blood cell counts. Cancer patients show a reduction in symptoms, a reduction in overall pain, better sleep, and higher daytime functioning. Relatively healthy adults see a decrease in blood pressure and lower liver enzyme levels. Arthritis and lupus sufferers report decreased fatigue. Physiological indicators of stress also show a decrease. Writing about past failures appears to decrease the stress we feel when we face a stressor in the future.[24]

One explanation for these results is that the writing may allow the writer to adapt both cognitively and behaviorally to a new, immediate stressor. Pennebaker was looking at stress levels at the beginning of his work. He found out, ironically, that writing about what stresses you actually de-stresses you.

Now, after almost 30 years of study, the list of benefits of expressive writing is so long that it makes you want to just go out and buy a bottle and chug that expressive writing right down. Here's a partial list:

- *Fewer stress-related visits to the doctor*
- *Improved immune system functioning*
- *Reduced blood pressure*
- *Fewer days in hospital*
- *Improved mood/aspect*

- *Feeling of greater psychological well-being*
- *Reduced depressive symptoms before examinations*
- *Fewer post-traumatic intrusions and avoidance*
- *Improved social and behavioral outcomes*
- *Reduced absenteeism from work*
- *Quicker re-employment after job loss*
- *Improved working memory*
- *Improved athletic performance*
- *Higher student grade point average*
- *Altered social and linguistic behavior*

Am I saying that a measly 80 minutes can change your life forever? I am completely dubious. If an hour and 20 minutes could change lives, wouldn't the entire population put in the time so we wouldn't have to talk about finding happiness because we would already have it? I had been trying to change my life for decades, the thought that a quick fix could work made me feel, well, stupid. And yet . . . .

One study followed 100 middle-aged engineers who were fired from long-term jobs with a company that was downsizing. Most of the men (yes, all men) had been with the company for many years, and all of them were at that certain stage in life when employment opportunities dry up. All the men were still unemployed six months after they were laid off.

At the six-month mark, the men were divided into an expressive writing group ("writers") and a control group composed of men who either did no writing or wrote about the emotionally flat concept of time management ("control group"). The writers and the control group were asked to write their deepest thoughts and feelings about getting fired. The men wrote for 30 minutes for five days in a row. Three months later, 27% of the writers group had landed jobs, but only 5% of the control group. Seven months later, 53% of the writers group had jobs, but only 18% of the control group.[25] For a majority of the writing group, the two and a half hours they spent writing changed their lives profoundly.

Two and a half hours!

You could do that tonight and still catch a movie.

It works!

UNDERSTANDING YOUR OWN WRITING RESULTS

If you aren't a middle-aged unemployed engineer, is there a way to look at your writing and gauge your own experience? Early on, researchers found that the more optimistic the writing, the more likely the exercise will have positive effects for the writer. Knowing this, try another expressive writing exercise:

You've already written for several days.

Today, look at the events you wrote about and try to see them from another perspective.

> Is there anything you missed that you want to cover today?
> Loose ends?
> Perhaps a different perspective or point in time?

Write for 15 minutes, four days in a row.

WHAT YOUR WRITING CAN TELL YOU

Take a look at your writing, literally, as though it were a picture.

What does your handwriting look like on the first day? Is it loose or tight? Big or small? Careful or explosive? Compare the first day with the last.

It's common for people to become more comfortable both with the exercise and the content of the event they are writing about, so the handwriting becomes looser. Did that happen to you? If it got tighter, did it happen as you went deeper into recalling an event? Did you correct your writing as you went? Did you cross out words, make corrections, or use good grammar? The more corrections, the more it indicates that the subject is concerned with the writing, as opposed to the content of the event.[26]

How was the *content* of the writing? Because this whole field was begun by social psychologists, there are algorithms for everything. How many happy words? How many sad words? And in what ratio? How about the number of pronouns? How many "thinking" words? Can we predict who will benefit from expressive writing before we go off wasting two hours of our life in the search for profound change? Consider these results:

The more *positive emotions* you include, the better. Positive words, like "love" and "joy" are indicators of an optimistic attitude, which is a fine thing to have all by itself. It also allows the writer to acknowledge positive emotions even when dealing with traumatic events and suggests a capacity for coping with setbacks.

Negative emotions? You're writing about things that bother you, so by definition, you are going to be negative. Try some moderation on for size. See if it sticks. People who use a lot of negative words like "afraid" or "hate" don't enjoy great benefits from expressive writing. People who use a moderate amount and acknowledge the feelings do well with expressive writing. It's as if putting it on the page and acknowledging it allows you to move on in your life.

Lots of *pronouns*. Really, pronouns? Yes. Lots of "I" and "me" at the beginning of the writing? Fine. Increasing the number of pronouns as you progress, lots of "you," "they," "she," and "he"? Great. That shift to more and different pronouns comes about when you change perspective. If you start out knowing it is all about you but end up viewing it through other people, that change in perspective gives you distance and context for viewing the experience. It breaks you out of a narcissistic or childish view of the event and forces you to be objective or more adult. It takes the sting out.

Stories help us. Now, I truly believe that the power of storytelling is the greatest power known to humankind, and I'll make my case for that later. For right now, let's acknowledge that the algorithm people agree on is that as you move toward building a story about a painful event, you do a few productive things. First, stories play out with a kind of universal structure and series of cause-and-effect moments. Building a story in this way means you are considering what caused the trauma and searching for ways to escape from the same situation in the future. Constructing a story builds hope. It builds a sense of efficacy because, as we work within the framework of story, we build our tools for overcoming obstacles.

If we use what are called "insight words" like "realize," "know," and "understand," we are indicating a stepping-back from immersion into the event and toward a third-person or objective point of view. Taken together, using story markers, insight words, and cause-and-effect words like "because," "reason," and "effect" show the greatest improvement after expressive writing. The more your writing pulls you toward story, the better writing will be to you in return.[27]

How did knowing which elements indicate positive results affect your writing? If you know that positive words or pronouns or any of the elements directly help you in gaining positive results, does that change anything? When I have taught this material, I tell students that the more positive their writing, the more likely they will have good results. The students then write more positively and have better results. Is this a good thing, or is it cheating on the test?

The answer is yes to both choices. Knowing that positive word choices give "better" results is a priming experience, leading us along the road we would want to go down anyway. It may be cheating, because you know what works, but it also helps you learn how to make it work.

THEORIES AND EXPLANATIONS

Pennebaker had initially theorized that expressive writing worked because inhibiting uncomfortable memories causes stress. Releasing those inhibitions would free up a lot of that energy and allow us to focus on more conscious and pleasant experiences. Confession releases the inhibitions, and catharsis results. Everyone feels all better. Eureka!

This preliminary explanation, called *disinhibition*, was elegant and simple. Suppressing memories causes stress on the body. Release the information, and emotions come pouring out of you. The stress-inducing thoughts appear on paper instead of in your brain, the inhibition is released, and the world is good.

For people who had never spoken of a hidden, dark secret, the theory can work. It's useful for those who have been repressed.

Getting it off your chest is good.

For some people.

For some of the time.

For a while.

It works.

Kinda.

Another explanatory theory for why writing works is that it causes a *cognitive change*, which is the social science way of saying we look at our experiences differently. As we get more comfortable with the writing and the experiences it expresses, we may change the voice we use (changing to third-person) and alter the overall tone (using more positive words).

When we repeat the exercises, we tend to put the events into a narrative form. From a subjective or random order, we tend to put the events into a chronological, and therefore more rational, order. Eventually the events may be presented in a cause-and-effect manner. Each of these changes brings us more consciously and objectively into seeing the experience in a more rational and less emotional way. That takes a lot of the sting out of bad memories—letting the past come into conscious awareness without all the stress.

So then, is expressive writing the silver bullet and now you can close this book, spend 20 minutes a day, four days in a row and completely transform your life?

If only.

The more research that was done, the less clear the results were.

First, the paradigm was developed, not in the real world but by social scientists working on campuses. We are talking academics in search of research money and tenured chairs. As a group, they are particularly defensive about being "social," not "real," scientists. They seek research money by proving that they have "results" and "measurables" and "data you can replicate." These are not the men and women of metaphor or transformational journeys. These are the measurers. They design experiments that can be populated with always-available college students, usually healthy, young, and of short attention span, who are willing to participate for a few hours for a few bucks or a few credits. The birthplace of this paradigm meant the results would be quantitative and limited—not deep, wide, or transformational. We can judge their results with their own tools: small, replicable, and often shallow.

Even with that proviso, the results of all that research were mixed. Yes, many people saw positive results. But while people high in the ability to write expressively about emotions had less anxiety three months after the end of a study, people who were not good at expressing emotional issues in writing showed a *significant increase* in anxiety. Expressive writing was *detrimental* to childhood abuse survivors and Vietnam War veterans with PTSD. Writing is ineffective when dealing with normal grief. People who just blew off steam in their writing without making other changes had negative results. The outcomes were mixed for victims of natural disasters and broken relationships. Pennebaker himself has concluded that "as you will see, writing doesn't work for everyone. The effects are typically modest but usually beneficial."[28] Like other social scientists, Pennebaker and his progeny's pursuit of the measurables leaves them without the deep, long immersion that fiction writers experience.

Is expressive writing just a baby step? Sophie Nicholls, the head of the Humanities Department at Teesside University and a novelist, sees expressive writing as a rung on a larger ladder of developmental writing. Nicholls knows what it means to spend more than a grand total of 80 minutes, but rather months and maybe years focused on writing a single complex story.

For Nichols, "In developmental creative writing, the writer gains some initial release from writing her feelings out onto the page and then moves on to begin to shape her material, learning to craft and redraft it, ultimately developing a new relationship with aspects of her self-experience, perhaps by experimentation with form, perhaps by fictionalizing or retelling the initially expressed material from a different point of view. . . . Significant insights and understandings are gained as the writer works through further phases, gradually becoming a "reader" of herself on the page and developing a greater reflexivity of self-understanding."[29]

I agree. Expressive writing can be just the appetizer for the delicious seven-course meal your writing can serve you.

WHY DOES EXPRESSIVE WRITING WORK?

So why does expressive writing work? I think that it helps non-natural writers to construct a story, and as any natural writer knows, constructing a story makes you make sense of the material. The closer Pennebaker's subjects came to writing a story or a narrative, the more positive were the results.

If you write out what happened to you, you are likely to move toward putting events in a chronological order. And if you have a chronological order, some events will become cause and some will become effect. Things will begin to have a reason for happening.

Maybe other participants in the event will make their presence known, thus changing the perspective of the writer. Adding another person's view gives us distance on the event, which has a defusing quality. Over time, as we develop a narrative, we have a comprehensible explanation and, because our brains have limited real estate, we can take the explanation, tuck it away in a nice, efficient place in our memory, and *stop ruminating about it*. Because it makes sense, it takes up a lot less room in our heads and frees us (and in particular, our brain's working memory) to either think other thoughts or, best of all, have some free space to just be present in the moment.

In the end, expressive writing can produce some miracles and many a smaller change, but the meta-analysis is decidedly mixed. The Pennebaker branch of the writing tree can confuse writing and typing. There are benefits to be gained by sitting down and putting a lot of words on a page, but it isn't qualitatively the same as throwing down a garbage draft and then working the structure to create a well-developed story.

What can we conclude about expressive writing? Sometimes it works. Sometimes it doesn't. Expressive writing doesn't alchemically change your life, though, boy, I wish it did.

SONS OF PENNEBAKER

Pennebaker published his findings, and the floodgates opened. A swarm of social scientists followed in his wake. The movement started with a search for the health benefits of relieving stress and widened to become a search for any benefits, period. Writing emerged as a practice and swirled through the "positive psychology" movement.

Timothy Wilson has made a major contribution to the study of how writing affects us. In his wonderful book, *Strangers to Ourselves*,[30] he introduces his view of the "adaptive unconscious." According to Wilson, in any given second, our senses are taking in 11 million bits of information. No, we definitely cannot make sense of all that stuff at one time. We are so limited in focus, that we actually only use 40 pieces of the 11 million in that same second.[31]

Where does all the other stuff go? Well, without paying much attention to it (that is, non-consciously), we file huge quantities of it in our "adaptive unconscious." It is an evolutionary adaptation in our brain that takes in all the data and sorts through it by patterns, constructs, and paradigms—a trait known as *patternicity*. When needed, it springs into action as gut instincts or flash decisions. It's adaptive because the development of quick responses helped us survive predators and other risks.

Wilson also wrote, "True enough, we are the only species (as far as we know) endowed with consciousness, that navel gazing, contemplative, sometimes angst-ridden ability to introspect about ourselves and our place in the world. But it turns out that consciousness is a small part of the human mental repertoire. We are strangers to ourselves, the owners of highly sophisticated unconscious minds that hum along parallel to our conscious mind, interpreting the world and constructing narratives about our place in it. It is these unconscious narratives that social psychologists target."[32] In effect, most of our opinions and actions spring from below our own radar.

Wilson and other social psychologists are acutely aware of the limitations of *conscious* processing because of the deep well of *non-conscious* material.[33] Their work requires data and measurable results, two qualities that simply cannot swim in the deep waters of the unconscious. These researchers have looked for measurable ways to increase the incremental well-being that can be achieved by the combination of writing and consciousness. In effect, they have given up on finding the transformative because the more primordial material is unavailable to the writer and to the measurer.

Pennebaker's results show we can make changes in ourselves, largely through changing our perspective on past events and thus changing our perspective on our own lives. Many a social psychologist wondered if there was some bigger or deeper way to use writing. Wilson's follow up book, *Redirect*, presents a focused way to use writing to make the life of the writer better.[34] If we can help people by just having them write, what would happen if we direct the writers in specific, beneficial directions?

Could small changes of narrative tone or perspective about an event change the writer and bring greater happiness? If we can we make small, targeted changes and increase our benefits, we can line up a series of small changes and get a truly changed life.

Wilson's approach is called "story-editing," which is defined as "a set of techniques designed to redirect people's narratives about themselves and the social world in a way that leads to lasting changes in behavior."[35]

Wilson suggests three basic exercises in story-editing. The first is the Pennebaker paradigm we've already examined. The second is "story-prompting," in which adults are given a real nudge to get them to view their own stories more positively. For example, a college student who has just failed an important test might think he is a failure or doesn't really understand the subject. What if he could be nudged to believe that if he studied a little harder, he'd do better? If you change that narrative of failure into one of needing to work harder, you have prodded the subject to work harder and, likely, his grades and his self-image will improve. Now he will have a narrative of success and hard work—surely a better adaptation to college than believing he just can't understand the materials.

The third technique is "do good, be good," which is social science talk for "fake it till you make it." Change your behavior first, and your attitude will change later. As any member of Alcoholics Anonymous will tell you, it works.

Taken together, Wilson's techniques are good, solid ways to make small changes in our self-narrative that are aimed at building sustained changes over time. Is this any more than a series of baby steps? Non-replicable results and studies without the deliverable measurables are inherently suspect to the scientific mind. Wilson is suspicious of non-scientific results, seeing them as merely anecdotal bromides. His analysis of happiness and meaningfulness are broad, perhaps even visionary, but his exercises are incremental.

I think of this approach as a kind of "Applied Pennebaker," using the stories we carry about ourselves as the raw material we can use to improve with a good, surgical rewrite to bring us that much closer to the ever-elusive happiness. It delivers the measurables. But, again, it leaves me hungry. Were my problems too big, or were the solutions too small? I wanted more.

HAPPINESS, INCORPORATED

People like psychologists Dan Gilbert and Martin Seligman revolutionized our view of both psychology and happiness by wedding the two.

Seligman is the Thomas Edison of positive psychology and the happiness business. The origination story of positive psychology is that

Seligman and his then five-year-old daughter were in a garden, where the girl tried, unsuccessfully, to get her father's attention. Seligman growled at her and, no slouch, his child confronted him. Did he remember when she was four and used to whine? Yes, he did. Well, she supposedly told him, she decided to stop whining when she was four, and if she could make that change, then he could stop being cranky.

Cue the lightbulbs. Instead of obsessively studying pathology, what if psychologists studied beneficial behavior? Put differently: Stop studying what is wrong. Start studying what is right. Out with the neurosis! In with the smiley faces!

Every psych student could tell you that they weren't interested in the pathology of other people or themselves. They wanted to be happy. That simple. Emphasizing what works makes people happier.

Happiness burst into the culture. Everybody wanted it. Studies were funded. Institutes established. Books published. The measurables came pouring in. And business kept growing and growing and growing. "How to" programs sprouted like dandelions on the front lawn.

In Seligman's own words, happiness had become "Happiology." Happiness was a box office hit. Number one with a bullet. It measured momentary joy or cheerfulness. It became a measure of emotion in the particular instant and not a lifelong or long-term concept.

In popular culture, happiness was a series of hedonic moments. Happiness became a series of quick and easy fixes. But that wasn't what the people I knew were seeking. They wanted something deeper.

Seligman, too, felt the need for *more*. Positive psychology became *Authentic Happiness*,[36] and he found that *Happiness Is Not Enough*[37] because we need to *Flourish*[38] using *PERMA*: positive emotion, engagement, relationships, meaning, and accomplishment.[39]

The social psychology experiments have given us some straight-up bizarre results. For example, we've proved that, contrary to long-held cultural values, having children doesn't make you happy. Some studies indicate that it makes you positively miserable. There's no question that if you test the average parent just at the moment when the kids are screaming at each other, you will get negative results. But our lived experience is that we humans know that our children are extremely important to each of us and all of us. Our children have a singular place in our souls, but the social science metrics told us they made us miserable. Having and raising children can be deeply meaningful. The tests failed to measure *meaning*. And *purpose*. And *connection*. And a lot of other attributes that are prominent in the long haul.

The Hedonic Treadmill

Ever bought something new, only to want the next better one months later? The Hedonic Treadmill is our tendency to revert to previous levels of happiness whether things have just gone extremely well or extremely badly. It is, effectively, the fine art of forever chasing more. Whether it's a new iPhone or a car or a house or spouse, we chase the illusive "more." If you are a car person, a new Mazda is good, but a new Acura is better. After driving the Acura for a while, the joy of having it returns to the mean. It's just your car, not good or bad, just itself. But the new Beemer, wow, that would be great. So you buy the new Beemer, drive it everywhere, handles great, friends are impressed. At first. Then, six months later, the newness has leveled off. At a year, it's a good car, not necessarily a great car. The rumbles start in your head. You like the Beemer; it's a good car. But too big, maybe. Not sporty enough. Yeah, that's it. More sport. A Porsche, that's the one. You buy the Porsche. Six months later, it's a good car, maybe even a great car, but, but, but . . . welcome to the Hedonic Treadmill, where lofty goals and hard work lead to . . . another trip on the treadmill going nowhere.

How ironic that Happiness Inc. was stuck on its own Hedonic Treadmill.

We wanted *more*. More meaning, flow, joy, soul, contentedness, satisfaction, bliss, serenity, fulfillment, levity, jubilation, enthusiasm, and sunshine. We wanted *effectance,* the sense that we are active in our world and making progress toward our goals. We need *grit*, "the power of passion and perseverance" that psychologist Angela Duckworth describes. We needed *PERMA*.

Happiness became an algorithm. A formula. Digitized. Data-farmed.

Most of the major factors in your personal happiness are completely out of your individual control. Here are a few facts: Mostly, you're born with a set point on happiness that isn't subject to tactical interventions. We can't choose to be born with a high IQ or a gorgeous face or a rich family. We can't choose our genes, and we can't choose where we are born or under what social, political, and familial circumstances. If we could choose, we'd probably choose the wrong things anyway. Most people would choose to be rich or beautiful, neither of which turns out to be useful. We only control a small amount of the territory known as our happiness, so we had better concentrate on the things we can affect.

What can we work on to achieve the deeper happiness that we all desire? My personal big four are:

- Optimism
- Attitude
- Meaning
- Purpose

OPTIMISM

Optimism is the expectation that things will go well. Pennebaker saw that more optimistic words meant more positive change. The more hopeful your outlook, the happier your attitude. Wait, if I slap a smile on my face, I'll be happier? That's it, just imitate an emoji? If you are optimistic, then you are happier and if you are happier, then you are more optimistic? It's that simple?

Umm . . . mostly, yes.

Your optimism base line is set long before you were old enough to understand that you have one. If you are wondering where you fall on the optimism scale, take the Life Orientation Test-Revised (LOT-R) or comparable tests and inventories online.

Wherever you are on the scale today, this minute, the good news is you can improve your score because optimism is a mental muscle that you can exercise and build. The more you practice, the better/stronger/ faster you get at being optimistic.

Optimists aren't better at getting through the day just because they can slap a smile on their faces. They are better at finding positive adaptations to life's obstacles. Perhaps because they start out less fearfully, they can engage in problem solving without too much baggage slowing them down. They find solutions faster than pessimists. They get through obstacles more easily because they formulate plans quickly.

More recent research tells us that optimism works because optimists:

- have better coping strategies
- face and confront problems directly
- plan better for the future
- focus on things they can control
- are persistent[40]

ATTITUDE IS MORE THAN A POSTURE

Just how important is a good attitude? Imagine the worst circumstances. Now make them even worse. Can a good attitude change everything? Is "putting on a happy face" a trite cliché or the road to survival of the soul?

Eleven days before I wrote these words, I stood at the entry to Yad Vashem, the Holocaust Memorial in Jerusalem. I was in the middle of a wonderful trip to Israel with my husband to visit my beloved nephew Robert, his wife, and their two gorgeous and lively children. All of us had fallen into a joint familial love, filling our hearts with the joy of reunion. My attitude was "good." As a Jew who grew up hearing stories of the Holocaust, I had to go to Yad Vashem. I didn't expect it to feel good or make me happy, but it's an important passage. I was resigned to the necessity of that moment. My soul was front and center.

I asked everyone what to expect, as I had seen my share of Holocaust displays, and each had reminded me of philosopher Hannah Arendt's description of evil as banal. Everyone assured me that the Israeli monument was triumphant, an expression of the enduring strength of the human soul. It sits on a hilltop in Jerusalem. The day was glorious, with a crystalline blue sky that reminded me of the California desert, with brilliant sunlight and air filled with the scent of rosemary. The entrance feels like a tunnel with blazing sunshine waiting for you at the far end. There's a zig-zag pattern of rooms that begin with bland photos and text from the 1930s in Germany. No camps, no atrocities. They simply covered the earliest political events, all in unengaging black and white.

I lasted through the first two rooms. Even in this most sterile presentation, I was overwhelmed by a depth of sorrow I felt coming face-to-face with the brutality and suffering depicted there.

Could a good attitude help anyone survive such ineffably horrific circumstances? Viktor Frankl said yes. He was a neurologist and psychiatrist who studied what it takes to survive our most challenging human events. Frankl believed that to survive difficult circumstances, we must have a purpose in life. It can be anything, but in particular the love of another person can give you a reason to live. Frankl believed that we can be in circumstances over which we have little or no control, but we always have some control over our *attitude* about those circumstances. With a purpose and a willingness to control our own attitudes, we each find and live the meaning in our lives. Frankl embraced this philosophy and lived to the ripe age of 92.

Could that philosophy possibly survive what I had seen at Yad Vashem? Frankl would know. He wrote *Man's Search for Meaning*[41] while he was enslaved at the Nazi concentration camp at Dachau. His purpose was to survive to see his beloveds again.

When he was finally freed, he found out that his wife, mother, and brother had been killed in the camps. Yet he made it through and contributed seminal works on the power of the human spirit.

Viktor Frankl demonstrated that perspective can, indeed, be everything. His determination to see his loved ones again helped him persevere through horror and later provide a depth of understanding that has been a great boon to many millions of lives. That's the value of perspective and attitude. His own life proves the truth of his work. His opus is challenging to read, yet 12 million copies have been circulated worldwide because of the strength and depth of his message.

Changing your perspective is not like putting on a new lipstick and calling your strut a new attitude. This is soul work.

MEANING

S**t happens.

Then what?

Meaning is how we explain to ourselves what just happened. My closest friend, Nancy, was diagnosed with stage-four breast cancer. My immediate reaction, of course, was outrage that such a brilliant and vivacious person could be struck down so very early in her life. No, I couldn't rely on a religious palliative. That is not a meaningful paradigm for me. But Nancy was a practicing Buddhist who believed in reincarnation, though with some rather idiosyncratic interpretations. In the two years between the diagnosis and her death, Nancy went through repeated chemo treatments and hospitalizations.

She viewed her extensive treatments as if they were a job she was intent on finishing. She never mentioned death or mortality or limitations or regrets. She gave no sign that she knew she was dying. She refused to talk about it. I never saw her rail against her disease or cry. She believed she should live her life to the fullest until she couldn't, and that when the end came, she would rest up and get ready for her next life.

Of course, all her clucking girlfriends worried that she was "in denial," which we were sure was a terrible thing. A few friends wondered whether we should stage an intervention so that she would be "prepared" for her death.

Once, when I walked in her hospital room, she almost jumped out of bed, thrilled to share a juicy moment with me. "Can you believe it?! They sent a chaplain to talk to me!! Like I'm dying or something!" Three days after her utter surprise that a chaplain had visited her, I sat at her bedside for hours. Eventually I had to go home and told her I would be back in the morning. She looked like she was sleeping, but her eyes popped open. With a twinkle in her deep blue eyes and a cheerful smile, she said, "I'll see you in the next life, my sister." She waved goodbye. She died an hour later.

Nancy didn't suffer. She showed us how to face death with grace and acceptance. She believed that she must have learned everything she needed to learn in this life, so she could leave it for the next. Nancy saw her death as a part of a larger process. Her core beliefs gave a context to her experience and allowed her to explain it to herself. She left smiling.

That is an accomplishment. That is meaning.

Meaning is a set of core narratives that explain the ineffables in life: Why are we here? What is the meaning of life? Meaning is the construct that helps you get through the overwhelming questions of life. Religions are the most prominent constructs for giving meaning to our big questions, telling us a story of how the universe works and where we fit in it and providing a set of instructions, for example, the Ten Commandments. If religion isn't a comfortable road for you, consider some other examples of core narratives: Communism. Astrology. Rock and roll. Technology. Each is a belief system that could explain for you why we are here and where we do or don't go when we die. Meaning keeps the existential wolves at bay.

Whichever narratives we individually subscribe to gives meaning to the choices we make in our lives. If you believe that if you live a good and kind life you will go to heaven, then you won't suffer the existential grief of wondering what will happen to you when you die. You don't have to consider whether to be kind or cruel, compassionate or criminal. Your core narrative tells you to be good, kind, and honest—and you won't have to worry. That narrative answers a wide swath of questions we would otherwise spend a lifetime and enormous resources to resolve. These core narratives explain painful events in a way that eases the existential grief and let you move on. Bad events make sense. It's like the drug your doctor would give you for unnecessary rumination. "Here, take this and move on in the morning." Or, "Here, it makes sense, so let it go."

PURPOSE

Purpose means having goals that are worthy of our pursuit—and then pursuing them. The emphasis is on whether, at the end of the long day, you judge your efforts to be directed toward something you truly value.

I repeat, you need *worthy* goals.

Raising well-adjusted children is a worthy goal. Helping others is a worthy goal. Teaching well, getting healthy, personal kindness, all worthy goals.

Big bank accounts, fast cars, promotion at work? Not worthy.

If you were planning on going down the money road, don't waste your time. In movies, we can make up something to have as a goal, like "a Maltese Falcon." It's called a MacGuffin, a stand-in for a real goal. We can all believe that the black ornament is a worthy goal because it is symbolic and metaphoric. Money is never the actual goal at the end of a movie. It's not because, God forbid, Hollywood is virtuous. It's that movies with "heroes" who want money will bomb at the box office. We know for sure that the audience doesn't like main characters who just care about money. As producer David Geffen said to Barbara Walters in an interview, "Anyone who thinks money makes you happy doesn't have a lot of money."[42]

Geffen would know. As of this writing, his net worth is $8.2 billion.

If you want to make money to pay for your daughter's surgery, the goal is helping your child, and that is worthy indeed. Money used as a tool for another person's medical or mental health is worthy.

Money for a Tesla isn't. The Tesla is pretty good for impressing people you already don't care about, say, that driver in the Honda next to you at the traffic light. You wouldn't trade your kid for a Tesla, but you would definitely trade that expensive piece of tin for your kid, hands down. You may say you want a Tesla, but you value your child. The only way money makes you happy is if you consciously give it away to bring a benefit to another. And yes, there's research on that.[43]

Pursuing a goal focuses the mind and the heart. It gives us a reason to wake up. It makes us stop thinking and start doing. We know that doing kind acts for others makes us happier. We know that volunteering is a sure way to purpose and life satisfaction. Pursuing a career for the practice itself (as opposed to the paycheck) works, and so does creativity. So are grandchildren and travel. These are real purposes. Being an accountant because your parents think it will be a good living isn't your purpose; it's theirs. Listening to the parents you carry around in your head to find purpose is a sure way to have a crack-up about purpose when you are 28 or in mid-life.

Goals and purpose matter because they give us a sense of effectiveness and autonomy. Choose your goals, and mark your progress.

TOOLS OF THE HAPPINESS TRADE

Herein the best of the best: the most effective writing exercises to increase your feeling goodness, reduced to the bare minimum few pages, complete with jokes, lyrics, and an ironic turn of phrase or two.

GRATITUDE JOURNALS

These take many forms, but it comes down to this: Write down 10 things a day that you are grateful for. Do it every day. The more you do it, the more likely when something good comes by, you'll notice it and add it to your bank of good things, and each time, you'll reinforce the positive habit of seeing the bright side. The results of gratitude journals are pretty good in the short term.

The long-term is less sanguine. My friend Stella cheerfully became a gratitude journaler. After a month of doing it, I asked her, "How's the gratitude journal going?"

"Great! It really makes you think about how many good things happen!"

A year later, I asked Stella, "How's the gratitude journal going?"

"Great."

"You're still doing it?"

"Nope."

"Why not?"

"I got bored."

Did I say I had this conversation with one of my friends? Make that 10 of my friends. Same conversation, word for word.

Gratitude journaling works for a lot of people. It's a great starter kit. For others, the journaling becomes homework, and the joy of feeling grateful gets linked to the misery of having yet another chore to do every day—and a boring one at that.

Should you do it? Definitely. Will it make you more optimistic? Probably. Will it change your entire life? No. It's an incremental, not global, change. Try it for a few months.

BACK TO THE FUTURE

What would happen if you thought about a future in which everything went right in your life? Sit down and journal for a few days about what your perfect future would look like. Then journal on what you did to get to that perfect place. If you contemplate the actions you took to get to your best future self, you will set out, loosely speaking, a series of steps that will take you to where you want to go—and have the additional benefit of avoiding having to dredge up all the things in your past that you just don't want to deal with. This practice encourages you to change your behavior first, with the hope that you establish a fortuitous beneficial cycle. It works.

WRITE YOURSELF SOME LETTERS

In 1935, Fred E. Ahlert (music) and Joe Young (lyrics) wrote a little ditty called, "I'm Gonna Sit Right Down and Write Myself a Letter." I know this little factoid because when I was a kid and hanging out in my father's office, a guy named Freddie Ahlert Jr. would often be there schmoozing away. Freddie's claim to fame was that he collected the royalties from his father's song. The song was recorded by everyone in a particular generation, among them Fats Waller, Frank Sinatra, Dean Martin, Ella Fitzgerald and . . . wait for it . . . Paul McCartney. I knew it by heart at the age of four and remember it as very '30s, lots of piano rolls, no guitar. Because of this peculiar personal connection, it remained categorized in my brain under "Freddie's little ditties." It was pretty shocking to look at the lyrics decades later and realize I had to move them from "little ditties" to the "wisdom" category.

What would happen if, as the song suggests, you wrote some kind letters to yourself, ladelling out affection and joy for yourself? There are no known studies on the effects of the Freddie Ahlert Song Test in modern social science, but I found it intuitively attractive.

When I was 15 and completely miserable, I would sit right down and write myself a letter. I addressed it to 15-year-old me, from a future happy me 20 years hence. I would explain the things that my future self was enjoying, the great things I had done recently, and my plans for my even more distant future happiness. I signed the letters, sealed each one in an envelope, and put it in a drawer for future perusal and reassurance. When the drawer was closed, I felt that everything was going to come out alright and, indeed, would think about how I would get from the miserable here to the happy there. It was a form of enforced optimism.

Many decades later, a heavy downpour wiped out the back of the garage that held my stash of keepsakes. I pulled out my most treasured shoe box and opened it. Inside the box were the last few pictures of my first true love and those letters written to my miserable 15-year-old self from a happier place in my fictionalized future. Everything in the box had turned into black liquefied gunk. Like a Pennebaker subject, I was momentarily saddened. I even got maudlin. I was in the rose garden of my Hollywood bungalow-style house in Southern California, the thick scent of orange blossoms picked up by the Santa Ana winds, the temperature that California perfect 72 or so. My only obligation that day was to love my daughter and maybe, just maybe, spend some time alone in front of the computer fantasizing about the imaginary people in my inchoate next script. I wondered what I had thought my life would be like in the letters. There I was, standing in the sweet sunshine, in that future I had dreamt of, and I was happier than I had ever imagined. The letters had done a good job. My first true love was still nowhere to be found, and I definitely hadn't traded up from him. But I had written my letters to me and that was quite good enough.

Try writing to your present self from your happier future self. It worked for me. And it's fun. Where else can you be the All Powerful One of your own life and feel guilt-free?

If you write it down, you are more likely to take the necessary actions to achieve the best possible you. These exercises put more than a smile on our faces. They help us change perspective and thus change our interpretation of events so that we take action that will more positively affect us.

READ A BOOK

"Go read a book," said the book writer to the book reader holding her book. Really. An easy sell, don't you think? But why should you read a book?

For starters, you'll live a few years longer. And no, reading the newspaper on your iPad isn't the same. Reading a book increases your life expectancy. "Book reading contributed to a survival advantage that was significantly greater than that observed for reading newspapers or magazines. . . . These findings suggest that the benefits of reading books include a longer life in which to read them."[44]

One teensy-weensy caveat: Read *fiction*. Enter imaginary worlds.

Remember when you were feeling cuddled up on a couch or in pajamas in bed and getting transported into the world of a novel? That joy of leaving your own world and entering a world created just to entertain you is like a soft pillow infused with lavender? Just the thought of it makes my heart feel yummy.

Can you remember the glorious cloud that floats under you as you flow through the journey in that book? Your cares and concerns dwindle as the real world gives way to the fictional one. You get a peaceful time-out from your own life when you enter another's. As cognitive psychologist and novelist Keith Oatley aptly says, "We need not lead just one life: By means of fiction, we can lead many lives."[45] If you can recall such a moment resting softly in your memories, you'll want to find another wonderful book. Reading is self-reinforcing.

Reading makes you happier because it has genuine benefits in the real world.[46] Reading:

- Reduces stress levels
- Defends against cognitive decline
- Increases your empathy; increased empathy creates better, stronger, healthier relationships
- Increases your vocabulary
- Increases your sense of efficacy and relationships
- Stimulates your creativity
- Improves your brain
- Improves memory
- Improves imagination
- Develops critical thinking skills
- Improves communication skills
- Improves focus and concentration
- Builds self-esteem
- Helps you sleep better
- Makes you smarter

Reading fiction makes you a better neighbor and citizen, including having higher levels of donating, voting, and volunteering than non-readers.[47]

If sometimes you pick up a novel just to leave your ordinary world, you are not alone. The burdens of self-regulation can make you want to take a vacation from yourself. By picking up a book and taking on the views and concerns of the fictional character, you leave the stresses of your own world behind. When we are reading, our constant self-monitoring takes a vacation from us.[48] That's why reading a novel reduces stress.

Reading presents a virtual or simulated reality. Keith Oatley wrote, "Think of it like this. If you learn to fly a plane, you would do well to spend some time in a flight simulator because, in the simulator, you can experience a wider range of contingencies, in a safer and more reflective way, than you could if you were aloft."[49]

I did learn to fly, I did spend a lot of time in a flight simulator, and it is like reading a book. Imagine sitting in a thing that looks a lot like a single-seat Fiat 500 with the windows painted grey so you can't see outside. You close the door and look out, and there is nothing there. I didn't think about the windows being painted. I immediately thought, "Wow, this is what it's like in really heavy weather." I was conscious that it wasn't really an airplane, but I was also aware that it was like being in the soup and I better pay attention because I would face this very situation someday for real, and my life would depend on how I responded.

Nothing in the simulator is exactly like what I'm used to. The wheel is shaped differently, the instruments are visually simpler, the instrument panel is higher than on the Cessna I usually fly. It's as if I can experience reality at a 50% setting. It's not real, and it's not make-believe either. It's reality-lite. If I crash, I won't have any injuries, but I'll know it's an unacceptable failure and that I better do better the next time and the time after that until I get it right.

It's just like reading a novel. "If fiction is a simulation of the social world, one can become more skilled in that world by engaging with more fiction. The physical world, of course, is not without its problems, but the world of agents who have different goals and plans than we do is more complex. We operate by making models (simulations) of such agents. The making of these models is a principal function of human consciousness. In our models, we conceptualize these others as both like and unlike ourselves. We are good at operating in this way, but not that good. Engagement in the simulations of fiction enables us to improve our model-making of others and to become more skilled in our interactions."[50]

Simulation theory hypothesizes that we engage in fiction, play, and daydreaming for the same reason: to practice our skills for use in the real world. We go into a 50% setting to prepare ourselves for the possibility of facing the full 100% when we are flying and the soup is real. We become more skilled because we spend time both in the flight and the fiction simulators.

What if we can still have a simulator, but the setting goes to 80% or 90% or real life? Wouldn't that be a much more powerful way to learn and prepare and change? There is a way.

It's not called reading.

It's called writing.

WRITE A STORY

The language of story-telling is often invoked on this trip to Happyland.

We are to be strong protagonists on our own journey. The parallel between the language of story and the language of self-development is a rich vein to pursue. I suspect it is often used as a Tony Robbins–type pep talk, "Be the Protagonist in Your Life! Start Today!" The depth of the parallel is belittled by the clichés.

Narratives put events in an order for us. If you begin writing with a chaotic view, once there are a few events in a sequence, the order of the scenes develops an organizing principle. Perhaps the events are chronological. If you write a story told in the first person, the order may not be the chronological order of events, but rather the order in which they are discovered by your protagonist. Action and reaction follow each other. A change in perspective is comparable to *reframing* a situation, and we can look at it not as the irrational event that made us feel powerless and victimized, but rather as a rational, empowered individual in an objective, rational situation. When we include other characters' points of view, we necessarily change our subjective perspective.

Someone else's perspective can change you deeply. If you or your main character is busy whining about some injustice and another character says, "Hey, you are just whining. Grow up," then in the process of writing the next line of dialogue, you will have to answer that charge. How does your character respond? "I'm not whining!!!!" tells us the character is too defensive. What gives? Or if the character says, "I sound like my mother," well, that's a very different way for the character to view herself. No matter what the response your character gives, you've been engaged to question what's really going on with your character, and you'll have to answer that question to continue in the scene.

When we write a story, we take a series of events and explain them in a way we think someone else could understand them. As we explain these events to someone else, we explain them to ourselves. Conversely, we can't explain to someone else if we don't understand it ourselves. Writing a story makes us explain it to ourselves.

Go write a story.

Follow the rules of good storytelling: a first act that explains the world as it is; a second act filled with plans, obstacles, and setbacks; and a third act that requires a new integration of knowledge and a resolution. Make sure your protagonist learns something, so you can learn it, too.

Write a great story.

GO BIG

Wilson posits that "Good narratives have a strong protagonist—a leading woman or man who takes charge and works toward a desired goal."[51] He explains that we can't all be Indiana Jones or Lara Croft and offers some baby steps to help make teensy-weensy changes that will make us *just a little bit more* like Indy and Lara.

If tiny steps will get you where you want to go, *mazel tov!* How great!

If your life is like mine was, it's a total mess. I hated myself and the world. I had no romantic relationships, deeply dysfunctional family relationships, hardly slept at night, and found my only peace sitting alone in a room in the dark with the computer screen on. A little fluff around the edges wasn't going to help me enough. I didn't want to be a little bit more like a fictional character. I need the complete renovation, the page-one rewrite, the full Monty. My life was a mess and nothing *teensy* was going to do the job. Fictional characters, strong protagonists, heroic journeys, fiction and the Self. These are Big, Fat, Juicy materials. Atomic materials. I had to go big.

Researchers like Pennebaker and Wilson brought together reliable findings on writing and happiness, but my sense is that their scientific method brought real limitations with it. Wasn't there a greater goal than "measurable improvement"? If we want to lead happy, fulfilling lives, are all these measurables enough to fill the very center of us? Is there more—by quality or quantity? I wanted something else. Something whole. Something kinda *om*. I wanted to feel good in my skin. Did we lose that big simplicity when we got lost in the ever-measurable social sciences?

All these approaches make important advances in the pursuit of one's better life. I tried all of them, plus a few thousand more, and I am certain that every one of them is beneficial and that if I kept at it, eventually I would reach my goal of having a really good life and knowing it. But it might take three or four lifetimes to get there, and I just wasn't that sure about the reincarnation thing. I didn't have a long-enough life to work it out with little steps.

10% Percent Happier was a great approach for Dan Harris,[52] but I was starting from a very low baseline, and 10% less miserable just wasn't enough.

I wanted more.

I wanted Happier.

Happiest.

I wanted Transformation.

I wanted Bliss.

JOSEPH CAMPBELL

Joseph Campbell believed that it was our job, as humans, to go out there and live the biggest, juiciest, fullest life possible. He said a lot more than "follow your bliss."

"We save the world by being alive ourselves."[53]

"The experience of eternity right here, and right now is the function of life. Heaven is not the place to have the experience; here is the place to have the experience."[54]

"We're so engaged in doing things to achieve purposes of outer value that we forget the inner value, the rapture that is associated with being alive, is what it is all about."[55]

"I always feel uncomfortable when people speak about ordinary mortals because I've never met an ordinary man, woman, or child."[56]

If you're a writer, someone with a low voice probably has whispered to you to "Go study the Hero's Journey." Campbell invented the paradigm. He was an academic of voracious intellect who studied, well, everything, but concentrated on mythology and came to revolutionize his field.

If you make a three-circle Venn diagram of mythology, psychology, and spirituality, then Campbell would be sitting right in the center, in the overlap of all three worlds. He was a great reader and intellect, and, Thoreau-like, spent five years during the depths of the Great Depression in a cabin in Woodstock, New York, devouring books on philosophy, religion, myth, literature, mysticism, and pretty much anything else he could get his hands on. He then took a teaching position at Sarah Lawrence College.

His book *The Hero with a Thousand Faces*[57] brought his interpretation of many of the sustaining myths of world culture into focus. The archetype Hero, who is an innocent at the beginning of the story, goes forth and faces a series of trials until an ultimate ordeal tests his ability to transform into a stronger, wiser being. If successful, the hero must then return to his original community with the magic elixir—the wisdom he has achieved. This is the "universal structure" of myth and story. Its aim is not just to entertain, but to draw its audience into a world of growth and transformation.

Campbell studied the history of story, and what he found was a universal structure to all stories that lasted through time. If thousands of years of stories through innumerable cultures have the same architecture, then there is something deeply significant in that form.

Campbell thought that the symbols and metaphors of myth were the doorway to spiritual transformation. He didn't see them as literature, but rather a cosmic map of inner and outer worlds. He challenged us to see the biggest view of each life, especially one's own, and to reject the small and the literal.

My favorite Campbell quote comes from his refutation of people who see the world of myth as symbolic or small. If you can't see beyond the literal and to the symbolic richness of the universe, he said, you are "like diners going into a restaurant and eating the menu."[58] To reduce Campbell to the hero's journey is to eat the menu and forgo the meal.

While Campbell's study of mythology revolutionized his own field and several others, *his own* journey was spiritual. Philosophically, Campbell spent his entire life exploring the meaning of a full, abundant life. "Follow your bliss" had many meanings, all ways of finding the fullest spiritual expression for your life. "Get out of your own way" is a pretty accurate rewording. Your *purpose* is to live your life so fully that you are at one with the greatness of God/The Universe/The Mysterium. "If you are falling . . . dive."[59] Throw out all the shoulds, all the proscriptions and prescriptions of others—and their plans and agendas—and be fully in your own life.

Journalist Bill Moyers recorded a series of lengthy interviews with Campbell that were edited down to six hours of film titled *The Power of Myth*. Together with the transcripts of the interviews, they were released as a book of the same title. It all made Campbell famous.

It also made the hero's journey the universal bullet-point list for good storytelling, the formula for successful story writing, the way to make it in the industry, the road to riches, and a lot of other sludge. If you Google "The Hero's Journey," you'll find more than 11,400,00 citations, including myriad sites that will lay out your 10, or 12, or 17, or 22 absolutely required steps of the hero's journey—in diagrams, drawings, spreadsheets, the works. It's as if the less creative among us just *had* to reduce Joseph Campbell's great work on spiritual transformation into an algorithm.

Just in case you weren't sure, Campbell did not write "be sure your Threshold Guardians are placed at page 22." He didn't know what had to happen on page 67, and he didn't think there were 17 necessary elements in a salable story. These hoary commercial overlays have feathered many a nest, and they might work for selling a story, but they reduce his philosophy to the trivial. And trivial he was not. Campbell wasn't seeking a 10% improvement, an incremental increase, a measurable result. He wanted the full glory, the Mysterium Tremendum, the Bliss.

What about the hero's journey? Campbell said, "The standard path of the mythological adventure of the hero is a magnification of the formula represented in the rites of passage: *separation-initiation-return, which might be named the nuclear unit of the monomyth. A hero ventures forth from the world of common day into a region of supernatural wonder. Fabulous forces are there encountered, and a decisive victory is won. The hero comes back from this mysterious adventure with the power to bestow boons on his fellow man."*[60]

Okay, what does that mean? The easiest way to conceptualize it is to think of tribal initiations. The hero, who is an innocent kid, must become a man and a full member of the community. His happy home with mom and the tribe must be left behind, whether he likes it or not, and he is thrown into the jungle of the initiation rite. He's in a forest with no tools and no food, and he has to stay for a week. He has no idea how to do it . . . and no one is going to help him. He will learn, or he will die.

Under Campbell's formulation, progressively more and more bad things will happen, and he will face his own loss or symbolic death. In the Supreme Ordeal when the hero must either figure it out or die, he'll figure out *something*. He'll figure out how to use a hunting skill he's known forever but put it to a different use, or he'll use cunning that he never before had to employ. Whatever the skill that he now understands in a larger way, he comes through this test both the same person and a very different one. He comes through the test not as an innocent boy, but a man. Now his challenge is to return to his tribe and bring with him the wisdom that he has earned.

In our stories, the hero faces a Supreme Ordeal in which her old ways are simply not enough. This is the golden moment in story and in life. The main character of this story is trapped. In previous iterations of the conflict, the character has used previous solutions to the challenge, but the challenge is bigger and the solutions are those of childhood. Old solutions are inadequate and useless. This is the very moment our protagonist is *stuck*. In this moment, if she only tries what she tried before, she will fail again.

In our writing, this is often the moment when we writers quit. We always have a convenient rationalization, like "I have no more time" or "I think it's boring" or "That's what actually happened so the writing of the story is done." If we stop now, we have failed as writers.

A hero knows that this is the ultimate challenge and the she's never succeeded this late in the game, *yet she plunges forward anyway.* On this journey, the hero has faced a series of obstacles, and she has *learned* something. There are new perspectives and skills. There is no assurance she will succeed, but she brings with her the knowledge and perspectives of her previous trials. This is the Golden Moment.

The hero goes forward with only the knowledge and experiences she has gained on her journey and *creates* something new: a new perspective or action or ability, made not of whole cloth but of all her fears and talents gained before and through the journey. This is the particular instant when the hero *transforms* from an innocent or a youth into an adult, when the lessons of childhood become applied wisdom, when there is growth. It is when she, and we, are one with God or the Universe or Whatever That Spirit is, a single being merged with Being.

This is the moment of *Alchemy*. It is the moment when *Everything Changes*. Or we *Get It*. Or we *Grow*. This is the moment of true transformation, from child to adult, from innocence to wisdom, from character to hero. Because it is so individual and transformative, none of the algorithms can measure it. But it is there and it is *the Goal*.

If we go on *that* journey, then we may believe, as Campbell did, that "the privilege of a lifetime is being who you are,"[61] and that "the inner value, the rapture that is associated with being alive, is what it's all about."[62]

Your job is to find and follow your own pathway. "No one in the world was ever you before, with your particular gifts and abilities and possibilities. It's a shame to waste them by doing what someone else has done"—or told you to do, or expected you to do, or the voice inside your head that sounds just like mom or dad tells you to do. No. Your job is finding the deepest best *you*.[63]

"People say that what we are all seeking is a meaning for life. I don't think that's what we're really seeking. I think that what we're seeking is an experience of being alive, so that our life experiences on the purely physical plane will have resonances with their own innermost being in reality, so that we actually feel the rapture of being alive."[64]

What if we are stuck or childish or unable to find our way to that point of bliss? Lucky us. The hero's journey is the map that shows us how to get from our innocence of today to our wiser self of tomorrow. Each journey travels through different territory, but the stages are the same. If we use the hero's journey as the template and don't give up on our fictional story, we will inevitably find both our main character and ourselves transformed and wiser at the end.

Campbell's greatness comes from his philosophical depth, but along the way he taught us two incredible lessons. First, he demonstrated that all the stories we need for our own growth and experience have the same *structure*. Second, he showed us that the wisdom of human history comes to us not on golden tablets, but through a *unique tool—Story*.

The job of each of us is to find the bliss of our life, and the tools of that endeavor are story and structure. The focus of the philosopher kings, like Campbell, is not on the words you choose, but rather the story you tell. The vast scope of a vision that seeks not just the Platonic meme of a well-lived life, but rather a blissful one, requires the great leap from words and language to Story.

Is Story so important it changed the way we all live?

Is it possible that making up stories is so important we humans changed our souls to do it? Maybe.

Is it possible that making up stories is so important that we changed our brains to do it? Let's find out. . . .

THE HARD SCIENCES

D o we have a Storyopolis in our body? Is there an organ that makes and processes *story*? Let's consider the neighborhood pets.

SAVE THE CAT

My dog Bozie spends the night sleeping at the foot of the bed snoring. Sometimes he straightens out and his feet start moving as if he's running. Does he have a muscular disorder like restless leg syndrome? Or is he dreaming of chasing a bird outside at full speed? What is going on in the mind of a pet?

Pets dream. Aristotle observed that "it would appear that not only do men dream, but horses also, and dogs, and oxen, aye, and sheep, and goats, and all viviparous quadrupeds; and dogs show their dreaming by barking in their sleep."[65]

What about cats? Didn't all the bad boys in middle school want to open up a cat to see what was going inside? French sleep researcher Michel Jouvet did exactly that. In the 1960s, scientists believed that all dreaming took place during rapid eye movement (REM) sleep when we are essentially paralyzed, but there was increasing evidence that people moved in particular patterns while in REM sleep. Jouvet knew, as Aristotle had observed, that animals seem to dream and also that the animals experienced REM sleep and the muscle paralysis, called atonia, that goes along with it. To study what was going on in the brain of the sleeping cats during REM, he had to reverse the atonia. He split the cats' brains open and damaged the brain stems sufficiently to defeat the atonia. The research team watched and filmed the cats as they went into a REM state called REM-A, which is REM sleep without the atonia.

The cats were asleep and impervious to the attractions of stimuli such as food or light. But in REM-A sleep, the cats would pop up and meander around, sniffing, smelling, and then, remarkably, cowering as if they were the prey. They also stalked imaginary victims and devoured imaginary mice. They moved defensively, hunted invisible dream-prey, and acted aggressively. They were dreaming in cat-land. And their dreams were filled with problems and fears. While they were sleeping, the cats created scenarios based on their real, awake problems. Then they rehearsed reactions to the scenarios while they were asleep. If they were faced in real life with those same risks, they had already practiced how to react and survive.[66]

These early experiments present several important ideas. First, the cats acted out fear and avoidance behaviors. The cats, like humans, had scary dreams.

Second, and more broadly, the cats were pursuing organized behavior like hunting, hiding, and eating, with no hope of fulfilling the behaviors while asleep. Cat dreams had a lot in common with human dreams, indicating that in both species, the dream state in the brain creates chemicals that in turn help the brain cope with actual, foreseeable future challenges.

Was a dream state a way to practice behavior and reaction to specific stimuli?

With the advance of technology, we have better ways to peer into the brains of animals. MIT scientists Kenway Louie and Matthew A. Wilson monitored the neurons in the brains of rats when they were awake and running in mazes. Then they monitored the rats when they were in REM sleep. The same neurons that fired when the rats were actually running the maze also fired when they were dreaming, and in the same order. The rats were forming a map of the maze and creating new memories in the hippocampus. They were rehearsing their non-sleep behavior.[67]

Zebra finches are birds known for their melodious singing. Researchers wanted to find out whether the birds are born with a song in their brains. The simple answer is that they are not. When the birds are awake, they listen to other birds singing and learn the songs, note for note. University of Chicago researchers Amish Dave and Daniel Margoliash mapped the brains of the birds while they were learning their song, then mapped the same section of their brains while the birds were asleep.[68] The same neurons that were firing when the birds were awake and studying the song also fired when they were asleep. The finches learned their songs by rehearsing them silently in their sleep.

Were the birds "paralyzed" in sleep, unable to do more than fire the same neurons? Some 18 years later, the results are in. Researchers attached electrodes to the finches' vocal muscles and found that the muscles move the same way as they would while awake and singing the songs. The birds can also create new songs by *improvising* versions of the song and can anticipate future notes *in their sleep*.[69]

We know that humans sleep and dream, and many of those dreams are hypothetical scenarios of real-world challenges. Like stories, dreams are about problems. Cat dreams had a lot in common with human dreams, indicating that the dream state in the brain creates chemicals that in turn help the brain cope with actual, foreseeable future challenges. For zebra finches, memorized songs are the key means of communication and survival in their waking lives. We know that zebra finches use their minds and their bodies while they are sleeping to rehearse and memorize the songs.

We know, too, that during sleep, animals mentally rehearse in scenarios they may face in the real world. The brain fires neurons in networks that embody the reactions to those scenarios. Those patterns are learned, and the reactions rehearsed in sleep are available if needed in the real world.

These studies suggest a powerful way to view our human dreams. When we dream, we present ourselves with versions of real-world problems, and our brains fire neurons in a pattern or network that embodies reactions to these challenges. We practice and learn optimal reactions to actual threats. We are *training* our responses to real-life challenges while we are asleep. The more we train, the better and more efficient we get and the more likely we will succeed in real life.

We have a physiological mechanism that creates scenarios and narratives when there are no significant inputs from the external world. Our brains are *story machines* that go to work when we are asleep.

This research suggests two important conclusions. First, our dreams are a form of simulation of the real world where we rehearse our behaviors to improve our skills in real life.

Second, we generate these valuable simulations with the basic units of universal story structure from deep within our non-conscious brain. We are generating stories in which we are the main characters, the protagonists, and we are facing the obstacles we ourselves envision we must overcome. No wonder stories are so powerful. We have a Storyopolis in our brains.

What else is going on up there?

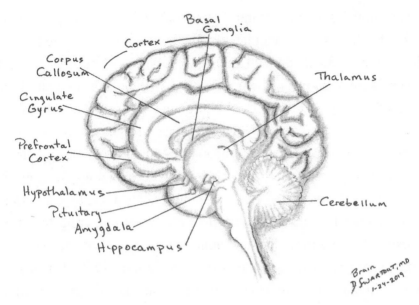

The Brain. Drawing by Dennis Swartout, M.D.

MEET YOUR BRAIN

Is there a little man up at the top of your head giving directions and running the internal show? Each historical age envisions the brain in its contemporary terms. During the Victorian era, it was seen as a bunch of pipes in a big house. During the later Industrial Age, we believed that the human brain was an overburdened bureaucratic office run by a slightly overweight guy with a large bald spot and a big file cabinet.

An extension of this fantasy was that somehow our memories were kept in those file cabinets. When we remembered something, the file was opened and a detailed, perfect re-creation of a past time was available. Once we people reached maturity, we had our given set of neurons that would last us throughout our lives, never to change. We believed in the perfection of recall, the power of the little man, and the mechanical organization of the brain. We believed in a hardwired brain.

Then we learned a thing or two and threw out all that junk thinking. So, what's going on in your brain?

Your brain is not your mind. Your mind may live in your brain, or not, but by "brain" we mean the organic material that is in your skull. What you individually do with all that matter is a very different subject.

The human brain is comprised of a few pounds of soft tissue contained in and protected by the structure of the head, your skull. Until the late 1800s, the only way to research human brains was to harvest dead people, crack open their skulls, and look at the goo inside. We historically had a good time inventing explanations for how the goo affected our lives (*see*, e.g., phrenology). Then one day, a railroad worker named Phineas Gage and his crew were preparing to set off explosives to break through rock. Phineas turned his head, the explosion sparked unexpectedly, and a three-foot-long, one-and-a-half-inch-wide iron javelin blasted through the front of his brain and lodged itself in his skull the way William Tell's arrow split an apple. And Phineas lived.

Phineas was a walking science project, allowing us to see what happens when that particular piece of the brain ceases to function in an otherwise normal person. Phineas became detached, rude, and a general pain in the butt. He left his wife and family and wandered around the countryside.

Because we could see both where the brain was damaged and what behaviors changed, we could see that different functions were localized into specific areas of the brain. Phineas lost what we now call the "prefrontal cortex." That area of the brain controls "executive functioning," which helps make decisions and filters emotional impulses.

Phineas was a pain in the butt because his prefrontal cortex was damaged and couldn't do its job. His injury showed us that brain functions can be *localized* into specialized areas and that injuries to the brain can change personality. His case also illustrates how few tools we had to research the functioning of the human brain. Well into the 20th century, scientists still had to await the "happy accidents" of patients getting specific physical injuries which doctors could connect with specific brain areas in order to make any advances in our knowledge. What have we learned?

Your brain weights about three pounds and has about 1.1 trillion cells. The most important cells are the neurons. The function of the neurons is to encode or register information and pass it along into a network of neurons in the brain. Neurons transmit information by electrochemical processes over a junction between neurons called a "synapse."

A neuron is like a tree: It has a body or trunk, but the work of the neuron is done by an extensive tangle of dendrites that look like the branches and twigs of a tree and which stretch out to make connections with other neurons that similarly look like the branches and twigs of the next closest neuron-tree.

A neuron can fire or not fire. That's it. Like the zeros and ones in computer coding, each neuron is either firing or not firing. When a particular group of neurons fire, a sequence of neuronal firings creates a particular pattern that, for our purposes, is the specific piece of information in your brain. When a child first puts his or her hand on a hot stove, a lot of things happen, among them the firing of neurons that register something like "stove hot!" It's an intense, traumatic sensation for the child, and plenty of neurons fire off, sending the message to get that hand off the stove and also to make the connection that stove hot means pain, let's not do that again. That set of information spreads through a network of neurons in the brain.

In order for our brains to process all the information we use, we need enormous numbers of neurons to make enormous numbers of different patterns.

We each have about a hundred billion neurons.

Each neuron makes between 1,000 and 10,000 connections.

Each neuron has about 10,000 synaptic inputs, or about a quadrillion synapses.

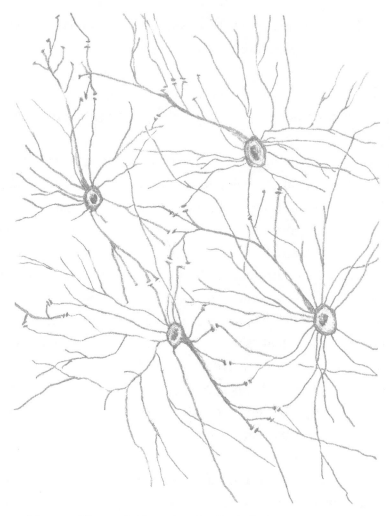

Neuron Network. Drawing by Dennis Swartout, M.D.

Each neuron fires between five and 50 times a second.

A moment for the math. One hundred billion neurons with 10,000 synaptic connections firing, say, 25 times per second, 60 seconds per minute, 24 hours a day. *The number of possible combinations of neural firings is 10 to the millionth power.* And each one of those firings carries layers of significant information in your brain. If the numbers are incomprehensible, here's a visual of the number of neuronal connections in your brain: If each connection was a grain of sand, your brain has enough connections, or grains of sand, to fill a beach 100 meters long by 50 meters wide by 25 meters deep,[70] or 328 feet long by 164 feet wide by 82 feet deep.

The power of the neurons comes from the number and strength of the connections to other neurons. The firing of the neurons establishes patterns or networks firing together, and those patterns in effect represent the *things* or *thoughts* in your brain. So all of those neurons have all of those potential connections in all of those patterns. That's how we *think* and *remember* and *learn*.

The area between two dendrites reaching for each other is empty space. The cells release chemicals to move the *message* from one cell to another. To help the process along, neurotransmitters shoot out from the sending cell toward the receiving cell. Think of the neurotransmitters as chemical couriers. They shoot out, land their message, and are reabsorbed back into the original neuron. Neurotransmitters are singularly important not only in understanding the brain, but in understanding why writing can change your life. When your friend says the chemicals in his head made him do this or think that, he's probably talking about neurotransmitters.

Our autonomic nervous system has a *sympathetic branch* and a *parasympathetic branch*. The sympathetic branch is the arousal department. Your great-great-great forefather walking in the hot jungle hears the soft sound of an animal stepping on deep grass. It could be the wind. It could be a tiger. If it's a tiger, he has to get his act together really fast or he is dinner. What happens in your brain? Your sympathetic nervous system shoots out the neurotransmitter norepinephrine, which turns on your fight-or-flight reaction, sending your body into full alert. Heartbeat up, blood circulation up, attention up.

The other branch is the parasympathetic branch, and its job is to monitor and keep your normal physical functions like digestion running smoothly. When the norepinephrine gets shot out, your parasympathetic system slows down. If the tiger runs away from us, we think "oh, good!" and we calm down. The parasympathetic system shoots some acetylchonline out, and your normal body regulators come back online.

Under stress, your hypothalamus dumps a dose or two of adrenaline into the chemical stew. You feel a surge of energy because you've triggered a fight-or-flight state. Then cortisol flies out. You're ready to respond to an immediate threat for a short period of time.

What happens when your brain receives a Story or an event from outside of you? A series of chemicals are discharged.

First cortisol is released. When something happens that warrants our attention like a scary sound or thunder in the distance, the cortisol makes us pay attention. Writers often begin stories with action or tension sequences. We do this because we want the reader to pay attention and those sequences cause the cortisol to spray out.

Next some dopamine gets excreted. Dopamine is the pleasure pill, the "Hey, I like this" juice in the reward system. Dopamine tells you to take action. If you are engaged with a story, the dopamine tells the brain to follow the story, that it matters, and that it's fun. It rewards you for keeping on task.

If there is a character we like, we might get a shot of oxytocin. This little gem of a chemical tells you that you are connected to someone. When mothers and fathers first see their brand-new baby, boom! Oxytocin takes over the brain. Falling in love, human-to-human, and just want to cuddle all day? Thank your oxytocin.

Our brains respond to external stimuli as varied as lions and stories, with exquisitely intricate, almost symphonic chemical responses. Our brains started out quite simply and developed into this complex system.

How did that complexity develop?

Very slowly.

TRIPLEX BRAIN

Over enormous expanses of time, the human brain evolved in structure, in functionality, and from bottom to top.

The first area is the brain stem, or *lizard brain*. It keeps your body functioning by regulating your basic physiological functions like heartbeat, breath, and sleep. When the girlfriend insults her idiot boyfriend for acting from his lizard brain, she's saying he's on automatic pilot, breathing but not thinking, and his brain stem is in charge. Because we are born with a fully operational brain stem, our instincts are loaded and ready to go.

Sitting atop the brain stem is the *mammalian brain*, a structure found in many mammals, including your dog or cat. My dog Bozie isn't that bright in human terms. But he has superb hearing, can feel a thunder storm coming from three hours away, and has a perfect memory of every human who has ever given him a treat. His brain is exquisitely tuned to address his physical needs. He knows everything he needs to about getting food, fighting off aggressors, and fleeing danger. He hones his skills by practicing while he is dreaming. He's a survival machine.

In humans, the mammalian brain includes the amygdala, which is sensitized to expressions of emotion like anger, rage, and pleasure and the formation of memories generated by or through these emotions. The hippocampus turns the momentary events we experience (short-term or working memory) into long-term memories. The thalamus is the control room for all your senses. These are fundamental and emotional functions that reside below our conscious brain and have major implications for how we consciously approach our world.

The functions of the mammalian brain are not conscious, and we civilians think of them as reactive: The world appears to us to act upon us, and we react without thought or understanding. Bozie doesn't know how a thunderstorm is created, but he knows his best response is to run under the bed.

In humans, as this area of the brain is developing, it takes in experiences and emotions from the outside, forming the patterns to be used in the future. This is called *conditioned learning*. Once it has developed, we use those patterns to act and react to the outside world. In short, we create emotion and memory in a basic brain structure that is developmentally achieved in our pets. As adults, we will experience and regulate emotions from this non-cognitive, Pavlovian space. We react "irrationally" because our reactions were formed before we had a rational brain. When mature adults "act out" and "behave like children," this part of the brain has taken over.

The third part of the brain is the *cortex*, the most recent and most elegant part of the human brain. The cortex sits at the top of the brain and is reflexively credited for what makes us human. This is where we *think* and *reason*. It takes decades to grow to full functioning.

The way the brain evolved has important implications for our efforts to improve our own lives. Timothy Wilson explains that "the architecture of the mind is such that a great deal of mental processing occurs outside of conscious awareness, not because thoughts and feelings are threatening to people, but because that is how the mind has evolved to work. The specific theories differ in their descriptions of the exact nature of the two systems (e.g., unconscious, automatic, slow learning, associative, implicit for one [and] conscious, controlled, fast learning, propositional, explicit for the other). For our purposes, the key distinction is that one system is less available to introspection, and it is up to the other to make conscious inferences about oneself that may or may not be accurate."[71]

This evolution of the brain was progressive. With each new development, our brains got physically larger. The birth canal did not grow in a similar fashion. Lower species develop their brains before birth and are born ready to face the world and its survival challenges. At some point, our developed brain was simply too big to make the journey out of the birth canal. What to do?

One possible adaption that could accommodate larger brain size would be a larger birth canal, although that would present its own challenges. Another possibility would be for offspring to leave the mother's body when the brain was still a manageable size and let it grow to full size after birth. Over time, the course of childbirth adapted to the challenge by humans giving birth to offspring who had underdeveloped brains and were not ready to survive on their own at birth. Our brains continue to grow well after birth and, as any parent can tell you, the brains of human offspring aren't fully developed until into their 20s.

Our physical adaptation to the larger human brain was for the brain to grow after it left the birth canal. The unintended consequence? We invented childhood. That's right, fish are born ready to swim, cows are born ready to walk, humans are born ready to . . . be taken care of.

Another consequence of this adaptation was that we invented beings we call children who simply cannot survive without an attached caretaker adult. Their brains were not ready for prime time. And their bodies weren't, either. The ordinary traumas of survival were visited upon these beings before they had the equipment to deal with them. Those traumas were incomprehensible to their undeveloped brains. Another unintended consequence of the evolution of the brain? We invented neurosis.

Why is the triplex brain of any interest to us in our quest for a better life? Because the nature and structure of how our brains developed tells us crucial information about how we can survive and thrive. Our pets dream from their mammalian brains . . . and so do we. Our dreams have relevant content for us, but our reasoning facilities, located in our cortex, aren't available during the dream state. Dreams can be difficult to understand because the "understanding equipment" in the cortex is offline when the "creating-the-dream equipment" in the mammalian brain is at work.

Traumas that occur before the full development of the cortex become fixed and operative in the primitive sections of our brain. We can apply all the reasoning we may want, but the trauma and the reaction to it are already fixed in a place where words and reasoning essentially don't work. It's not a bad place—it's a rich repository of memories and facilities—but it is *non-conscious*, so our conscious efforts to deal with the material are like bringing a dictionary to a knife fight. It's just the wrong tool for the job.

To the extent that we want to work with material stored in the more primitive areas of our brains, we need to consider less verbal, less focused, less reasoned approaches. Meditation can work this way. Fiction can work this way.

When we are writing, the materials we use—the protagonist, the problem, or the terrible obstacle—will come from this non-rational place, if we let them. Unconscious traumas come forward as dreams or ideas not apparently tethered to reality. We can call it fiction or a story. In this creative space, the issues that were formed before we had a consciousness to address them come bubbling up and present themselves for our conscious consideration as authors.

Then we work to discover answers. We think about it, map it, brainstorm it, and apply our finest cognitive tools to address the obstacles our unconscious has sent us as *ideas*. If we write fiction, we are forced to find resolutions to these previously non-conscious problems.

The solutions we find rationally were not available to us when the traumas were formed. We are writing fiction, and we can choose to believe that everything we are facing in the story is make-believe. Whether fact or fiction, your job as the author is to finish the story, and to do so, you must find the resolution to the problem. When you find the solutions in fiction, you have found answers to problems that are similar to problems you had before you had a rational mind. When we solve the dilemma for our protagonist, we apply our highest cognitive functioning to solving a problem we generated from deep in our own non-conscious minds.

TECHNOLOGY

Neuroscience is relatively new. For centuries, we studied how brains worked mostly by waiting for people to die and then cracking open their skulls and examining the then detached grey matter. But people kept dying from unrelated problems in inconvenient places. The cracked-head business was slow, and research hardly advanced. For example, it took until 1904 for the first scientists to even conceive that a thought or a memory had a physical state at all. Well into 1950s, scientists, both mad and otherwise, were placing electrodes into animal brains and hoping that if they watched carefully enough for long enough, they would find out something about how the brain "learned."

Karl Lashley was a prominent psychologist and researcher who spent 30 years recording information from rats in mazes, searching for the place in the brain where the groups of neurons that held a memory, called an "engram" or "memory trace," were formed and stored. Lashley was both brilliant and possessing of an intoxicating sense of humor. After decades of tireless research to find the physical evidence of a memory trace, he made his concluding report to the ever-sober scientific community: "This series of experiments has yielded a good bit of information about what and where the memory trace is not. It has discovered nothing directly of the real nature of the memory trace. I sometimes feel, in reviewing the evidence of the localization of the memory trace, that the necessary conclusion is that learning is just not possible. It is difficult to conceive of a mechanism that can satisfy the conditions set for it. Nevertheless, in spite of such evidence against it, learning sometimes does occur."[72] Lashley concluded that there wasn't a memory factory located in a specific site in the brain, but a network widely distributed in the brain. He was partially right.

Donald Hebb was a scientist exploring how rats learned to run a maze. Hebb had plenty of rats in the lab and would bring a few home for his kids to play with as pets. When those pet rats were returned to the lab, Hebb noticed that they out-performed their in-lab colleagues. He concluded that the pet rats had been in a richer environment and therefore had more developed skills to face their life tasks. He hypothesized that the memories that were encoded as connections between the neurons were reinforced by simultaneous firing, but he said it better: Hebb's rule is that *neurons that fire together wire together*. The more we do the same act or think the same thought, the stronger the neuronal network representing or creating that act or thought becomes. The more you do it, the stronger it is. Hebb was way ahead of his own colleagues because he had touched on rich environments, brains that wire together fire together, and the inklings of plasticity. Hebb's rule is important in memory and in neuroplasticity.[73]

Positron-emission tomography (PET scan) was the first major leap in brain research because it allowed us to look into the brain without cracking the skull open. A "tracer" is introduced into the body, usually intravenously. As the tracer is metabolized in the body, the PET scanner detects the tracer's distribution through the body, giving us a picture of where the tracer has gone within the body. By the 1990s, PET scans were common in research.

Magnetic resonance imaging (MRI) brought a major advance in the technology. The MRI makes use of strong magnets to change the orientation of water molecules in our bodies, which in turn produces weak radio signals. The basis for the workings of the MRI is that any time a charged particle (proton or electron) undergoes acceleration, a radio wave is emitted. The human body is made up mostly of water, which is made up of one negatively-charged oxygen atom and two positively-charged hydrogen atoms. Applying a strong magnetic field causes the water molecules to align with that field: The positively-charged hydrogen atoms orient toward the negatively-charged magnetic pole, and vice versa. As the magnets in the MRI machine change polarity, which we recognize as the loud clatter made by the machine, the water molecules spin to realign with the fields. This results in acceleration and deceleration of the charged atoms of the molecule, causing radio waves to be produced, which the machine detects, and through computer manipulation, constructs into an image of, for example, the brain or the lungs.

Functional MRI (fMRI) uses the same principles and takes advantage of the fact that red blood cells with and without oxygen are different by about 20% in their response to a magnetic field. This results in differences in the amount of signal from the two states of red blood cells in an fMRI. The areas that have changes in blood flow and which are deoxygenating the blood faster show up more intensely. Therefore, in an fMRI, areas that are using more oxygen and creating more red blood cells without oxygen show up more intensely. Since we know that oxygen use and activity in the brain are related, areas that are more active show up more intensely. This allows us to map the activity in the brain.

MAKING MEMORIES

To most of us, a *memory* is our recall of an event or fact from our past. To our strange neuro-scientific sisters and brothers, memory is the ability to encode, store, retain and recall information within the brain. *Learning* is the process of taking in information and turning it into a memory. How does that happen? New information comes into your brain through all of your senses. First your brain has to *encode* it into a form useable within the brain. This encoding is roughly comparable to inputting computer information into zeros and ones. Then the information is *stored away* for future use. If you need the information at a later time, it is *retrieved*. Lastly, there is a spectacular *surprise ending*, but let's forget about that for now.

Imagine you are at a gathering at a friend's house. Your friend has just been fired and a few people come over to offer support. You see an interesting guy talking with your friend Joe over near a potted ficus tree with dead leaves on it. There's a table stacked with beers and a jar labelled "donations" with a few singles in it next to the ficus. It's warm and dry in the backyard, there's pizza sitting on a table getting eaten by flies, and some aggressive music is screeching out of a small speaker with no bass. This spray of information, the smell, the sound, the sight of the guy, the fabric of friendships, and all the other details come in through your senses into your brain.

Sensory information is processed in many different areas of the brain. Each area is highly specialized, and they are distributed throughout the brain. To get each tiny bit of information to the right processing point for encoding, all the information is essentially thrown into a Cuisinart food processor, chopped to smithereens, and thrown out to the processing centers throughout the brain. The point of the Cuisinart effect is to separate the information into the most exact bits possible so the highly specialized centers can encode it that precisely.

It moves along the neuronal networks made up of those gazillions of connections.

This mechanism is so specific that, for example, the notecard that said "donations" that you didn't pay any attention to, would be processed by the color of card, by the curves in the handwriting, the meanings of "donations," the colors of the background and foreground, the ink, lighting, shadow, words. Even the vowels and the consonants in "donations" are stored in separate parts of your brain. This highly specialized system ensures that encoding is spread all over your brain.[74]

Your brain takes in each little bit of information and encodes it electrochemically onto the appropriate neurons and communicates it to other neurons via the synapses. The synapses in turn connect with innumerable other neurons.

What happens next? As soon as the information is encoded, it goes into what is known as *working or short-term memory*. By either name, it's your friend. Although it sounds like it is a place, it is actually a process that takes place in a variety of centers in your brain. It lives entirely in the *now*, can last 20 to 30 seconds, and holds about seven pieces of discreet information. If something significant happens to you, you might tell a friend that you "need to process it," which means you need to put it together in a way that makes it meaningful to you. That may take a minute or two, after which you can tuck it away and move on. Your working memory needs to process the stimuli it receives in the same way.

Once you've finished processing the data, it departs the short-term memory. It either gets thrown away or it goes into *long-term memory*.

The new *neuronal pattern* of firings in the areas throughout the brain *is* the memory. New learning is wired in the form of a web of electrochemical connections.

Memories come in a multitude of shapes, strengths, sizes, and classifications. Here are a few ways to categorize memories:

- Conscious
- Non-conscious
- Declarative
- Implicit
- Explicit
- Procedural
- Episodic
- and many more

Most of us learned a very simple model of memory: conscious and unconscious. "Conscious memory" is stuff you can recall at will. "Unconscious memory" is the stuff that you mostly are unaware of, and when it hits your conscious awareness, you think, "Where the heck did that come from!?"

Another model for memory is the Freudian holy trinity, in which the *superego* stores all the shoulds and rules of decent behavior. The *ego* rules our conscious decision making and interaction with the real world. The *id* is the repository of unconscious desires and instincts.

The Freudian approach fostered the belief that the unconscious was the land of sordid desires and unspeakable hungers. It was where our socially reprehensible cravings waited for a chance to bubble up into our behavior. If you wanted to sleep with your mother or kill your brother, those desires were supposed to stay in the unconscious. To protect yourself from the unspeakable, your ego and superego had the job of repressing those desires, thus keeping them unconscious. The result of the Freudian influence is that we all came to view our unconscious as a frightening, risky piece of business, and our job, throughout our lives, was to keep that nasty stuff down in the deep, unknowable swamp of our unfindable thoughts.

Fortunately, we've made some real progress on this. Remember Wilson's 11 million bits of information that our brains take in every second?[75] Remember that we process only about 40 bits of that information? What happens to the other 10,999,960 bits of information? Say hello to your non-conscious memory, adaptive unconscious, and, well, your post-Freudian unconscious. All that material gets run through the brain machine and gets sorted out and filed away for use when we need it. But it doesn't become conscious memory. It becomes the stuff we use all the time but never think about—like how to drive a car or ride a bike. Directions to the office. Two times two. Putting on eyeliner. Think of *unconscious memory* as where you store the behaviors that you had to learn how to do but which you now just do without thinking.

We don't think about it because . . . that's right, *it isn't conscious*. It's there. It's useful. It just isn't stuff we ordinarily bring to awareness. It's non-conscious, but it isn't the cesspool Freud predicted. It's much friendlier than that, and it allows us to function in the real world while we are focusing consciously on more important stuff.

Those millions of bits of information cause all those kazillions of neurons to fire chemicals and electricity down through the synapses, forming networks of cells switching momentarily on. And then off. The key to understanding the brain, for us non-science people, is to see the brain as an infinite number of networks of information that are held in instantaneous patterns of networks. Neurons are ineffably small, but they come in groups of millions and billions.

If we have kazillions of neurons, how many neurons do we need to make a memory?

Back in the 1960s, before we were good at seeing the inside of our own brains, a cognitive scientist named Jerry Lettvin theorized that our neurons were so specific that a single neuron could contain the memory of a familiar person, say your grandmother. That cell became known as "the grandmother cell" because Lettvin thought that a single cell could specifically be "memories of this specific person, Grammy."

The grandmother theory—one neuron, one vote—didn't make it to the 1970s before the ridicule ensued. Simplistic! Stupid!

Then Jennifer Aniston arrived. Yes, that Jen. Good hair, good house, and her very own Jennifer Aniston Neuron. Researchers investigating brain activity in epileptic seizures mapped and implanted about 100 electrodes in patients' brains. They showed the subjects a total of 993 photos of famous people and then reduced the array down to 132 and showed the subjects between three and seven photos of the same person along with 80 pictures of other famous people, animals, and scenes. In some subjects, Jennifer Aniston was recognized and a particular neuron fired. They tested again and again. That specific neuron didn't fire for any other pictures. When Jen appeared, the same neuron fired. There it was: A single neuron carried around the subject's memory of Jen.[76]

We have a hundred billion neurons each making thousands of connections each second, a quadrillion synapses in our highly complex brain, and yet we can fit our memory of Jennifer Aniston on a single neuron? How much about Jen can be carried on that one neuron that says "Jen? Is there a picture of her? Just one picture? Does she have *Friends*? An eponymous hairdo? An ex-husband?" What is on that single neuron and how much more is needed to "remember" Jennifer Aniston?

Let's ask the folks that like actress Halle Berry. The researchers showed subjects not an information-rich photograph, but a simple line drawing of the Catwoman used in the artwork for Halle Berry's film. The subjects recognized the drawing as being of Halle Berry, and the Halle Berry neuron fired. It also fired when the subject saw a picture of Halle with her Catwoman makeup almost entirely obscuring her face, and it also fired with other representations of Halle. So the neuron was not firing only when it recognized a single picture of Halle Berry. It fired for a variety of representations including just the letters "H A L L E B E R R Y," because, miraculously, it had not learned the line drawing representation, but rather *the concept of Halle Berry—loosely, the personhood of Halle Berry.*

Same person, different representations and the single cell knows it's firing in recognition of something bigger than a single picture, but rather a single person in many representations. What if we show the same person with different associations, say the Eiffel Tower or Jen's friend from *Friends,* Lisa Kudrow? One subject's Jen neuron also fired when the subject saw a picture of Lisa Kudrow. That one little neuron within the subject's brain carried not just a picture of Jen but also her environment, the larger view of Jen, and the connection to other social aspects of Jen's life.

If I asked you who Halle is, you would probably tell me what she looks like, that she is a movie actor, the kinds of movies she is in, perhaps a few roles, and a few things about her social life. You would present a picture of her personality and personal history, in an order that pleased you because you would have ordered it in a way you think I would most likely understand. You would tell me the story of Halle Berry as you have come to know it.

Even at the single-cell level, we have memories that are *contextual.* It's not a simple file that says "That's a picture of Jen," but rather a neuron that says "that's Jen, sometimes she played this woman on *Friends*, she had that great ex-husband," and we'll connect with other memories of other concepts, environments, characters and actors from that environment, and even the enviable New York apartment that NBC thought was "typical for young New Yorkers." That single neuron, the memory of Jen, brings forth the full tableau from our memory, showing us the richness of the memories we hold, the strong associations that are linked to people and places, and the interconnected way we hold memories.[77]

Memories call on whole networks to bring us information we've sewn together from every part of the brain, yet one single cell among the 1.1 trillion we have can carry a map of our personal universe.

The same thing happens when we remember a thing. Recently a friend asked me about my first car. I took a second to recall the car, and then my brain provided the following information: *"I remember a picture of the car; it was red and fast and filled with special speakers because my father liked listening to demos in it, and it smelled like leather. And I remembered the photograph I had of the car and me and my then-young nephew plunked on the hood of the car parked in front of my parent's house. Yes, I remember that picture, and I'm going to see that nephew next week. He's grown up, has a kid I never met."*

I had that car for two years and had many a great time in it, but my most immediate memory of it is a photograph, and not the myriad times I saw it in my driveway. I've seen the photo a few times in the past few years, but I haven't seen the car in real life for decades. So the photo is the most recent memory—the image is on top of the memory stack, and it comes up first. I also remember my nephew, who hasn't been a baby propped up on a car in a very long time. I remember it was fall because the air was crisp that day. It smelled like fall, with leaves fluttering and, though I don't recall specifically, I'll bet there were lawnmowers making noise nearby.

I remember a multi-sensory show of smell, touch, sight. I remember interactions: loved the car, nephew looked oh-so-cute, must be fall, look at the trees. In short, I remember a tapestry, a series of interactions and senses, all of which come up at the same time, because they are all connected with the specific object, my first car. We humans don't pull up a file of "the car," a physical object. We remember the interactions, environments, and the context of the car. We remember our interaction with the car, not just a picture of it.

The research on Jennifer Aniston and the picture of my first car tell us crucial information. We remember context: not just the person or the thing, but the person as part of a larger construct. We remember items as they are associated with other people or things. We remember Jen in a variety of settings and with the *context* of her and her friends. I remember and associate my first car with the house I grew up in and my nephew as a young child.

The idea of perfect memory or the file that contains an exact reproduction of an event is a fantasy. It's a party trick. What is useful is remembering the *context* or *connective tissue* of a memory because it holds *meaning*. So, too, we don't remember facts per se because they are lists. We remember the connective tissue and full context of facts, which we call Story. *The difference between a list of events and a story is so fundamental it is played out in the very neurons of our brains.*

THE MYTH OF MEMORY

Remember how your brain encoded the memory of going to a party? A few years after the party with the guy, the ficus tree, and the donations card, you and the interesting guy who is now your partner are sitting at dinner with some friends. One of them asks you, "How did you two meet?" You react by entering the third stage of memory, *memory retrieval,* bringing the stored data back into present consciousness. This stage is what we civilians usually mean when we throw around the word "memory." What happens?

We think that somewhere upstairs in our brain, there is a file that has a perfect reproduction of specific events and when we call it up, we get a perfectly faithful digital reproduction from the cranial file cabinet. Science, of course, says otherwise. Preeminent neuroscientist Antonio Damasio reminds us that "perfectly faithful memory is a myth."[78]

All of the bits of data that are the memory of the way you two met are spread out over the vast neuronal network of the brain. When you want to remember meeting your partner to tell the story of how you met, the kazillions of data points now dispersed throughout your brain have to be *retrieved*. On their journey back to the central station, a lot of things can happen. Like a trip back to your home town: The roads have changed, the lights flash in different patterns, and there are new buildings everywhere. The path back to the central station is filled with pot holes. And even when all the roads or neuronal networks have been traveled back, is that the memory? No, it's a pile of data points that have to be put back together the way they used to be.

Herein lies the fallible memory. Each step along the way from storage to reconstituted memory is amenable to myriad other influences. Faithful memory must yield to the imperfect functioning of the cells.

"Many scientists question the entire notion of stability in human memory," according to neuroscientist John Medina. The modern theory is that whenever we call up a memory, the millions of tiny pieces spun out of the Cuisinart come back from the four corners of our brain and have to be reconstructed into a coherent memory. Each time we call it up, it is reconstructed, and it changes. If memory has to be reconfigured in short-term memory every time we bring it up, then "it means permanent storage exists in our brains only for those memories we choose not to recall!"[79] Ah, the irony.

Understanding memory is a rabbit hole right out of *Alice in Wonderland*. Memory has an elastic relationship with time, space, truth, and accuracy. Yes, memory can come to your consciousness as it is in the present, as it was in the past, as you alter it to meet your emotional requirements, and as it is changed in a variety of ways well beyond your conscious control. Memory is spread throughout vast stretches of complex neuronal networks. Memory *varies in time*. Memories *change* in the space *in your head*. Memory has *quirks*. Memory is *geographically biased*. An application of Hebb's wire together–fire together model is that neurons close to each other get in the habit of firing together, so they become fixed with each other. Another geographic anomaly is that when you seek to retrieve a memory, the most recently accessed memory will be sitting on the top of the memory stack and will be the most likely retrieved, even if it isn't the most accurate or pertinent.

"If it's not one thing, it's your mother," Robin Williams said. Is there a neurological reason for the myriad mommy jokes? For good or bad, our mothers are our first and most persistent stimulus when our brains are at their very earliest formulation. Mommy sits front and center from birth through childhood as our brains grow from the reptilian state to our cortex-rich consciousness. As a result, she is especially available. She has been sitting on the very top of the memory stack for so very long and at such fundamental times that—for better or worse—she is *chronically accessible.*

Significant others are also so well-established at the top of the memory stack non-consciously that they are automatically brought up when we meet new people. Psychologists call it "transference," and the neurology supports our understanding that significant others are so deeply ingrained and so often retrieved non-consciously from our memory that they are regularly the template or pattern we use when we meet new people or characters. Our characters are often like our real-life family because mom, dad, and sibs sit atop the stack as our perennially accessible templates.

We remember *selectively.* What we remember depends on many factors, but initially it depends on how recent, how salient, how emotional, and how focused we were on an event.[80]

New memories can sit on older memories and *reshape or wear away* older memories.[81] Sometimes new memories intermingle with the old, creating a more variable *blend.* Adding new memories can perform a kind of mental alchemy. *New memories alter old memories. New memories of the present change the memory of past.* Consider that for a moment: To your brain, what happened today changes what happened yesterday. Those interactions between the past as it happened and the past as you remember it today are valuable for emotional growth, but make accurate memory a joke.

Your brain has a *negativity bias*. Something bad is more likely to be remembered than something good. In the evolutionary sense, it was more important to remember threats to our survival than happy interludes along the way. If you are out on the savannah and a lion wanders in front of you and then attacks someone just a bit ahead of you, you definitely want to remember everything about the lion: the sound of the grass as it approaches, the smell it gives off, the sound of its breath, the pause it takes before it leaps. If later that season you think you see a lion, your brain will receive all of the input it received before to help you avoid being eaten. The purpose of the negativity bias is to use as much brain space as you have available for the details of life that will increase your chances of survival. Negativity bias helps us avoid animals in the jungle.

It also means we remember perceived risks beyond their utility. It means we remember and give more brain space to negative events than to positive or neutral ones. It also means those memories are inaccurate. Memories formed in childhood, when the world is a risky and unmanageable place, are coated in negativity. If these memories are reinforced as we grow, then as we mature, they are hardened, largely unconsciously. They are characteristically fear-inducing. *They become trauma.*

Memories *consolidate*. They become more *fixed*, but both very quickly and very slowly. A new memory may go right to the top of the pile, but a memory is usually not fixed or set for about 10 years. And anything can happen during those 10 years. Memory is *variable* and *unreliable*. Old memories *combine with new ones to change the present and the past*.

If memories are spectacularly unreliable, what if we could shift how we use the land in our brain so we have more room for accurate memory? A few people do have immensely more accurate memories than you and I. How do they fare?

THE GRACE OF THE FORGETFUL BRAIN

After encoding, storing, and retrieving memories, what's that fourth stage again? I forget. Oh yeah. It's *forgetting*.

Comedian Steve Martin wrote a great little piece that goes roughly like this:

How to have lunch with a friend:

1. Find your keys.
2. Call your friend.
3. Make reservations.
4. Find your keys.

I say it goes roughly that way because frankly I can't remember it exactly. Yes, the irony of forgetting the details of a joke about forgetting the details is not lost on me . . . until I forget that, too.

We all want better memory. In fact, we want perfect memory, the ability to read a book and store the whole thing in our heads, go to lectures and not have to take notes, see an old friend and remember every single thing about them. Studying wouldn't exist, you'd just know everything you had read and heard for every course you ever took. Getting that PhD would be a breeze. Or would it?

Imagine if you could have an almost unlimited memory. Solomon Shereshevskii was a Russian mnemonist active in the 1920s; he had such a good memory that he made his living demonstrating it. As molecular biologist John Medina explains it, Shereshevskii remembered pretty much *everything* he came across. Names, facts, lists of numbers. Everything. Psychologist Alexander Luria once showed Shereshevskii a complex formula of 30 letters and numbers. Shereshevskii recalled the formula perfectly. Without telling his subject, Luria put the formula in a safe. Fifteen years later Luria found Shereshevskii and asked him to repeat the formula. Without seeing it or any other coaching, Shereshevskii repeated it perfectly.[82]

Kim Peek, the real life model for the main character of *Rainman*, could read two pages at the same time, one with each eye, comprehending and remembering perfectly everything contained in the pages. Forever.[83] Peek reportedly could recall, with great accuracy, the contents of 12,000 books.

People with Highly Superior Autobiographical Memory (HSAM)—or *hyperthymesia*—have almost perfect memory of their personal lives and connect those memories with dates. Ask one of them what happened on, say, July 21st seven years ago, and the movie of that day in their life runs in their head. In fact, movies of days in their past run all the time, and some sufferers feel like their days are divided as if on two screens—one with Now and one with Another Date—running next to each other, and their focus is divided. Having HSAM is reported to be exhausting because memories of the past are always running in their heads. It's particularly painful with regard to negative memories, which simply won't go away. Imagine how hard it would be to never forget any of the times you were foolish or acted shamefully or were traumatized.

What do these lives—and others with apparently endless memory capacity—tell us? The lesson I draw is that perfect memory really messes up your life. Kim Peek was both physically disabled and unable to form meaningful associations or relationships. He was dependent upon his father for his entire lifetime.

Shereshevskii also held vast amounts of information in his brain but was so overwhelmed by it all that he was unable to find any meaning or discern patterns in all that so-called knowledge. It's as if all the information was encoded into zeros and ones and left that way forever. In one test, Luria gave Shereshevskii a long list of numbers and he remembered them perfectly . . . but didn't see that the numbers were perfectly sequential.

Neither Peek, nor Shereshevskii, nor other notable people with extraordinary memories seem able to *use* the information well. They *remember* well but can't *think* well. The best explanation for this is quite simple: They lack the grace of forgetting. Our limited capacity for memory normally means we get rid of a lot of memories that aren't useful. We ignore things that we think won't matter. We prioritize because our memories are limited, and a lot of the excess goes to the trash folder. We use our memories to hold what matters, putting it together in the much more efficient package of contexts and meanings. To some degree, we filter memories for quality over quantity. We are not overwhelmed, as Shereshevskii and Peek were, with floods of unprocessed data. We hold onto the treasures of our memories, without all the surplus.

What is a memory? Memory is made of *people, places, smells, sounds, environments, and contexts—all associated with more of the same. Memory is vital, broad, and ever-changing. Memory is malleable. Memory is a function of use. The more recent memories come back to us first simply because they are on top of the stack. The more often we bring up a particular memory, the more quickly it fires because it has more practice with firing. The more times it is fired, the more times it will bring up related material because neurons that fire together wire together. Memory throws huge swaths of knowledge and personal history into the trash. Memories call on whole networks in our brain, bringing us large quantities of information we've sewn together in our brains. Yet a single cell can bring up Jennifer Aniston or Grammy or any of the people who have impacted us in any way—and bring with them the map of our personal universe.*

The true lesson of memory is that it is its own Mysterium.

How do we remember all the information we receive at the rate of 11 million bits per second? As neuroscientist Rodridgo Quiroga explained, "The surprising answer is that we basically do not. We remember almost nothing. The idea that we remember a great deal of the subtleties and details of our experiences, as if we are playing back a movie, is nothing more than an illusion, a construct of the brain. And this is perhaps the greatest secret in the study of memory: the astounding truth that, starting from very little information, the brain generates a reality and a past that makes us who we are, despite the fact that this past, this collection of memories, is extremely slippery; despite the fact that the mere act of bringing a memory to our consciousness inevitably changes it; despite the fact that what underlies my awareness of a unique, immutable "self" that makes me who I am is constantly changing."[84]

Memory is magnificent, complicated, precise, fuzzy, unstable, unreliable, elaborate, and labile. Most importantly, our memories are *always changing*.

Is there some way to utilize that mutable quality to our benefit?

NEUROPLASTICITY

Can the brain change itself? Of course it can! You and I call it learning. Stimuli come in through our senses and get encoded on our neurons. Neuroscientists knew that we learned. They also believed that the brain was hardwired and unchanging. While we civilians had an intuitive knowledge that we can change our minds, neuroscience only recently discovered that we do it by changing our brains.

"Neuro" refers to our neurons. "Plastic" refers to change. "Neuroplasticity" refers to the brain's ability to restructure itself after training, repetition, or practice. We have long been aware that the brain changes during childhood as it learns and grows. Scientists thought that once adulthood was reached, the brain became static and the existing connections between cells became fixed and unchangeable. For example, the messages from the tip of your left pinkie always went to a particular set of neurons in your brain. Each part of each body was attached permanently to specific locations in the brain. The number of neurons was set forever. The pathways were set forever.

The "machine" model was all set, ready to run until the last neuron died. This was the universally accepted *hardwired* model. Why is this model important? Because it essentially meant that once you *made up your mind* you couldn't *change your mind*.

Nevertheless, scientists continued putting electrodes into the brains of cats and making interesting discoveries. Nobel Prize winners David Hubel and Torsten Wiesel used micromapping, a process of connecting microelectrodes to *individual neurons* to determine which ones light up when a particular stimulus is involved. Essentially, when this labor-intensive means of mapping the brain is carried out, we can determine which neuron(s) controls which specific action in the body. Hubel and Wiesel discovered, for example, the specificity with which the kitten brains processed visual stimuli: Different areas processed "lines, orientations, and movement." They sewed one eye closed on a set of kittens. They found that if the kittens couldn't see out of that sewn-closed eye during a particular period, then after the stitches were removed, the kitten would never learn to see using that eye. The area had been fully plastic earlier in the kitten's life, but for some crucial period of time when the area was ready to encode stimuli, the eye was sewn closed. Nothing came in from its dedicated source, so nothing from the dedicated source was encoded. Neurons within the brain have optimal periods of growth, which explains, for example, how easily kids can learn a foreign language but adults struggle. The brain changes during these optimal periods by learning the skill presented to it. The plasticity is turned on at critical stages and then turned off.[85] This is *change* and *plasticity*, but the scientific community still held onto the hardwired model. The reasoning was that the brains of kittens and kids were immature and plastic until the brain matured. The hardwired brain model still ruled.

What happens to the area in the brain that was supposed to work with the eye that was shut? It began to work on input from the open eye. During critical times in brain development, the brain is plastic, and it doesn't waste that valuable cortical real estate. It *wires or rewires itself for nearby tasks*. The area wasn't hardwired to the shut eye. It adapted. It changed. This *plastic change* might make those hardwire fundamentalists reconsider, but not much of the scientific community did change.

Neuroscientist Michael Merzenich tested the *localization theory* by cutting the nerves that connected the middle area of the hand of a monkey to its brain. Localization theory would posit that the site in the brain that processed input from that nerve would be unresponsive. Because that connection was broken, that area of the brain could not receive input. But the brain area was responsive to input from the sides of the monkey's hand, which was unexpected. Up in the brain's mission control, the area that had served the central nerve of the monkey's hand had been invaded by nerve stimuli from the two other areas of the monkey's hand. The brain areas didn't sit on the sidelines when there was no input. Use of those brain areas wasn't hardwired. The real estate was too valuable, and the use of it was open to competition. When it comes to brain power, it's use it or lose it. It's not that the brain loses the power of the area, but rather that the function to which it had been dedicated loses it to other areas of the brain. There is competition for space in the brain. Necessarily, the brain is plastic beyond the "critical periods" of learning.[86]

The late American neuroscientist Paul Bach-y-Rita attached electronics to a type of television camera and transmitted the information from the camera to the tongues of congenitally blind subjects. The subjects "learned to see" through their tongues. From these efforts in the middle of the 20th century, we knew that some changes to the use of the neurons in the brain were possible.[87]

As we learn, the brain is able to and routinely does change the pattern of connections among the neurons to form new networks. This is "neuroplasticity"—the ability to change our brain, and thus, to change our mind. Given the right motivation and upon exposure to new motor or sensory activity, the areas of the brain associated with that activity can increase by two to three times in the first two days. The areas will continue to expand and refine with repeated activity but will disappear without repetition of the activity. As the neurons refire, they function better, faster, and more efficiently. As Donald Hebb said, "Neurons that fire together wire together and neurons that fire apart wire apart."[88] Although the neuronal changes can happen rapidly, they are temporary and have to be reinforced by practice or repetition to become fixed. If they aren't regularly reinforced, they can disappear as the brain continues to remodel. Use it or lose it.

We knew that we could achieve the results of neuroplasticity by altering the connectivity between existing neurons and also by increasing the number of neurons. We knew neuronal change was possible.

The big leap came in the 1990s: We found neural *stem cells* in the brain. Rough translation: *The brain could grow new neurons*. That's the sweet spot: The brain can generate new cells. The cells can learn. In effect, the brain can get rid of the useless stuff by just forgetting it, thus increasing the amount of available real estate for more important, newer information. *The brain can get a regularly scheduled software update*. It's a fantastic advance, but it's not automatic. The golden rule of neuroplasticity is that you use it or lose it. Like going to the gym, the less you push the brain, the worse shape it's in. To keep it in good shape, you have to work it.

Neuroplasticity swings both ways. On the negative side, if you have had the same thought, perhaps reliving a trauma, over and over and over again, that path in your brain is well-traveled and established. The more you repeat that journey, the more practice you've had and the less malleable the path becomes. Same for addictions and fears. Keep going down the road, and the road becomes an inflexible superhighway. Similarly, persistent childhood trauma has an impact on the brain because the trauma creates "massive plastic change in the hippocampus, shrinking it so that new, long-term explicit memories cannot form."[89] This stress-induced change can persist throughout life, though it can also be reversed over the long haul.

In a more positive vein, neuroscientists and some psychologists view psychotherapy as *plasticity in motion*. Repeated discussions of particular experiences open up the memory to more recent input. We loosen the hold of the old interpretation of, say, a trauma by adding new possibilities in interpretation.

Neuroplasticity occurs when we block a particular route or thought pattern around a particular memory. In so doing, the brain seeks out less-used paths. We find new outlooks. Over time, those new paths gain traction. Our brain learns a new perspective, breaking the hold of the older view. This is not a spectacular moment of insight but rather the slow reorganizing of perception and interpretation.

Neuroplasticity matters because without it, we would be stuck in whatever mental state we were in when we reached adulthood. Neuroplasticity is your brain's way of growing your knowledge, adjusting your behaviors, toning your mental muscles, and staving off the degeneration of your mind. It is what changing your life looks like in your brain. If you are changing your life for the better, it's a very, very good thing. We can change what and how we think. But it takes effort.

Just as we saw in memory formation, what we remember depends on how recent, how salient, how emotional, and how focused we were on an event."[90] Neuroplasticity is optimized when we are focused, attentive, and determined and put in the work. If it's a significant challenge and we determine to meet it, we can turn our neuroplasticity to "on." The more we repeat an activity, the more the neural networks associated with that activity fire and the more stable they become. Basically, practice makes perfect.

The same Michael Merzenich who did the pioneering work on neuroplasticity also wrote a user's guide for your brain. In his lovely book, *Soft-Wired: How the Science of Brain Plasticity Can Change Your Life*, he explains the 10 basic rules of neuroplasticity.[91] They can be summarized as:

1. Change mostly happens when the brain's learning switches are turned on. The brain releases "chemical modulatory neurotransmitters that enable the brain to change." They are on and off switches. If you aren't focused and alert, the switch stays in the off position.
2. The harder you try, the more motivated and alert you are, the better the outcome, and the bigger the brain change.
3. What actually changes in the brain are the strengths of the connections of the neurons that are engaged together, moment by moment.
4. Learning-driven changes in connections increase cell-to-cell cooperation, which is crucial for increasing reliability.
5. The brain also strengthens its connections between those teams of neurons representing separate moments of activity that represent each little part of an action or thought. The brain strengthens its connections between its neurological representations of successive things that reliably occur in serial time.
6. Initial changes are just temporary.

7. The brain is changed by internal mental rehearsal in the same ways and involving precisely the same processes that control all changes achieved through interaction with the external world.

8. Memory guides and controls most learning. Progressive learning requires many successful, remembered attempts toward the goal.

9. Every moment of learning provides a moment of opportunity for the brain to stabilize and reduce the disruptive, potentially interfering backgrounds or noises. Every new event that strengthens the new connections also weakens the old connections. Positive and negative plasticity work together.

10. Brain plasticity is a two-way street. It is just as easy to generate negative changes as positive ones.

One more thing: Sleep on it. Yup, just as Jouvet's cats practiced in their sleep, we humans improve our learning by dream-state simulations. Sleep helps incorporate neuroplastic change. Without physically moving your body, your brain practices new behaviors in your sleep, and as it fires and refires the new circuits, it is strengthening the neural connections for later use in your awake state. Those dream-state repetitions count. For parts of your brain, real life and fiction are equally beneficial.

Athletes do this when they mentally go through their routines. They can improve the brain activity and cell connections associated with the muscle movements they will perform in real life and thereby improve their actual performance. Same for writers. When you are dreaming about the piece you are working on, you can be looking for, finding, and consolidating solutions to the obstacles you and your protagonist face.

While you dream, the part of your brain that allows you to think broadly and to confront fears is stimulated, while the part of the brain that inhibits those thoughts is toned down. You are more brave in your sleep, and you learn that quality, too. Because of these modulations of brain activity in dreams, we can create long-lasting changes in the brain's functioning and in behavior.

What are the lessons of neuroplasticity? Our brain is always in a state of change. The more we focus on a new activity, the greater the impact of neuroplasticity. Merzenich counsels that "the key to brain change is close, serious, highly attentive engagement at a level on which you are continuously challenging yourself."[92]

Focusing on the task and doing the work is the formula for success at neuroplasticity and in writing. *Writing is applied neuroplasticity.* We change our brain when we work hard on a writing piece and stick with it. We have the necessary focus. We have the effort. We face our obstacles. And we *resolve* the problems our characters face. We rewrite again and again, changing the new gravel road into a superhighway as our brain incorporates these changes. These resolutions are hard-earned and hardwired and fired together. *When our characters work to get out of bad situations, they take us along for the resolution.*

THEORY OF MIND

"I wonder what she's thinking." "Why is he doing that?" "I wish I knew what was going on in her mind." We all try to figure out what someone else is thinking, because then we can figure out what we want to do in response to their thoughts to further our own ends. What do we call that?

The neuroscientists and cognitive social psychologists could have called it "mind reading," but that would be too easily understood. They sometimes call it "mentalizing,"[93] which sounds suspiciously like a television show. They took the fact that I know that what is in your mind is not exactly the same as what's in my mind and called it "theory of mind." It is terrible branding, but the actual concept is great: *I theorize that your mind is separate from my mind.* Therefore, your mind can hold a completely separate and distinct idea of any particular reality than my mind holds.

The classic experiment, loosely adapted here, is with a child observing two dolls in a room. Doll Alice has a box of toys. Alice puts a candy in the box while Doll Zelda is watching. Then Doll Zelda is taken out of the room. Doll Alice takes the candy out of the box and puts it behind the bookshelf. Doll Zelda is brought back in and is told to get the candy. At three years old, the subject child will predict that Zelda will look for the candy behind the bookshelf because the three-year-old knows that the candy is behind the bookshelf. At five years old, the child will predict that Zelda will look for the candy in the box because the child knows that Zelda saw the candy in the box the last time Zelda saw the candy, even though the child also knows that the candy is in fact behind the bookshelf. At five, the child knows that what Zelda is thinking is not the same as what the child is thinking. At five, we have theory of mind, the belief that what you are thinking is not the same as what I am thinking. At three, we simply don't understand that what we are thinking isn't universal.

The ability to predict what someone else is thinking is crucial to our individual survival. It allows us to gauge whether another person is a threat or friend to us. Without it, pure brute force would be the controlling factor in interactions among people, tribes, and countries. When we understand the motivation of others, we can negotiate and cooperate. Our predictions are more likely to be accurate. We avoid mistakes, like assuming that the nice guy over there is our friend—when he suddenly pulls out his gun and shoots. These are examples of a theory of mind of two people: I know what I think, and I know what I think you think.

Theory of mind gets more complicated when applied to more than two people. This morning I came across the following headline:

HOW SKIP BAYLESS THINKS
TOM BRADY WILL REACT TO
ANTONIO BROWN'S
AARON RODGERS REMARK[94]

This could well be called the Theory of Mind Test. This article asks us to imagine how SKIP BAYLESS (1) thinks TOM BRADY (2) will think and behave in response to what ANTONIO BROWN (3) thought and said about what AARON RODGERS (4) thought and said. Four different internal dialogues, being tracked by a fifth internal network, the reader. Whew! Your dog can't do that. In fact, some very smart people think that skill is what makes us human . . . or at least what makes a great writer.[95]

How is this useful? It helps us interact more effectively. Here's an example from my own life. I walk into a meeting with a studio vice president. I've been told that the studio has some sci-fi script with a strong female angle, and I toss out some ideas that might work. The studio exec stares at her phone screen. You and I know this is a bad sign. What is in my mind ("Hey, this is a really great take; you should buy it!") is not what is in her mind. She may be thinking, "Gee, that other pitch I heard this morning was pretty good; I wonder what price we'd need to pay" or possibly "Joe wasn't really paying attention last night; am I getting fat?"

What is it that I have just experienced? I've observed the exec's behavior, and I interpret the staring into the phone as not paying attention to me and my pitch, so to survive, I have to do something. I am "mentalizing" or processing the intentions of someone else. I have taken a small gesture (where her eyes are focused), interpreted a larger meaning (she is paying attention to something else), and processed it into behavior (I will do something). If I determine that the first thing I need is to get her back into the conversation in the room, I ask her some questions about what I've been talking about. She doesn't know, and I know she doesn't know what I have been talking about, but asking her brings her focus back into the conversation and maybe now her mind is connected with my mind. I lay out more of the pitch. Her eyes cloud over again—but not completely.

"How would we shoot it?" she might ask. I evaluate what she said. Does she actually wonder how to shoot it, was it just a conversation filler, or is there something bigger in there? I roll that over and remember that this exec rides a heavy hand on budgets. She's not really asking how to shoot it; she's asking what it will cost. The better I am at predicting what she is thinking, the more likely I will get what I want out of the meeting, but it's too soon for me to suggest a budget level because I am not certain that that's what she's looking for. I talk more about the story. I push the romantic plot. She seems to warm a bit. What part of the pitch is bothering her? Wait, is it the sci-fi angle? Is that why she thinks it will cost too much? She's not big on sci-fi, but she did that huge chick movie. That's it, she doesn't like the budget and the sci-fi, but she's good on the romance part. Do I say "Hey, the budget is low, it's not sci-fi, and there's a big romance"? Definitely not, because I know her mind well enough to know that that's too direct. Instead, I say, "You know, we can do it for a dime because, really, it's Romeo and Juliet in Space, and it will be all interiors!"

I've perceived that the eyes going to the screen meant her mind isn't focused on my pitch. I've used my best antennae to sort out what is going on in her brain that is not going on in my brain, and I act on that with a plan to bring our thoughts back into concordance with my goals. This is a working model of what you and I might call *mind-reading* but our scientific friends call *theory of mind*.

When you were very young and utterly narcissistic, you made no distinction between your inner world and the outside world. As you developed, you learned that the outside world had its own ways. For example, if you put a cookie on the table, then left the room, you knew it would be there when you walked back into the room, until one day you walked back in, and the cookie was gone, and your older sister was standing there with cookie crumbs on her face. You asked her where the cookie went, and she told you boldly that she had absolutely no idea. You make the great discovery that what you believed (serially, that the cookie was constant and that what you thought and what your sibling thought were the same) was not in her head. Her mind was different than your mind. And what one person thinks is not what another person thinks. In a nutshell, that's theory of mind.

But what about Thanksgiving dinner when 10 people are at the table having cross conversations? On your end, Alan says, "I hear Joe is getting a divorce." Then Bob says, "Oh, that's too bad." Charlie reacts by looking at Bob, and Bob is smirking, and Charlie's wife Debra notices Charlie's reaction and looks over to Ellen, who looks away. You conclude that Ellen is having an affair with Charlie.

To make that conclusion (which is correct!) you had to follow what Allen thinks, what Bob thinks about what Alan thinks, what Charlie thinks about what Bob is thinking about what Alan thinks, what Debra thinks about Charlie's reaction to what Bob was thinking about what Alan thinks, and finally what Ellen's reaction shows you about what Ellen thinks about what Debra thinks about Charlie's reaction to what Bob was thinking about what Alan said about Joe. You would have to *mind read*—that is, peer into the mind of each of the five other people to find out what each one is thinking

If all you saw was Ellen's reaction, you could guess that she didn't like something about Debra, that Ellen was hungry, or that Ellen heard the phone ring. Or did Ellen look away because she could put together that the ultimate meaning of the lies and obfuscations of that instant of communication was that someone was having an affair and she didn't want anyone to think she was having an affair with Charlie because that would make her feel guilty and gain her the disapproval of the other members of the group (except Charlie, we predict)? To follow that chain of behavior, you have to follow not just what each person is thinking, but also what each one is *thinking about the previous person's thoughts*. There are five people in this particular conversation, so five consciousnesses, plus you, the observer, so that is the sixth level of theory of mind.

Perhaps this is just family gossip. It's not significant. But what if the family is the Romanovs? Or the Caesars? If you were watching as the line of information went up to the Czar or down from Julius through the family, knowing who said what at the right moment—and why—would give you important insight into what was going on inside the minds of people who had a fair amount of control over the lives of millions. This information was valuable in every sense of the term.

Why do humans read *People* magazine, watch royal weddings, and gossip about everyone in their grade/class/college/company? Tracking information about our social groups helps us navigate the waters of social interaction. Knowing what the king said is valuable, knowing *why* he said it is even more valuable, and predicting what he will do based on that information is even more important. We humans evolved to refine our ability to accurately decode and interpret the thoughts of those around us both for the direct task of staying alive and for the more complicated tasks of manipulating and cooperating among our kin/friends/countrymen so that we prosper. Theory of mind allows inferences. Coordination. And the fine-tuning of the social group. As Robin Dunbar explains, "Social cognition (typically exemplified by theory of mind) plays an important role in human relationships. The ability to see the world from another person's point of view is a fundamental prerequisite for successful social interaction."[96] In other words, theory of mind is essential to the development of social groups and society itself.

I have a friend, Margaret, who is smart, quick, and funny, and she writes that way. Margaret also has a unique gift. She's a walking continuity machine. She can read my writing and tell me exactly where it fails in verisimilitude. She is a genius at finding the bumps because somewhere in her mind she tracks each of my characters as I have presented them, and when one the four characters in my crucial scene has not made an adjustment to information they received five scenes ago, Margaret's hair will go all frizzy when she stops and says, "No, he wouldn't say that because 20 pages ago, he said something else, and he would feel differently when he sees the picture of the girl you think he liked 40 pages ago." It doesn't make any sense to me, either, when she says that. So I slow her down and follow as she tells me what each of my characters must be thinking in each of the scenes before the scene we are in now and how those all get you to a place where one of the characters I've invented isn't acting consistent with how I invented them. A bump. She has tracked the inner consciousness of each of my characters through a series of scenes. I can't do that, even with my own characters in my own scenes in my own story.

Margaret has a gift for theory of mind. High IQ is also a great gift, but they are not the same. Theory of mind is its own special skill or capacity. It's proven useful in the courts of the Caesars, the Romanovs, and many an executive suite. It has supplied Margaret with incredible job security. Margaret will always have a good job as long as there is a soap opera shooting somewhere in the world because she is the one person on a soap who actually remembers what each of the characters has been thinking from time immemorial.

People with highly developed theory of mind have a high aptitude for social interaction and prosper from that skill. It is particularly valued in storytellers. One of the reasons we like stories is that we can be presented with complex social situations with the guidance of a lead intellect—the writer—to help sort through the cognitively taxing work of understanding the unstated levels of motivation and emotion in multi-character situations comparable to the situations that we experience in our own real lives. It's as if the writers have the decoder ring on the human interaction game that takes place 24/7.

Much of the benefit of reading fiction comes from our transportation into the mind of a writer who is gifted at navigating social interactions so that we the audience can simulate that navigation and learn from it. As British anthropologist and evolutionary psychologist Robin Dunbar pointedly asked, "Why are there so few great writers?"[97] One answer is that to enter that very exclusive club, that person must present complex social situations usually up to four characters (four levels of theory of mind) to an audience (the fifth level) and still maintain her own perspective, making a grand total of six levels of theory of mind. Storytelling is valuable because it presents complex social situations that the audience takes in to sharpen their own tools for coping in a complex social reality. The ability to follow four levels of theory of mind is rare and highly taxing. Six levels are about as high as we can go. An answer to Dunbar's inquiry is that great writers have to have six levels of theory of mind and effectively communicate to five levels— which is a very rare level of skill.

Theory of mind is the jargon way of saying, "I know what you're thinking." Theory of mind greases the path of social interaction. Add in mirror neurons, and it becomes "I know what you feel." If we put them together, I know what you think and what you feel, and we make a quantum leap: We know what is going on in your head and your heart. We have a tool of an entirely higher magnitude: We have *empathy*.

Is theory of mind just a theory? A construct of squishy conjecture? I thought so, too, until I came across the default mode network, a spot in your brain that does your theory of mind homework for you. It's a lovely piece of brain software. Sit back, day dream, and I'll take you there.

DEFAULT MODE NETWORK

What happens when we *aren't* thinking? When we are falling asleep, when we are driving down the same highway we've driven for five years, when we are in the shower, or when we are riding our bike? And where, exactly, is my unconscious? I want to find it, so I can make sure it just shuts up for a while.

Join me in my perfect world. Staring out the window is the most productive time of my day. No one interrupts me when I am doing nothing. Doing nothing is sacred. Doing nothing is the very best way to have and keep good friends. Also, gabbing about nothing with my friends is a great way to share important information and make plans. In my perfect world there is a physical place in my head where my unconscious is located! It's a place that makes good ideas, bakes them into daydreams and sends them up to me. In my perfect world, doing nothing is the way to happiness. In my perfect world, doing nothing built cultures and nations and societies and conquered the Earth.

My perfect world is real. So is yours.

What's going on upstairs when we are "doing nothing"? For a long time, we just didn't know. Our best guess was that our brains have an on-off switch. When you are working, it's on. When you are not working, it's off. So for me at this very moment when I am at my desk writing this paragraph, my brain is working to select concepts and words to best express the ideas that have been floating around up there since I woke up this morning. That would be "on." Later I will take a nap, and the switch will go to "off."

The experts believed that there were specific file cabinets or neuronal places where each function existed in our brains. We had speech centers, visual centers, auditory controllers, and the like. We later called them nodes, modules, networks, and schema. The assumption was that the brain functioned something like attention: It was on when we were thinking—and off the rest of the time.

We didn't understand what actually happened when we were thinking or whether thinking had any physicality. What does a thought look like? How can we find out where the thought lives? We didn't know.

Early neuroscientists connected electrodes to pets' brains to research what—if anything—goes on in there. Adolf Beck favored rabbits and dogs, and in 1890, he published the first paper that noted that the brains of the animals showed rhythmic oscillations. He then put the electrodes directly on the brain surface and concluded that the oscillations were brain "waves." He is the source of all those "being on the same wave length," phrases but otherwise he was reduced to the "interesting but irrelevant" neuroscientific slush pile.

Hans Berger invented the electroencephalogram (EEG) in 1924. The EEG records the electrical activity in the brain, and an EEG reading looks the same as an earthquake or stock market chart. Berger's readouts showed that when his subjects were at rest, their brains kept sending off electrical signals. In a world where there were only on and off positions on the brain-o-meter, his conclusion made no sense and was disregarded.

The model of the working brain as either absolutely on or absolutely off rolled forward, but as the technology developed, there were clues that something was going on when the brain was off. We expected that the metabolism of the brain would decrease when it was doing nothing but found out that the metabolism remains constant. In the 1970s, scientists discovered that blood flow to the prefrontal cortex of the brain *increased* when the brain was off.

We developed the now-familiar technology, the PET scan, the CT scan, and the MRI. Scientists were able to "look" inside the brain to see what areas were activated when the person was exposed to different stimuli. What area of the brain "lights up" when you see a picture of a puppy? Hear the sound of a gunshot? Smell a rose?

In order to figure out what areas were activated, researchers had to know what "not activated" looked like. They needed a baseline for what the brain looked like when it was "off."

How do you test the difference between *brain on* and *brain off?* Researchers assigned subjects to perform two tasks, which were designed to demonstrate the two states of the brain, on and off.

The active task (task positive) required that the subject follow a moving dot or read words. The subject's brain had to process information that was changing. During the active task, the brain should be "on."

A passive task (task negative) asked the subject to focus on a stationery dot. Because the dot was unchanging it did not require processing and the brain should be "off."

The theory was that during an active task, the brain was on, and during a passive task, the brain was "off" or at baseline.

Except that's not what happened.

They found that when the brain does an active task, parts of the brain are "on." So far, so good. When it switches to a passive activity, the part of the brain that was on turns off, as expected . . . and turns on another completely different network. The brain isn't unitary. It isn't all on or all off. It's either-or. One network is on, and another off. Change the task and the networks toggle.

The "no activity" or task negative setting turned on a separate network of its own and, lacking much of a sense of humor, they called it the "task negative network." This network turned on when everything else was off, as a kind of low-power default mode, and was later aptly renamed the "default mode network" (DMN).

What happened when we were doing nothing? The DMN turned on.

What happened when we were doing something? The DMN turned off.

Now this is a curious thing, because areas of the brain tend to be additive. The number of areas that are working on a task tend to increase when the task gets more complicated. But the default network mostly does not. It's on when everything else is off, and off when the rest are on. It's not additive.

When we finish a focused task, the DMN turns on instantaneously.[98] It does this over and over again, all day, every day. It is the *default* setting of your brain.

But what is it doing when it is doing nothing?

At first it looked like the neuroscientists had actually found the unconscious. Wouldn't it be great if there was a defined place or network that was your unconscious? Instead of being some post-Freudian fuzzy thing, it would have neurons and synapses and regions in the brain. It would have physical reality and would be oh-so-much better for those of us who are good friends with our unconscious. It would be more real.

It turns out that the DMN is kinda-sorta our unconscious. It isn't a direct embodiment, but it covers many of the tasks we believe our unconscious does. It is the network in the brain that turns on when we daydream or otherwise enter a non-real view of the world. It seems to play out scenarios or possibilities focused on ourselves or other people. It processes theory of mind.

What does the DMN do? It daydreams and remembers. It has "me" and "you," and therefore it has a perspective.[99] Technically, "the regions of the DMN appear to synthesize a sensory experience of the body and internal world that allows us to have a conscious experience of ourselves in imaginal space within the flow of time. This function, so vital to the experience of self and the development of culture, suggests that the adaptive functions of the DMN have exerted strong selection bias on both neural and sociocultural evolution."[100]

Let's decode. The DMN runs when the rest of your brain is resting. Think of it as running in the background most of the time. It is the network that processes your autobiographical self, which is your memory of you. It also works with your memory of other people and social interactions, theory of mind, memories of others in comparison with the self, social evaluations, and the emotions of others. It remembers the past and imputes the future. It remembers old narratives and creates future narratives. It is the engine of your theory of mind.

Your brain is functioning all the time (we hope!). Sometimes we are concentrating on a specific task. When that happens, your DMN powers down. When you aren't working on a particular cognitive task, your DMN steps up. It turns on. It is highly organized. It uses a huge amount of resources, consuming most of the energy your brain has available. It organizes the functions of the brain so your mind and your body are working compatibly. It functions to help you understand what might happen next. To do that job, it keeps tabs on a huge swath of our experiences: our relationships with others, our memories of our self, our past, and our projected future.

The default mode network turns on when we engage in self-reflection, when we are thinking about others, and when we create and explore scenarios with others.[101] It is where we create and practice social interaction. When we daydream, we aren't focused on anything outside our minds, and the DMN is activated.

When you're reading fiction, your default mode network is on.[102] It's also very busy when you are focused on working creatively.[103]

More simply, the default mode network does two things. It processes your *self* and it processes information *about other people*. It is the *social junction box* in your brain. The DMN processes story and finds correlates in your autobiographical and social mind. Your *self* has physical reality here in the neurons and signals. When you take in—or write—a story, it happens here, right next to your social junction box, your memories of yourself and others, and the social world you live in and refine. Your consciousness isn't "on." Your default network is.

This odd mental state is beautifully represented in an old Burt Reynolds movie entitled *Best Friends*, which was written by and based upon the relationship of Barry Levinson and Valerie Curtin. It opens on a shot of an IBM Selectric typewriter with a blank page in it. We wait for something to happen . . . and wait . . . and wait while we stare at the blank page. Still, nothing happens. Finally from off-screen, a character says, "Let's take a break." The audience laughs at the irony of taking a break from getting nothing done. I happened to have seen this film with a group of screenwriters. No one laughed. The room filled with groans of agony. Each of them knew what was really going on in that room in the movie: Writers had been laying on couches staring up at the ceiling, desperate for an idea to float into their awareness and even then, in the perfect quiet of the perfect room with no distractions and plenty of time to wait, even then, nothing came up. It is an agony. In neurological terms, even their DMN wasn't producing. Groan.

Writers love their DMNs though they don't call them that. Creative types use their DMNs so much and so often that they have significantly more grey matter than non-creatives, which is to say that creatives have bigger DMNs.[104] Here's the ringer: For most brain processes, the DMN is on or off. *For creative writing, the DMN is on at the same time as conscious functioning is on. When you are writing a narrative, your focused and non-focused attention all light up at the same time.[105] Your brain really is on fire.*

Doing nothing is a very productive activity. Have you ever had a breakthrough thought while you were taking a shower; or driving on a road so familiar that it bores you; or just walking, gardening, even just vacuuming? Thank your DMN. What about riding a bike? One man credited a bike ride for his big idea. It was Einstein, and the very big idea was the Special Theory of Relativity.

When our focus is off and the DMN is bubbling along, new ideas float from our blobbing brain to our consciousness. Give it a lot of room.

When I was a newbie writer, a veteran screenwriter came to visit me. I had my feet up on the desk when he walked in. He said, "What are you doing?"

"Staring out the window."

"Oh! So you're working. I'll come back later."

It was a beautiful moment. He slipped back out of the room. He understood.

MIRROR NEURONS

In the 1920s, the phrase "monkey see, monkey do" became popular in song, dance, theatre, comic books, poems, cartoons, and everyday parlance. The idea was simple: The first monkey does something. The second monkey watches . . . and does the same thing. Seventy years later, neuroscientists replicated "monkey see, monkey do," and the scientific world hailed it as the key to human development. Go figure.

Neurophysiologist Giacomo Rizzolatti is a professor at the University of Palma studying the neurons that carry out motor (movement) commands in monkeys. He and his research team placed electrodes on the cortex of macaque monkeys. The team then watched as the first monkey was offered a nut by a researcher. The first monkey's neurons fired when the monkey reached out for the nut. That was expected. The second monkey was sitting on the side watching. When the first monkey reached for the nut, the neurons in the same region in the second monkey's brain also fired. To be clear, the neurons in the watching monkey fired *as if* it was reaching for the nut, though the second monkey didn't move. There were neurons in the watching monkey's brain whose job appeared to be to mirror or mimic the action of the first monkey—but without the physical movement. They are called "mirror neurons." The second monkey was rehearsing the brain pattern for the movement without actually moving.

Apes and other mammals seem to have mirror neurons that work the same way as Rizzolatti's monkeys, mimicking the brain patterns while watching the physical actions of others. If humans have mirror neurons, the implications are enormous.

Rizzolatti's discovery set off the hype machines in science as exceptional thinkers competed for the most cosmic interpretation of the importance of mirror neurons. For example, the brilliant and thoroughly entertaining V. S. Ramachandran calls these cells "the neurons that shaped civilization" because they uniquely gave humans the ability to learn from others through time and space, use tools, cook with fire, organize in large groups, and communicate to vast numbers throughout the globe.[106]

The analysis goes like this: Because we humans have mirror neurons, our brains can practice behaviors without physically having to do anything. Therefore, we can learn advanced behaviors just by observing. Because our brains automatically *do* what we see, we automatically *feel* what the other person feels, so we have the biological system to create new perspectives and empathy. Because we have empathy and the ability to learn from watching, we can cooperate with each other and coordinate social behavior for larger and larger groups. Mirror neurons are thus responsible for the unique ability of humans to cooperate, communicate, and learn. These skills allowed us to create art, technology, advanced global culture, and institutions. Therefore, mirror neurons (watch out below!) are the reason humans dominate the planet.

Then came the rush of experiments, mixed results, and the predictable backlash. While the really smart people argue over the true meaning of mirror neurons, let me summarize what we civilians know. We have mirror neurons, a specialized kind of neuron. We are born with some and develop a lot more. They allow us to practice behaviors without acting out and to feel what it is like to do those behaviors as if we are the person doing them. We therefore go into a different mental state because we inhabit the *feelings* of another. We likely have what is dubbed the "phi complex," which is a brain rhythm that syncs up with the brain rhythms of other people. "Mirror neurons are the brain cells that fill the gap between self and other by enabling some sort of simulation or inner imitation of the actions of others."[107]

Whether it's due to mirror neurons, phi waves, or magical mystery dust, our ability to feel what another is feeling is a crucial skill that affects each human each day in important ways. It allows us to step into someone else's shoes . . . or eyes. It is a way we change perspective, and that is transformative.

To demonstrate how important a change of perspective can be, consider the camera technique you've seen in lots of movies, the "point of view" (POV) shot. We are accustomed to seeing movies photographed in either a master shot that takes in all the action in the visual field, or in close-up shots where we are, yup, close to one actor and then another. Both of these shots are from an objective point of view. We see the action from the outside observer's position. It's a passive experience. For example, if we are watching a scene in an emergency room, we might see a gurney with a patient lying in it. Doctors and nurses hold onto the gurney while they roll blood pressure and oxygen machines toward the distant door into surgery. That's an objective point of view. We are bystanders.

If we switch to the patient's POV, the camera is placed as if it's in the patient's head and we see the ceiling. It rushes by. We see the tops of IV polls, a few hands and faces coming in and out of view, and we feel slightly nauseous speeding down the hallway. We viewers experience these two perspectives in very different ways. When we go into the POV of the patient on the gurney, we don't see the patient's body because we understand that we are *in* that body. Everything becomes first person and intimate. We feel what the patient feels. When the ceiling seems to fly by, we feel panic because we don't know how to judge speed by how fast the ceiling tiles go by. We know our orientation to the world is off, and the noises around us are disembodied because we can't focus on faces. We are disoriented. It's a subjective shot because we can feel what the character is feeling. We change who the *self* is in the scene. It is powerful because there is no distance between us and what is happening. We are the patient. Take a moment to experience how different we *feel* with this small change of camera angles.

Another example of change of perspective is in the first act of the classic film *Jaws*. We see a young boy swimming in the ocean off the same beach where there was a shark attack. The camera goes underwater and swims toward his kicking feet. We viewers are now looking at the world from the view of the shark, and it is indeed a frightening perspective. We feel an instinctual, non-rational drive as we move through the water. The audience sees only moving water and kicking feet, and we hear a few musical notes, yet it is terrifying. That is the power of the change in perspective. If we watched this scene through an objective point of view, we would be frightened for the swimmer. When we watch it through the eyes of the shark, the emotion is more like sorrow for the inevitable. The shark is far more powerful in the subjective view.

When we change POV in film, we change the way the events are experienced. Similarly, in real life, a change of perspective can glibly seem small, but if we go through an event from a truly different perspective, then *everything* changes in our experience. We change the *self* from an observer to a participant. The experience of another becomes *personal* to us when we change perspective. We humans can see the world through the eyes of another being, and that experience is uniquely social. The power of storytelling comes, in part, from its ability to transform us in two ways. First, it allows us to experience events as if we are participants, when in fact we are merely watching, powerless to affect the outcome. Second, it takes an individual experience and makes it a social one in which our imagined participation requires interaction with others. We experience the skills and benefits of a network of action instead of acting solo. It changes our mind.

Movies are magical for allowing us to experience what a character experiences. If you were one of the subjects wired up to an fMRI machine and watching Clint Eastwood in *The Good, the Bad, and the Ugly*, your brain would have lit up in a way that mirrors Clint Eastwood's in the movie.[108] If you were in a theatre, your brain and the brains of the other audience members would light up simultaneously.

We know that people can feel "as if" they are the character they are watching in a movie or reading about in a novel, but what is happening inside our brains when that happens? Our mirror neurons may act as if we are making the same physical movements as Clint is. When the character feels anger, are our brains turning on the "I'm angry" circuits? Yes. Not as strong as if we actually were the person portrayed by the actor in the movie, but yes, the fMRI machine would light up in all the same places as if you were actually experiencing whatever *action and emotions* you were watching or reading. When you watch Clint Eastwood move, your brain lights up as if you were moving. When Clint feels an emotion, you feel the same emotion. This is the biology of *empathy*.

You can experience this effect if you watch a movie about Ben and his father, www.youtube.com/watch?v=q1a7tiA1Qzo, which Paul Zak has used in his research.[109] It shows a father and son at play in a local park. That's all. What is the experience of the viewer? Frankly, not much. Very little cortisol is released and the audience members don't pay attention. Let's say the filmmakers grab their digital "reels" and go back to the editing room to reorder the movie and get some emotion going. The new edit shows a really happy child playing, but a less cheerful father watching his son wistfully. The narrator tells the audience that the father knows his son has cancer and will be dead in a few months. The dad struggles to feel any happiness at all, but then, seeing his son's joy in the moment, the father, too, smiles with happiness.

What happens to the viewer this time? As soon as we know the happy child has cancer, cortisol is released in the brain, and the viewers pay attention. In this state, the viewers watch the father and feel what he feels. And what does the father feel? The father's sadness dissipates when he looks at his son and shares the son's emotion of happiness. The father is sharing the child's joy. Oxytocin is released in the father's brain. The father is feeling what his son is feeling. Does the audience feel sad watching a boy with cancer? The audience watches the father, and experiences the father's emotion when he watches what his son is feeling. The son feels happiness. The father watches the son and experiences the son's happiness. The audience takes on the father's emotion of feeling the son's happiness. This is a form of theory of mind. It is empathy. We feel what the father feels that the son feels. And our brain chemicals made us do it. Thank goodness.

Oxytocin is a chemical made in the hypothalamus that was first associated with the contractions of childbirth. It is now associated with trust, sympathy, and bonding. When oxytocin is released, we are more generally trusting in interaction with another. It says, in effect, "You are not a threat to me, I have faith in you, let's get together." It promotes bonding, and, very broadly, social interaction and connection. And it starts with those molecules in the hypothalamus.[110]

In a nutshell, when we see or read something that gains our attention, cortisol is released and, if it is a positively affecting image or person, the oxytocin helps us bond with that character, which in turn promotes a positive, caring change in our behavior toward that character. We empathize with that person. We see what they see. We feel what they feel. We are changing our *self.*

How important are mirror neurons and this ability to change perspective?

First, it means that humans can learn, and *learn a lot,* by watching. Trial and error is an inefficient way to gain expertise across generations. Learning through watching allows generations of expertise to be passed on quickly and efficiently. The ability to pass along masses of information in efficient packages does, indeed, set us apart from all other species. This proficiency uniquely allows us to build ever progressively on previous knowledge.

Second, it allows a very different kind of consciousness. If you can watch someone else feeling an emotion and both feel it yourself and know it is happening to someone else, you have a deep link to another person at the same time that you know it isn't your own experience. Put another way, you have consciousness *and* you know that the other person has a consciousness that is different from yours. Humans have the unique ability to change perspective. It allows us a far deeper understanding of other people's minds . . . and needs and wants and plans and pains—and all the rest. It gives us the power to comprehend and effectuate a social network. It makes it possible to build a common culture. No other species does that.

Third, the ability to be in someone else's mind or perspective also allows us to look back at the *self* from another person's viewpoint. We can experience our *self* from the inside out—*and from the outside in.* If having a *self* is essential to the creation of consciousness, then truly having the ability to see ourselves from the outside looking in is a crucial step.

VULCAN MIND MELD

The original *Star Trek* looked like a black-and-white sci-fi television series made entirely of kitsch. It slid under the cultural radar for more than a year, but there were strong clues that it was more than it appeared. Consider, for a moment, Episode 9, which aired on November 3, 1966. It delivered three tasty cultural bon-bons. First, it had this sweet dialogue:

EVIL GUY VAN GELDER

(waving gun)

I want asylum!

CAPTAIN KIRK

At gunpoint?!

A lovely dab of satire, right up there with Dr. Strangelove's "Gentlemen! There's no fighting in the war room!"

The second joyous Christmas candy was delivered in the very title of the episode, "Dagger in the Mind." Yes, it's a lift from Shakespeare—*Macbeth*, in fact:

> *Is this a dagger which I see before me,*
> *The handle toward my hand? Come, let me clutch thee.*
> *I have thee not, and yet I see thee still.*
> *Art thou not, fatal vision, sensible*
> *To feeling as to sight? Or art thou but*
> *A dagger of the mind, a false creation,*
> *Proceeding from the heat-oppressed brain?*
> *I see thee yet, in form as palpable*
> *As this which now I draw.*
> *Thou marshall'st me the way that I was going,*
> *And such an instrument I was to use.*

I have to love a writers room that did that. Allow me this moment of inside baseball. The writers, producers, and network executives on *Star Trek* didn't think the audience was going to read the title of the episode, let alone read it and appreciate that it was a Shakespearean allusion. The writers in that room shared the quote, had a good time with it, and happily put it in the title because *they* enjoyed it. And if the audience enjoyed it also, well, they'd say then that it was *great*. Enjoy the allusion, or enjoy knowing that a few writers who were thought to be hacks were bringing Shakespearean jokes to what was then known as the idiot box. You, too, have to love that writers' room.

The third and absolutely sweetest piece of candy from the episode occurs when Dr. Spock lays hands on the face of evil Dr. Gelder. Spock whispers, "Your mind is my mind" as he performs his first Vulcan mind meld. "My mind to your mind. My thoughts to your thoughts," as Spock melds his own brain with Gelder's.[111] Oh those crazy guys in the writers' room! We've mimicked the Vulcan mind meld for decades! The Vulcan mind meld is an exuberant bit of cheap science fiction! It's fantastic! It's spectacular! It's fantasy!

Ummm. . . . Wait.

Thirty years later, scientists put two people in fMRI machines. One spoke, one listened, and the scientists watched what happened inside their brains as the speaker told a story about his life and the listener did nothing but listen. Were they on the same wavelength? Were they in sync? Did they have the same vibe? Were they both connected to the same bad cliché machine?

Yes, to everything but the bad cliché machine. When two people are talking, the neural circuits in one brain syncs up to the other person's neural circuits. "During successful communication, speakers' and listeners' brains exhibit joint, temporally coupled, response patterns. Such neural coupling substantially diminishes in the absence of communication, such as when listening to an unintelligible foreign language. Moreover, more extensive speaker-listener neural couplings result in more successful communications."[112]

The better the communication, the closer the sync is. Usually the listener's circuits are a little behind the speaker's. If the listener is deeply engaged in the communication, then the listener's brain becomes so well interfaced that the listener's brain will *predict* what the speaker is going to say. When we are gossiping with a girlfriend or listening to a good story, our brains are so engaged that they neurologically meld with each other. Your mind *is* my mind.

Other than making all those "wave length" clichés accurate, what good is this information? It changes our perspective. We usually think of speaking and listening as two separate activities taking place in two separate people. One person is speaking. The other is listening. Neuroscientist Uri Hasson suggests that these studies "look at interactions across two brains as a single shared process. Coupling is not the result of understanding. It is the neural basis on which we understand one another. *We are suggesting that communication is a single act performed by two brains.*"[113] He's also suggesting that our brains are already connected wirelessly to each other, a kind of Bluetooth for brains—no spoken words, hand signs, or other direct communication needed.

Miguel Nicolelis, a neurobiologist at Duke University, found that rats whose brains were linked via electrodes would *work together to solve tasks* even when they were in separate rooms.[114] To study this, the researchers implanted microelectrodes into the motor cortex—the part of the brain that deals with voluntary movement—of two rats. One rat was taught to hit a certain lever to get a reward, and the electrodes recorded the activity in the rat's brain when it got it right. This activity was "transferred" over to the microelectrodes in the second rat, which was set up in a room with an identical lever-reward system. The second rat, receiving brain input from its pal next door, hit the right lever 70%

of the time. This experiment continued to work even when the rats were thousands of miles apart and the brain signals were transferred over the Internet. Two rats who could share electrode information did two incredible things. First, with no visual input at all, they coordinated their behavior. Second, they understood a shared external goal without any direct communication. In effect, they shared their minds.

Not spooky enough? Nicolelis and his team have announced in the journal *Scientific Reports* that they can do the same thing but with *multiple* animals—creating a mind-meld network referred to as a "brainnet." They are building an organic computing device with multiple interconnected animal brains. This time, their experiments involved two or three rhesus macaques linked together via brain electrodes in separate rooms. The monkeys were tasked with controlling a single robotic monkey arm, but each of them had control over different dimensions. Over time, the monkey brainnet learned to work together to move the robotic arm toward a moving target, earning each of the monkeys a small reward of juice.

In another experiment, the researchers hooked up *five rats* via their brains. To create a sensory "cue" for the rats, the researchers then induced a tactile sensation in the rats by electrically stimulating the somatosensory cortex, which deals with the sense of touch. When presented with this cue, the rats learned that they would be rewarded with water if they managed to synchronize their brain activity.

Rats could pick up on different patterns of electrical stimulation—the brain cues—and modify their synchronized behavior in response. By teaching rats to associate certain brain patterns with changes in temperature and air pressure, researchers even managed to get the rats to predict the chance of rain. "The rats could divide tasks across animals, so their individual workload was much smaller," Nicolelis told *LiveScience*. "We didn't expect that in the beginning."[115]

The same group of scientists published the results of experiments with pairs of monkeys working on a social task. The monkeys' brains showed "high synchronization, in which pools of neurons in each animal's motor cortex tended to fire at the same time." They didn't call it a mind meld; they called it an "interbrain cortical synchronization." The coordination by the two monkeys was "heavily influenced by the type of social relationships among the animals participating" and "could predict another key social parameter—the rank of the monkeys in the colony."

Okay, let's decode. First, Nicolelis believes that the synchronization is the result of mirror neurons. Second, the synchronization reflects *social* connections—that is, rank in the colony for these monkeys. And he believes that similar correlations between brain synchrony and social interactions takes place among humans, also. This means that our human brains are synchronized for social tasks. "We may be able to quantify how well professional athletes, musicians, or dancers are working together, or if an audience is engaged in what they're seeing, listening, or imagining. This could be valuable for any social task that requires synchronization of many individuals to improve social cohesion."[116]

The further evidence is that *groups* of us synchronize *our brains and our actions*. In team sports like rowing and football, the brains of the players are linked up so that the physical efforts are timed with the magnificence of wireless communication. When my husband says, "Hey, the offensive line is really in sync" what he means is that the linemen on a football team are highly neurally coupled. And he's right!

We sync up not just with another human in another machine, but with other humans, individually or in groups, to share communication. This is well beyond a little Vulcan mind meld. This brainnet doesn't merely connect one consciousness to another. It connects *and coordinates* thoughts and behaviors in a social world that includes social rank, goals, and communitywide decision making. Consider that the next time you are in a movie and everyone laughs out loud at the same time. You are in a brainnet.

PATTERNICITY

> *We tell ourselves stories in order to live. . . . We live entirely, especially if we are writers, by the imposition of a narrative line upon disparate images, the 'ideas' which we have learned to freeze the shifting phantasmagoria which is our actual experience.*
>
> –Joan Didion,
> *The White Album*

In the most general sense, the job of the brain in every living organism is to keep the organism alive. It does this in two ways. First, it keeps the automatic systems like breathing and blood circulation operating. Second, it gathers whatever information it can from the outside world to protect itself. All animals have developed the capacity to bring in external information and process it. Taking in the stimuli and organizing them in patterns allows the brain to store a lot of information and also to access large numbers of individual incidents at the same time to use for decision making and sharing.[117] Putting these stimuli into patterns is an essential and valuable process. It allows us to efficiently synthesize information and to predict behavior, so we can plan for the future. For example, bird species learn the patterns of feeding grounds and remember the patterns of the landscape that lead them to the feeding grounds.

Language is an example of pattern recognition. First, we learn the sounds of language, and eventually we can put the sounds made by words in an order to express a meaning. What about the written word?

First we learn the order of the letters of the alphabet: A, B, C. Then we learn manipulated patterns, for example A-B-C can also be C-A-B and that this new pattern has a different meaning. Once we know what a cab is, we store it away almost permanently. The letters of the alphabet are used to make patterns with innumerable but specific meanings. We learn the pattern of letters which form words. We use patterns to process information for our own use and to pass it along to others.

Even though our brains have grown in size, the real estate up there is limited and valuable. When new data comes in through the senses, the human brain, programmed for efficiency, looks for patterns in the data so it can categorize and store it with the smallest use of the valuable real estate. We can see each bit of information, or we can see the common elements, identify the pattern, freeze-dry it down to its minimum size, throw out all the specific incidents and details in favor of the pattern, and store it in the smallest possible unit. But there's a price to pay.

When that information is brought up in the future, your brain will need to reconstitute it by putting each of the pieces back where they were originally located. Your brain is pretty good but not great at putting it back together again. Memories fray, splinter, disappear. But the pattern has probably been used before, and you can bring up the pattern. This strong desire to find patterns is called, yeah, here it comes, "patternicity." It represents our drive to find patterns so we can store the information. The more we remember patterns, the greater quantity of information we can store. Our brains have a patternicity bias because it uses less brain capacity than remembering each of the elements of the pattern, but we give up a good bit of specificity to do so.

Imagine holding a smiling picture of your best friend from high school. What happens in your brain? The picture is ready to be "put away"—that is, stored in memory. Your brain takes the picture, throws it in the Cuisinart and chops it into a kazillion pieces. Then the pieces go to their assigned places in your brain, smell going to smell, colors going to colors, a piece goes to facial recognition, another piece goes to where high school memories are stored, another to early beer-drinking memories, and another piece to the friend of your friend section. The yin to the yang of splintering memory in a kazillion pieces is that the brain is incredibly good at finding patterns to put the pieces back together. It revels in patterns.

If you think of patterns as the basis for such developments as language, you can understand why some neuroscientists believe that another pattern, Superior Pattern Processing (SPP) is the neurological basis for all of human culture.[118] SPP allows us to find patterns and change those patterns: We call it "progress" or "invention." It allows us to share the patterns, and we call that "language" and "writing." Most of that processing takes place in the default mode network.

We also see patterns in the thoughts and behaviors of others. Our ability to engage in social interaction depends, at least in part, on our ability to see patterns in the thinking of others, to use that information to predict future actions of those others, and to adjust our own behavior in interaction with those others. We remember the patterns demonstrated by the people we interact with particularly quickly. We use this mental faculty every single day. You are cranky in the morning. Your husband knows not to ask you why you didn't pay the bill you said you would until you've had two cups of coffee. He knows your pattern. You have a co-worker who loves getting out of the office, so she's the person you send to a meeting at a client's office. Your kid hates vegetables and loves jelly, so you promise the jelly sandwich if he eats the veggies. We learn the pattern and then use it to predict and manipulate future behavior.

Our pattern recognition as it applies to our fellow humans is both swift and acute. "We do not need to wait for multiple encounters before forming a response and do not have to dredge past memories to compute another's character at the moment we realize we need an assessment. We file a summary judgement effortlessly even on a first encounter, and we retain and recall this trait summary from semantic memory remarkably accurately."[119]

If you're wondering exactly how strong this instinct to find pattern is, consider the lowly *random numbers table*. At some point in high school or perhaps in Intro Psych, there was reference to the random number table and you wondered why some computer had to actually compose it. Wouldn't that be an easy thing to do, just randomly throw down some numbers? It turns out that it's very hard to do because our brains want patterns and when we try to create a random table, we wind up always making patterns instead.[120] *We can't be trusted to be random.*

Just as we tend to use pattern even when we intend to be random, when events truly are random, we'll search out the pattern anyway. Some of the patterns we perceive are accurate. Some aren't. We believe them all.

If you teach a child to recognize the difference between a square and a triangle, and then take out a puzzle, that child will know where to put the triangles and the squares to fill the puzzle. If we show that same child a video of two squares and a triangle moving, what pattern will she see? She will *not* describe it as two squares and a triangle moving. The kid will say something like "The mommy and the daddy are leaving and the little girl doesn't want them to go, so she follows them to the door." The child knows that *human relationships are patterns*. This example is a variation on the Heider-Simmel animations of geometric shapes moving,[121] and invariably we humans interpret the shapes as humans relating to each other. For a child, two identical objects and a third somewhat different object will be Mommy, Daddy, and kid because that is the most familiar alignment of human relationships to her. That is her pattern recognition. Two are moving? They must be leaving, because that's a world-shattering event to the child, and it comes right up as a fear response.

If there isn't a pattern, we'll make one up. And we'll give it meaning. Ever wonder about conspiracy theories?

Imagine that I am a frustrated middle-aged guy driving down my neighborhood street. I pass a pizza parlor where I once bought a slice of pizza and that the place was busy with a lot of annoying kids at the next table. It so happens that I think Hillary Clinton looks like a nasty or violent mother figure. I really don't like her; in fact, I think she's awful. I just heard that another cache of John Podesta emails will be released today, but no one knows what is in them. I am arguably a sane person. I'm driving and, as usual, I'm not paying much attention. In my "not paying much attention" space, my brain scans around for what to do with itself. It's looking for meaning or a pattern. It finds the pattern or relationship between the data points: The kids in the pizza parlor are enslaved, Hillary must be running the ring, and Podesta's emails have code on the child slavery ring that they are running from the pizza parlor. With that much evidence, and no more, on December 4, 2016, a man named Edgar Maddison Welch walked into the Comet Ping-Pong Pizzeria with an AR-15 type weapon and shot three times because he was apparently convinced that the pizza parlor was the center of a child slavery ring run by Hillary Clinton and needed immediate eradication. Three pieces of information pulled together into a false narrative.

A man in England in the 1960s noted that Paul McCartney had been out of sight for a while. In 1967, the Beatles released their *Sgt. Pepper's Lonely Hearts Club Band* album. On the cover, the band members, in fanciful uniforms, stand over a flower arrangement formed into stars and spelling out the band's name. Is there a pattern? Well, for some people, yes. Paul has disappeared and the album cover shows what could be interpreted as a funeral. Put them together as a pattern, and "Paul is dead!" The rumor spread around the world, with little tidbits of information reinterpreted to support the theory. Paul was just fine. Still is. But a false pattern would have it otherwise.

Conspiracy theories are false patterns that take non-associated events and weave a story together. We initially see a list of events: bad pizza place, Hillary is mean, emails leaked. These items have no connective tissue, no meaning. A conspiracy of child slaves run by Hillary with coded instructions? It's a pattern that has *meaning* and we can happily store it away for later use and retrieval. Haven't seen Paul McCartney lately plus funeral image? Paul is dead.

When we convert discrete items into a pattern, we create the connective tissue to hold the items together. We have converted a meaningless list to a meaningful pattern. In effect, we've given the list value. In reading, our desire for patternicity makes genres—like thrillers, murder mysteries, and romance novels—attractive to us. We know the pattern of the genre, so we can spend more time on the elements within the genre and less time and brain function trying to figure out what the genre or pattern is.

Patterns make it easier for our brains to process input. We don't normally have encyclopedic memory of past events, but rather we have highly available and efficient memory of *the gist* of situations and characters. We process out the details but retain easy access to the most important parts. It seems that we value our memories by their qualitative utility, not their specific accuracy.

How does patternicity affect writing? Genres are patterns. We understand what a mystery or a romance is, and we spend our attention on the content of the story, not its architecture. As writers, we can determine the elements our readers will want to experience within the genre, and we help our readers into the deeper meaning that we are trying to express.

As people who are writing for happiness, we are writing alternatives to our pre-existing, already embedded pattern. Each additional unit of attention is rewriting the existing pattern and changing the pattern for future use. Before we start a new story, some bit of our history is floating around in our unconscious, irritated and unsolved. When we write, we are changing the ending on that particular pattern. When a comparable situation arises in the future, we will bring up the new pattern, the one with the happier ending.

We love patterns, but what if there really isn't a pattern to be found? Do we just make them up?

Yup. Just ask the piece of your brain known as *The Interpreter*.

THE INTERPRETER

We have a part of our brain that just makes up stuff on the fly and then convinces us it's all true. We have an internal *truthiness machine*. An inner flim-flam man.

Thank goodness.

Our brains have two separate hemispheres—left and right. There's a road straight down the middle, called the *corpus collasum*. In experimental surgeries, neurosurgeons have cut the corpus collasum so that the hemispheres are not as directly connected. The results became known as the right brain-left brain split. The right brain is credited with, among other skills, all sorts of creativity. The left brain is your inner accountant or librarian, who keeps everything in neat and perfect order.

Michael Gazzaniga is a premier neuroscientist who led the research in discovering the right brain-left brain paradigm.[122] Imagine that the two hemispheres are independent of each other. If we show each separate hemisphere of the brain a list or set of pictures, what happens? Gazzaniga discovered that the right brain can keep an accurate list of the items that have been perceived. If there are blanks on that list or a spray of pictures, the right brain records it as a blank space. What does the left side do? The left side cannot tolerate the blanks. There is a module in the left hemisphere whose function is to reconcile new information with old information. It takes in the new data, finds the old data, and merges them. What if there is a blank or a place with no data? This module in the left side just fills in the blank creatively. It makes it up. It confabulates. The interpreter is like your lugubrious friend who is great at telling stories that entertain but not too particular about keeping the facts straight.

Importantly, the interpreter makes up new stories *and believes them*. To this essential part of your brain and therefore to you, the *connections* matter but the *truth* does not.

What does real life look like when the main road that connects the two hemispheres, the corpus collasum, is inadequate, damaged, or non-existent? It looks like the actual life of Kim Peek, the man *Rainman* was based on. He had agenesis of the corpus callosum—that is, the complete or partial absence of the corpus callosum. Peek could hold massive quantities of information but was unable to integrate the information into meaning. His father was his lifelong caretaker because Kim couldn't function on his own. He had no other meaningful relationships and could not do simple motor tasks like combing his hair. He had no connections between his vast knowledge of facts and his interpreter to help him understand the *significance* of the facts.

Remember those 11 million bits of information every second? The interpreter picks out what's worth keeping, finds a template from your memory to use for the new stuff, and stores it away. All the other input gets tossed out.

When something you've seen looks odd, but a moment later you realize "it makes sense," the time between the instant that the information comes in through your eye and the instant "it makes sense" is the time your interpreter has taken to process the information and find the pattern for it that you are willing to believe. As Gazzaniga says, "The interpreter [is] driven to infer cause and effect. It continually explains the world."[123] The right brain is literal and specific. Not so the left hemisphere. "So, when it comes to the interpreter, facts are cool, but not necessary. The left brain uses whatever is at hand and ad libs the rest. The first makes-sense explanation will do. It looks for cause and effect and creates order out of the chaos of inputs that have been presented to it by all the other processes spewing out information. *That is what our brain does all day long: It takes input from various areas of our brain and from the environment and synthesizes it into a story that makes sense*."[124]

Our brain takes in all the information and puts it into story form. It's not a list of facts. It's not the truth. It's a narrative or story made up of the truth and whatever else the interpreter needs to make it *meaningful* and *memorable*. Let's take another look at that. The brain takes in the information, rewrites it through the interpreter to have it make sense, and sends it into the memory pod.

As literary scholar Jonathan Gottschall explains, "The storytelling mind is a crucial evolutionary adaptation. It allows us to experience our lives as coherent, orderly, and meaningful. It is what makes life more than a blooming buzzing confusion. . . . The storytelling mind is allergic to uncertainty, randomness, and coincidence."[125]

Our narratives are inaccurate but highly efficient. We have a *confabulator in chief* in our brain because "This elaboration has a deleterious effect on accuracy but usually *makes it easier to process new information*."[126]

The best way for your left brain to remember information is to reduce it to a cause-and-effect narrative and store it away in a pattern for use later. We call these narratives "stories" and love them because so far it's the best way to organize information and keep it on the ready.

Why are stories so important to us? Your brain doesn't just hold stories; it *is* stories. If we want to make a change or improve at a task or write our way to happiness, we do it in the language of our brains and our minds. We do it by creating stories.

READ A BOOK, THE SEQUEL

Remember how reading a book helps your body and soul? Is anything happening in your brain to support the purported benefits of reading a novel? Yes, plenty.

Reading is like going to the gym for your brain. Areas of the brain concerned with language go to work, increasing the interactions of neuronal networks in the brain. Reading is learning, and neuroplastic change takes place. We can create more white matter. We exercise and expand our working memory. Unlike hearing or watching a story, while reading, we can stop and process it at our own speed, which lets us keep the elements in our working memory for as long as we want them there. We increase the connectivity in the brain, which means we are improving how different parts of the brain work with each other.[127]

When we curl up and read the latest from Kate Atkinson or John Grisham or Nicholas Sparks, we experience the fictional world as if it is the real world: All those areas of the brain, smell, touch, language—all of it lights up. We open the pages and let the real world around us fade away, which is the squishy way of saying that we activate our default mode network. An activated DMN decreases our attention to the external world, including cues and filters that reflect societal norms and physical truths. When we suspend disbelief, we close down our doubts about the experience we are reading or watching. We buy in.

Our mirror neurons fire up. When the character leans over a hot stove, we feel the heat, which is to say that the neurons in our brain that would interpret the stimulus of the heat from the stove activate. When a breeze carrying the scent of fresh jasmine wafts into the character's room, our mirror neurons feel the breeze and smell the jasmine. Our brains light up for all of the sensory stimuli the novel presents to our eyes.

The medial temporal lobe subnetwork of the DMN responds to sensory passages. The dorsomedial prefrontal cortex (dmPFC) lights up for social or abstract content.[128] The hippocampus works with spatial relationships and creates a sense for us of physically being in the scenes presented in the fiction. Identification with characters activates the dmPFC, which processes narrative and is thought to manage representations of the self in relation to imagined scenarios.[129]

The more involved we are in the novel, the more we identify with the main character. What do we mean by identifying with a character? We all know the feeling of reading a novel or watching a movie and feeling simpatico with the protagonist. Our DMN is now toggled to on. Our mirror neurons fire as if we are the character. *Identifying* has a physical reality in our brain: Our neural networks fire and wire, again and again, as if we are the protagonist. We *feel empathy*; we neuronally couple with the storyteller and become a pale mirror image of the protagonist. We always know we are not the protagonist, and yet her mind is our mind, and her feelings are our feelings. We are merged.

As the protagonist faces her obstacle, we readers replicate that emotional and physical moment: We *simulate* the situation of the protagonist. And just like sitting in a flight simulator to perfect our piloting skills, we are in a life simulator, perfecting our human skills by experiencing the protagonist's journey, choices, and victories. We are not evil Dr. Van Gelder acting cruelly, but rather Dr. Spock—so completely merged with Van Gelder that Spock can feel all of the emotions and thoughts of Van Gelder. In this mode of feeling the emotions and actions of another, we learn new actions and thoughts. By merging with a character, our brain neuroplastically encodes the experiences of the character in our own brain. It is not with so much strength as to overcome our *self*, but with a familiarity of emotions and behaviors as if taken by ourselves.

The brain builds neural models of the story.[130] The part of our brain that comprehends narrative overlaps substantially with the part of the brain that processes theory of mind.[131] In effect, the brain is taking in the fictional world as a simulation to prepare us for our own, personal, real world.

If you read some fiction, your brain uses that opportunity to merge with the fictional world and transfer the experience and the knowledge you gained to your own brain, without you ever having to go and actually have the experience. Reading fiction hotwires your brain for learning, empathy, and kindness.

What about non-fiction?

The answer isn't absolute, but the evidence is strong that when you take in facts, your brain files them in memory as rational information, without all the mirror neurons and identification and DMN firing. The more areas of the brain we use, the more important and more permanent the experience is. Facts just don't use that much of your brain.[132]

Are there levels of identification? Yes. The more intense the identification with the fictional world, *the more intense the changes in the audience member*.[133] We have some identification with the anthropomorphic robot in the *Transformers* movies, but when I watch a hardware movie, I catch myself wondering how the special effects were created and whether the narrative line has loosened at the beginning of the second act. Then I know I have the brain space to think about these things because I am simply not that engaged in the movie itself. We noted earlier that when subjects watched a Clint Eastwood movie, the emotions of the audience members reflected the emotions of the character Clint Eastwood is playing. It's a tighter identification than with a machine. But sometimes I find myself wondering how they lit the over-the-shoulder shot, and then I know I'm engaged in the craft of movie-making and not identifying with the story. Sometimes, though, I am enjoying a book or a film so much that I really don't have an awareness of the world around me. I've forgotten that I am consuming media and feel only that I care about the character and the dilemmas she faces. This would be a more intense level of identification.

At this level of engagement, the character is presenting a simulation of real life, and theory of mind jumps to the front of the cognitive line. We are passively flowing with the story, but our brain is analyzing everyone in the scene: what they want, what they fear, what is likely to happen next. We are in the flight simulator of a social environment, sharing the character's point of view in learning about the social world the character faces right now—one which we might face in real life tomorrow. We are honing our social skills.

Is there an even more intense level of involvement with fiction?

Yup. Cue the Star Trek theme, and beam me up, Scotty. We're off to the transporter deck.

WRITE A STORY REVISITED

If we are so involved with the story that our real world disappears and we project ourselves more fully into a story, psychologists say we are *transported*. "We conceptualized transportation into a narrative world as a distinct mental process, an integrative melding of attention, imagery, and feelings."[134]

"Transportation is defined as 'a convergent process, where all mental systems and capacities become focused on events occurring in the narrative.'"[135] "People lose track of time and fail to observe events going on around them; a loss of self-awareness may take place."[136] "The narrative world is distant from the world in which the reader lives and makes it possible that the events in the story are perceived as real within the story context, even when events would not be possible in reality."[137]

The most intense interaction of the reader and the protagonist that I have found in the literature is this transportation of the reader into the fictive world. At that level of involvement, the impact of the fiction is heightened yet again. Entering this imaginary world, we throw off even more of the restraints of the real world. We are even less likely to have concern for factual accuracy or critical analysis. We become oblivious to false notes. When we as audience members are transported into a story, we are ever more likely to experience the events as truly personal, and we are thereby more apt to be changed by what happens on the page to a fictional character.

We feel what the character feels. We learn what the character learns. In the real world, we reality-check all the time, running a doubt filter to make sure we don't get fooled. We turn it way down when we read. Because we accept the world as the story presents it, *we internalize the experience without doubt.*

We know that reading a book can change someone's life. By reading about someone else's journey, we have simulated that experience, and gained the benefits and wisdoms of that journey. If the protagonist comes out not just wiser but happier, then we, too, have absorbed the lessons of the journey and the happiness as well. Keep reading, and your little happiness bonus units will keep adding up.

Our absorption in story not only changes how we feel in that moment, but also *changes our behavior.*[138] The more involved we are with the fiction, the greater is our ability to change ourselves. We have made this progress simply by being couch potatoes and passively observing that journey by reading. If each level of involvement increases the power of the vicarious experience of the journey of the protagonist while you are passively reading, can you imagine the huge jump in impact when you go from passively viewing it to actively creating it?

Reading can light a lovely flame of change for us. If we want more than that, we have to use the magic fire accelerant. Let's light it up. What's the accelerant? Well, writing, of course.

When we looked at POV shots, we saw the famous *Jaws* scene from the points of view of the objective camera and also from inside the shark. It's a scene about a killer shark attacking a child. What happens if you are the writer instead of the passive audience member? The writer will start by going into the boy's mind. We experience the boy kicking away, maybe he gets a little seawater in his mouth, spits it out, looks up at the seashore to wave to mom and dad, and continues swimming. That's the first perspective.

To write the scene, we'll now go into the shark. We only have a shark brain, so all we think is "umm, hungry, umm, food." We close in on the prey and take a good bite. "Umm, good." The shark feels some satisfaction. That is the second perspective.

But we are in the shark's mind and we can see the results of our shark-action. We can observe the terror on the kid's face and the gruesome sight of the child's limb torn from the body, the blood in the water. We hear screams as the effects of the attack play out. Do we still feel "umm, hungry, umm, good"? Do we *also* have some empathy for the kid and some horror at the damage we have just caused?

We have experienced both being victimized by a man-eating shark and also victimizing the young boy. Haven't we, as the shark, just changed how we see our self because we feel empathy for the victim? If we "go inside" two characters in the same interaction, the experience is additive, and your empathic response changes you.

The writer has just experienced two levels of theory of mind, the shark and the kid. What if we add a third level of awareness?

This very question is dramatized in the movie *Disney's The Kid*. Bruce Willis plays Russ Duritz, an image consultant. Russ's childhood self, Rusty, played by Spencer Breslin, comes to visit Russ. Where

Russ is smooth, Rusty is a dork. The story asks, what can Rusty do to be less dorky? Or the reverse, what can Russ do to be more accepting of his flawed self? What event caused this transformation from dorky to cool? And is it a good thing? Russ is, after all, not just attractive but insensitive and repressed as well.

In the film, young Rusty gets to relive a traumatic event from his past while Russ looks on. Rusty has done something wrong, and his father reprimands him. Rusty starts to cry. Dad then yells at him. When Rusty tries to control his tears, he develops a twitch. We writers are in Rusty's mind and he is overwhelmed and frightened.

Now we have to go into Dad's mind. What's going on there? Dad is angry and tells Rusty that his mom is sick and "we could lose her." Does Rusty understand this? No, he's still a child with a narcissistic mindset, wondering how to not get yelled at.

Can Dad understand what this is doing to Rusty? No, he's overwhelmed by his fear of losing his wife. We have no synthesis of the points of view.

What do we do now? We writers need to create another perspective on this event. How about having Russ watch this interaction? Russ can watch and try to understand the experience from within the minds of both Rusty and Dad. Russ represents the next (third) level of consciousness. He can feel how frightened the kid is. He can feel how angry the dad is. He can also feel, as the kid cannot, how terrified the father is about the potential loss of his wife. This is information not available to the kid and not quite cognizable in the dad.

Russ thus provides an additional, more elevated and empathetic awareness or theory of mind. He can imagine the separate consciousness of the kid, who is frightened because Dad is yelling at him. He is also into Dad's mind while the man is shouting because the father is terrified, overwhelmed, and weak. From Russ's point of view, the dad, who has only been a tough disciplinarian in the past, is now *also* vulnerable and flawed. He isn't frightening to Russ anymore, but rather more nuanced and worthy of compassion.

This understanding transforms the relationship between Russ and Dad. Russ knows the father never intended to hurt his son; the father was just having a fully human moment of freaking out in front of his son because the man's wife is dying. And Rusty was scarred by the event because he couldn't experience his father's fear. We can understand the emotions of each of the two characters, but they are still at loggerheads. The two perspectives understand, but are too limited to resolve the situation. For that beneficial outcome, we need a third point of view. We need Russ. He gives us the compassionate outlook that synthesizes the event into an adult, empathetic perspective. Whew.

Russ's consciousness is different from, and wiser than, either of the previous levels of theory of mind. Adding Russ's POV makes the entire experience that much more intense, memorable, and transformative. That's the importance of the additional layer. It brings us more nuance, more depth, more opportunity to grow.

But who is watching this scene or reading this story? We writers must necessarily consider, and enter, yet another level of consciousness. Our job is to entertain and engage the audience. What's going on inside the folks sitting on the couch, watching the movie or reading the book about the three fictional characters? How the audience is processing the story is crucial to our job as writers. How are the actions of Rusty (1) and the reactions of Dad (2) integrated by Russ (3) and processed in the minds of the audience (4)? What benefit is that to us, this fourth level of theory of mind? By watching Russ integrate the information, we the audience learn how to integrate information, and that it has an impact on our ability to grow and change. Each additional level of consciousness brings with it additional benefits, if we can keep it all straight. We go into the mind of the reader or audience member because our job is to effectively communicate the story. When we review our writing and ask whether "it works," we are asking what is going on in the mind of our audience member. If it doesn't work, we have failed and have to try again. If it works, we've brought the message home to its target, that additional layer of mind.

But wait, can we add yet another beneficial level of understanding? Of course! Someone had to think up Rusty, the conflict with Dad, the observations of Russ, and the emotions of the audience! That's right, there's a fifth level of theory of mind, who keeps all this emotional analysis and learning going. It's us! It's the writers! The mind of the writer has to not just passively watch all this, but also must originate it. The writer's mind is always yet another level of consciousness. To adequately do our job, we are challenged to bring yet a further level of understanding, compassion, analysis and wisdom. We may be quiet about it, but we bring a lot of consciousness to the table, and *we receive a lot of benefit from it, if we so choose.*

For some number of years, the Writer's Guild tried to bring more respect to the lowly screen and television writers by taking out billboards on Sunset Boulevard with a picture and the written dialogue of famous scenes, with the headline "Someone wrote that." It's as if the Hollywood writers corps was standing on a soap box screaming, "Hey we're the smart ones! We thought it all up!" Or, perhaps they could have shouted, "Hey, we're the smart ones! We bring an additional level of theory of mind!" I grant you that it would be a terrible advertising slogan, but it would have the benefit of being true, at least the theory of mind part. When we write, we have the minds of all the characters in the scene before us. We go in and become each of them, with straight empathy and theory of mind.

But writing is different. Writing is *active*. We don't just watch these characters' minds; we choose, direct, and express their feelings and thoughts. We are transformed into all the characters and the synthesized content of the totality of the scene.

When we write, we are in the brain of a character when that character speaks. Then we switch to the brain of another character when that character speaks. We don't write dialogue from the outside. We compose dialogue from inside the mind of each character in the first person. We are the first person who speaks. Then we go into the second person, the listener, to see how it plays. We might have a third character in the scene, like Russ, who is a synthesizer or pure observer. Russ has the third level of consciousness, which the writer shares. But how is the audience feeling about the scene? The writer has to consider how the audience feels about Russ's synthesis of Dad's anger at Rusty.

We writers are the God-figure living in the head of each and all the characters, understanding all of them at the same time, synthesizing it all, and creating all their emotions and behaviors. We are the fifth level of theory of mind. Writing a story or scene like this requires that the writer exercises an extraordinary sensitivity to and understanding of the minds of all of these people simultaneously as they *react* to each other as they are *moving through time*. The process develops a daunting understanding of other people and of ourselves.

What does it mean for the writer to go inside everyone's mind? Like Russ, the writer will feel empathy *for all sides*. The writer *is* each of them. The bad guy isn't all bad. The good guy is flawed. We transform our emotions about the victimizers to have empathy for what drove them in the first place. We don't have to like them for it, but we will have a level of understanding, *and that takes the onus off your character for having the flaws in the first place*. Dad yelling at Rusty? Well, that third level of consciousness could say, Rusty got frightened because he was a kid, and dad was frightened because of mom. . . . Hey, look at that: Dad isn't a monster, he's just human. Rusty isn't a dork, he's just human. Great, we can love them both!

The benefit of the transportation? Do we have to love all our characters, and even like the child-eating shark? No, we don't. It still ate a child who could not defend himself. But in our horror at the event, we can also see that the shark was following an evolutionary mandate. It wasn't an intentional murder. It was a force of nature, with less malice than we would have expected. We can still hate the antagonist and yet learn from our changed perspective.

As writers and creators, we live in the minds of our characters as they interact with each other, and we learn the lessons they learn. We empathize with everyone. And since characters are pieces of ourselves projected onto the page, we can have more love and empathy for *ourselves*. We can love the pieces of us, not for prideful reasons, but because we have increased our acceptance, empathy, and compassion for others and ourselves.

WHY WRITING STORIES WORKS

We writers are not passive couch potatoes. We are creators. We choose the emotions, actions, and words of each of the characters. We are *actively* in the consciousness of all the characters involved. And we feel empathy and understanding for each and all of them. We choose each behavior of each person in the scene. To accomplish this amazing trick, we go into the mind of each of the characters and *simulate* all the possibilities for emotions and actions that we can think of for each of the characters. We aren't just simulating a perspective. We are a multi-dimensional interpersonal simulation super-consciousness. We have felt and thought through every possibility we could imagine, multiplied by the number of characters in the situation.

So let's review. You and I, the writers, let our sub-conscious come up with an idea about something that is bothering us. We write a story, following the basic rules. We experience the problem from every perspective we can think up. We try every solution we can imagine, for every character. We writers have had to experience the internal world of the bad guy or antagonist in the moment of victimizing

219

us, the protagonist. Our view of the antagonist must change. When that happens, our view of the protagonist—that is, some version of ourselves—also changes. When our hero realizes this new synthesis, we realize it, too. As the character is changed and victorious, so are we. We now have the all the knowledge gained from inside each person's head as they behaved in interaction with each other. We've absorbed the growth of the protagonist, the empathy of the fearsome but defeated antagonist, the synthesis by the observer, and the integration of the reader.

Remember our friend, the default mode network? It is that non-additive part of our brain which toggles on when we are doing nothing, but toggles off when we are focusing on a task. What happens when we turn our focus to working on a story or trying to figure out what our main character is going to say to the antagonist in the next confrontation? New research indicates that there are a few types of tasks relating to the self and social interactions that engage *both* the default mode and other, conscious operations of the brain. The DMN is activated ("on") during conscious tasks like episodic and working memory, forecasting, emotional processing, and, most importantly, the interpretation of narratives.[139] In other words, during the process of creating narratives, we use the DMN *plus* other networks. Creative writing is different than almost all our other activities because it adds more areas of the brain to the activity. More of our brain is engaged. More brain with fewer filters means more neuronal engagement, which in turn creates more connectivity, which causes more neuroplasticity, which means we have more learning, which means we have more change. Again, your brain is on fire in a way that is more intense and unique compared to all the other ways you use your brain.

That's why you can write to happiness. Because writing is that much more intense, active, and involving. While you are writing fiction, you are not just "like" the character before you, you <u>are</u> character. You ponder the choices, make the decisions, play out the scenarios, and gain or suffer the consequences. This is so much more than merely simulating some possibilities. This is *living the possibilities*, and the choices, the changes in perspective, the wisdom, the failures, and the rewards—all in the first person. When we write fiction, we throw Miracle-Gro on transportation theory . . . We <u>are</u> the character. What that character learns, we learn. Our brains change to include the new knowledge, the new wisdom, the new perspective. We write our way to a better us. And this is why our writing to happiness must follow the rules of good storytelling. We will be tempted to drop out early or take the easy way out. Good storytelling requires that you face the obstacles and surmount them. Good storytelling requires that you find a genuine resolution and write a real ending. And when you do, you—in the real world—have encoded those lessons and perspectives into your own mind, through the combined miracles of transportation, mirror neurons, simulations, and the great exercise of neuroplasticity. You have focused and reworked and paid so much attention to your writing that the highways of your brain have been rerouted and you are, indeed, the hero of the journey. You have managed to do this remarkable work from the comfort of your own desk, in your jammies, without breaking a sweat because it was always just fiction, you were never really physically at risk, and your interpreter sewed it all up. You believed it was real, so the *changes in your brain are real*. You emerge no longer an innocent with obstacles, but an adult who has resolved the problem of the past and integrated the information you may always have had into a new wisdom. You can throw off the old baggage that slowed you down. You've written yourself to greater skill, understanding, and happiness.

FURTHER MATERIALS
FOR WRITERS

STORYBONES

WORKSHEETS FOR
BUILDING YOUR STORY

Fill in the blanks to find the skeleton of your story.

1, The Spine

My character named _____ wants _____ but _____ stands in the way.

2, The Breaks

A, Meet my character, who lives in a place called _____.

B, Then one day, _____ happens.

C, And it's finally worked out when _____.

3, The Tale

Once upon a time, _____.

And then one day, _____.

And just when everything was going so well, _____.

When just at the last minute, _____.

And they all lived happily ever after.

4, The Spine

Once upon a time there was _____. Every day _____. One day _____. Because of that, _____. Because of that, _____. Finally, _____.

5, The Hero

What does she want? She wants _____.

What is stopping her? _____ is in her way.

What is she afraid of? She's afraid of _____.

6, The Opposition

What does the opposing force want? He wants _____.

What is he willing to do to get it? He's willing to _____.

What special assets or powers does he have to foil the Hero? _____.

What in his past that makes an ultimate battle over the problem inevitable? He _____.

7, More about The Hero

If she wants _____, then _____.

What happens if she doesn't get it? She'll _____.

Why now? Because if not now, she'll lose _____.

8, The Short Story

In the beginning, the hero named _____ lives in this place called _____ at a time when _____ and everything is fine, but we know there is a problem about _____ (theme). Another character/force/event makes our hero consider that this has become a problem. Then everything changes because _____ (Act One turn).

My Hero then plans _____, but _____ and, even worse, _____, until everything is lost.

Then my hero decides she must _____ and so she does this _____ and wins or loses, thus _____ (the resolution.)

9, The Lovely Bones

1, The Beginning: meet my hero, _____.

2, My hero is behaving in her normal world, with her normal life, which looks like _____.

3, Then _____ happens that causes the hero to know a choice will have to be made.

4, Then a really big thing, _____, happens, and the hero must act.

5, The hero plans and gathers skills and resources. The hero has this plan: _____.

6, It looks like it's going to work because _____.

7, But then things start to fall apart when _____ happens.

8, Until finally, everything is lost because _____ happens.

9, The hero realizes she must face the ultimate battle, which is _____.

10, The ultimate battle is engaged because the hero and the villain are face to face and _____.

11, And they live happily or unhappily ever after.

10, CLOSING EXERCISE

Revisit the spine of your story. Delete anything that doesn't directly relate to:

My character named _____ wants _____, but _____ stands in the way.

FURTHER READING FOR WRITERS

Bell, James S. *The Art of War for Writers: Fiction Writing Strategies, Tactics, and Exercises*. Cincinnati, OH: Writer's Digest, 2009.

Bettelheim, Bruno. *The Uses of Enchantment: The Meaning and Importance of Fairy Tales*. New York, NY: Vintage, 2010.

Bradbury, Ray. *Zen in the Art of Writing*. Santa Barbara, CA: Joshua Odell Editions, 2013.

Cameron, Julia. *The Artist's Way: A Spiritual Path to Higher Creativity*. New York, NY: Jeremy M. Tarcher/Perigree, 2002.

Campbell, Joseph. *The Hero with a Thousand Faces*. Princeton, NJ: Bollingen Foundation, 2004.

Cooney, Gus, Daniel T. Gilbert, and Timothy D. Wilson. "The Novelty Penalty: Why Do People Like Talking About New Experiences but Hearing About Old Ones?" *Psychological Science* 28, no. 3 (March 2017), 380–394. doi:10.1177/0956797616685870.

Csikszentmihalyi, Mihaly. *Finding Flow: The Psychology of Engagement with Everyday Life*. New York, NY: Basic Books, 1997.

DeSalvo, Louise A. *Writing as a Way of Healing: How Telling Our Stories Transforms Our Lives*. Boston, MA: Beacon Press, 2000.

Dunbar, Robin I. M. "Why Are Good Writers So Rare? An Evolutionary Perspective on Literature." *Journal of Cultural and Evolutionary Psychology*

3, no. 1 (March 2005), 7–21. doi:10.1556/jcep.3.2005.1.1.

Field, Syd. *Screenplay: The Foundations of Screenwriting*. New York, NY: Delta Trade Paperbacks, 2005.

Gardner, John. *The Art of Fiction: Notes on Craft for Young Writers*. New York, NY: Vintage, 1991.

Goldberg, Natalie. *The True Secret of Writing: Connecting Life with Language*. New York: Atria Books, 2013.

Goldberg, Natalie. *Writing Down the Bones: Freeing the Writer Within*. Boston, MA: Shambhala Press, 2006.

Goldberg, Natalie. *Wild Mind: Living the Writer's Life*. New York: Bantam, 1990.

Gornick, Vivian. *The Situation and the Story: The Art of Personal Narrative*. New York, NY: Farrar, Straus and Giroux, 2002.

Immordino-Yang, Mary Helen, Joanna A. Christodoulou, and Vanessa Singh. "Rest Is Not Idleness: Implications of the Brain's Default Mode for Human Development and Education." *Perspectives on Psychological Science* 7, no. 4 (2012), 352–364. doi:10.1177/1745691612447308.

Kaufman, Scott Barry, and Carolyn Gregoire. *Wired to Create: Unraveling the Mysteries of the Creative Mind*. New York, NY: Penguin, 2015.

King, Stephen. *On Writing: A Memoir of the Craft*. New York, NY: Simon & Schuster, 2002.

Lanouette, Jennine. "A History of Three-Act Structure." 1999. Screentakes. Last modified December 24, 2012. https://www.screentakes.com/an-evolutionary-study-of-the-three-act-structure-model-in-drama/.

Robley, Chris. "Kurt Vonnegut's 8 rules for writing a short story." BookBaby Blog. Last modified November 20, 2013. https://blog.bookbaby.com/2013/11/kurt-vonneguts-8-rules-for-writing-a-short-story/.

Mamet, David. *Bambi vs. Godzilla: On the Nature, Purpose, and Practice of the Movie Business*. New York, NY: Vintage Books, 2008.

Mamet, David. *Three Uses of the Knife: On the Nature and Purpose of Drama*. New York, NY: Vintage Books, 2000.

Maran, Meredith. *Why We Write: 20 Acclaimed Authors on How and Why They Do What They Do*. London, England: Penguin, 2013.

McDonnell, Jane Taylor. *Living to Tell the Tale: A Guide to Writing Memoir*. New

York, NY: Penguin Books, 1998.

McKee, Robert. *Story: Style, Structure, Substance, and the Principles of Screenwriting*, 1st ed. New York, NY: ReganBooks, 1997.

Mehl-Madrona, Lewis. *Healing the Mind through the Power of Story: The Promise of Narrative Psychiatry*. Rochester, VT: Bear & Company, 2010.

Merzenich, Michael. *Soft-Wired: How the New Science of Brain Plasticity Can Change Your Life*, 2nd ed. San Francisco, CA: Parnassus Publishing, 2013.

Murdock, Maureen. *The Heroine's Journey*. Boulder, CO: Shambhala Publications, 1990.

Oates, Joyce Carol. *The Faith of a Writer: Life, Craft, Art*. New York, NY: HarperCollins, 2003.

Pearson, Carol S. *The Hero Within: Six Archetypes We Live By*. Revised & expanded ed, 3rd ed. San Francisco, CA: HarperSanFrancisco, 2013.

Popova, Maria. "Neil Gaiman's 8 Rules of Writing." Last modified September 18, 2015. https://www.brainpickings.org/2012/09/28/neil-gaiman-8-rules-of-writing/.

Lamar, Cyriaque. "The 22 rules of storytelling, according to Pixar." Gizmodo. (Originally shared in 2011 as a series of tweets by Emma Coats, @lawnrocket). Last modified June 8, 2012. https://io9.gizmodo.com/the-22-rules-of-storytelling-according-to-pixar-5916970.

Robson, David. "Heroes and villains." *The Psychologist*, August 2016. https://thepsychologist.bps.org.uk/heroes-and-villains.

Seger, Linda. *Making a Good Script Great*. Hollywood, CA: Samuel French, 1987.

Seger, Linda. *Making a Good Writer Great: A Creativity Workbook for Screenwriters*. Los Angeles, CA: Silman James Press, 1999.

Vogler, Christopher. *The Writer's Journey: Mythic Structure for Writers*, 3rd ed. Studio City, CA: Michael Wiese Productions, 2007.

Wilfong, Cheryl. *The Meditative Gardener: Cultivating Mindfulness of Body, Feelings, and Mind*. Putney, VT: Heart Path Press, 2010.

REFERENCES

1   Michael Merzenich, *Soft-Wired: How the New Science of Brain Plasticity Can Change Your Life* (San Francisco, CA: Parnassus Publishing, 2013), 203.

2   David Mamet, *Three Uses of the Knife: On the Nature and Purpose of Drama* (New York, NY: Vintage Books, 2000), 30.

3   Stephen King, *On Writing: A Memoir of the Craft* (New York, NY: Simon & Schuster, 2002).

4   Linda Seger, *Making a Good Script Great* (Hollywood, CA: Samuel French, 1987), 125.

5   Syd Field, *Screenplay: The Foundations of Screenwriting* (New York, NY: Delta Trade Paperbacks, 2005), 246–247.

6   Chris Robley, "Kurt Vonnegut's 8 rules for writing a short story," BookBaby Blog, last modified November 20, 2013, https://blog.bookbaby.com/2013/11/kurt-vonneguts-8-rules-for-writing-a-short-story/.

7   David Mamet, *Bambi vs. Godzilla: On the Nature, Purpose, and Practice of the Movie Business* (New York, NY: Vintage Books, 2008), 112.

8   Maria Popova, "Neil Gaiman's 8 Rules of Writing," Brain Pickings, last modified September 18, 2015, https://www.brainpickings.org/2012/09/28/neil-gaiman-8-rules-of-writing/.

9   Jonathan Gottschall, *The Storytelling Animal: How Stories Make Us*

Human (Boston, MA: Houghton Mifflin Harcourt, 2012), 11.

10   Ibid., 11.

11   The commonly accepted ad exposure rate of 5,000 a day comes from a study by Yankelovich dating before the spread of social media. See, e.g., Louise Story, "Anywhere the Eye Can See, It's Likely to See an Ad," *New York Times*, February 15, 2007, https://www.nytimes.com/2007/01/15/business/media/15everywhere.html. More recent estimates now reach 10,000 ads per day, or more. See, e.g., Jon Simpson, "Finding brand success in the digital world," Forbes Agency Council, last modified August 25, 2017, https://www.forbes.com/sites/forbesagencycouncil/2017/08/25/finding-brand-success-in-the-digital-world/#3923c536626e.

12   Leo Widrich, "The Science of Storytelling: Why Telling a Story is the Most Powerful Way to Activate Our Brains," *Lifehacker*, December 5, 2012, https://lifehacker.com/the-science-of-storytelling-why-telling-a-story-is-the-5965703.

13   See, e.g., Jonathan Gottschall et al., "Patterns of characterization in folktales across geographic regions and levels of cultural complexity," *Human Nature* 14, no. 4 (December 2003): 365–382, doi:10.1007/s12110-003-1011-3.

14   Ibid.

15   Glen McBride, "Storytelling, Behavior Planning, and Language Evolution in Context," *Frontiers in Psychology* 5 (2014), doi:10.3389/fpsyg.2014.01131.

16   Brian Boyd, "The Evolution of Stories: From Mimesis to Language, from Fact to Fiction," *Wiley Interdisciplinary Reviews: Cognitive Science* 9, no. 1 (2017): 6, doi:10.1002/wcs.1444, citing Daniel Dor, *The Instruction of Imagination: Language as a Social Communication Technology* (New York: Oxford University Press, 2015), 31, 33, and 204, n. 2.

17   Ibid., 7.

18   See, generally, McBride, "Storytelling, Behavior Planning, and Language Evolution in Context," 4.

19   Ibid.

20   Jennifer Vanderbes, "The Evolutionary Case for Great Fiction," *The Atlantic*, September 5, 2013, https://www.theatlantic.com/entertainment/ar-

chive/2013/09/the-evolutionary-case-for-great-fiction/279311/.

21   James W. Pennebaker and Sandra K. Beall, "Confronting a Traumatic Event. Toward an Understanding of Inhibition and Disease," *Journal of Abnormal Psychology* 95, no. 3 (August 1986): 274–281, doi:10.1037//0021-843x.95.3.274.

22   Ibid.

23   James W. Pennebaker and John F. Evans, *Expressive Writing: Words that Heal* (Enumclaw, WA: Idyll Arbor, 2014), 3 et seq.

24   Brynne C. DiMenichi et al., "Writing About Past Failures Attenuates Cortisol Responses and Sustained Attention Deficits Following Psychosocial Stress," *Frontiers in Behavioral Neuroscience* 12 (2018), doi:10.3389/fnbeh.2018.00045.

25   James W. Pennebaker and Joshua M. Smyth, *Opening Up by Writing It Down: How Expressive Writing Improves Health and Eases Emotional Pain* (New York, NY: The Guilford Press, 2016), 23.

26   Pennebaker and Evans, *Expressive Writing*, 43 et seq.

27   Ibid., 48.

28   Ibid., x.

29   Sophie Nicholls, "Beyond Expressive Writing: Evolving Models of Developmental Creative Writing," *Journal of Health Psychology* 14, no. 2 (March 2009): 174, doi:10.1177/1359105308100201.

30   Timothy D. Wilson, *Strangers to Ourselves: Discovering the Adaptive Unconscious* (Cambridge, MA: Harvard University Press, 2004).

31   Ibid., 24 et seq.

32   Timothy D. Wilson, *Redirect: Changing the Stories We Live By* (New York, NY: Back Bay Books, 2015), 27.

33   Timothy D. Wilson and Elizabeth W. Dunn, "Self-Knowledge: Its Limits, Value, and Potential for Improvement," *Annual Review of Psychology* 55, no. 1 (2004): 493–518, doi:10.1146/annurev.psych.55.090902.141954.

34   Wilson, *Redirect*.

35   Ibid., 11.

36   Martin E. P. Seligman, *Authentic Happiness: Using the New Positive Psychology to Realize Your Potential for Lasting Fulfillment* (New York, NY: Simon & Schuster, 2002).

234

37   Martin E. P. Seligman, "Happiness Is Not Enough," Authentic Happiness, last modified April 2011, https://www.authentichappiness.sas.upenn.edu/newsletters/flourishnewsletters/newtheory.

38   Martin E. P. Seligman, *Flourish: A Visionary New Understanding of Happiness and Well-being* (New York, NY: Simon & Schuster, 2012), 16.

39   Ibid., 16. See also Martin E. P. Seligman, "The Original Theory: Authentic Happiness," Authentic Happiness, last modified April 2011, https://www.authentichappiness.sas.upenn.edu/learn/wellbeing.

40   Wilson, *Redirect*, 64 et seq.; Pennebaker, *Expressive Writing*, 60 et seq.

41   Viktor E. Frankl, *Man's Search for Meaning* (New York, NY: Simon & Schuster, 1984).

42   Cited everywhere, including on refrigerator magnets available at amazon.com.

43   Elizabeth W. Dunn, Daniel T. Gilbert, and Timothy D. Wilson, "If money doesn't make you happy, then you probably aren't spending it right," *Journal of Consumer Psychology* 21, no. 2 (2011): 115–125, doi:10.1016/j.jcps.2011.02.002.

44   Avni Bavishi, Martin D. Slade, and Becca R. Levy, "A Chapter a Day: Association of Book Reading with Longevity," *Social Science & Medicine* 164 (2016): 44–48, doi:10.1016/j.socscimed.2016.07.014. "(tT2 = 90.6, p < 0.001; tT3 = 67.9, p < 0.001)."

45   Keith Oatley, "Fiction: Simulation of Social Worlds," *Trends in Cognitive Sciences* 20, no. 8 (August 2016): 624, doi:10.1016/j.tics.2016.06.002.

46   Quick Reads and Josie Billington, "Reading Between the Lines: the Benefits of Reading for Pleasure," last modified 2015, http://letterpressproject.co.uk/media/file/The_Benefits_of_Reading_for_Pleasure.pdf.

47   "The Arts and Civic Engagement: Involved in Arts, Involved in Life," National Endowment for the Arts, last modified 2006, https://www.arts.gov/sites/default/files/CivicEngagement.pdf., cited in Diana I. Tamir et al., "Reading fiction and reading minds: the role of simulation in the default network," *Social Cognitive and Affective Neuroscience* 11, no. 2 (February 2016): 221–224, doi:10.1093/scan/nsv114.

48   Michael D. Slater et al., "Temporarily Expanding the Boundaries of the

Self: Motivations for Entering the Story World and Implications for Narrative Effects," *Journal of Communication* 64, no. 3 (2014): 439–455, doi:10.1111/jcom.12100.

49 Keith Oatley, "The Cognitive Science of Fiction," *Wiley Interdisciplinary Reviews: Cognitive Science* 3, no. 4 (2012): 427, doi:10.1002/wcs.1185.

50 Ibid., 427–428.

51 Wilson, *Redirect*, 69.

52 Dan Harris, *10% Happier: How I Tamed the Voice in My Head, Reduced Stress Without Losing My Edge, and Found Self-Help That Actually Works–A True Story* (New York, NY: HarperCollins, 2014).

53 J. P. Morgan, "Follow Your Bliss: A Collection of Joseph Campbell Quotes," J. P. Morgan Creating, last modified September 26, 2012, http://jp-morganjr.com/follow-your-bliss-a-collection-of-joseph-campbell-quotes/.

54 Joseph Campbell and Bill Moyers, *The Power of Myth* (New York, NY: Anchor, 1991), 85.

55 Ibid., 5.

56 Ibid., 205.

57 Joseph Campbell, *The Hero with a Thousand Faces* (Princeton, NJ: Princeton University Press, 1968).

58 Diane K. Osbon, ed., *Reflections on the Art of Living: A Joseph Campbell Companion* (New York, NY: HarperCollins, 1991), 9.

59 Morgan, "Follow Your Bliss: A Collection of Joseph Campbell Quotes."

60 Ibid., 30.

61 Ibid., 15.

62 Campbell and Moyers, *The Power of Myth*, 5.

63 Nakul Grover, "24 Joseph Campbell Quotes To Inspire Your Life," Positive Life Project, last modified December 25, 2018, https://positivelifeproject.com/joseph-campbell/.

64 Campbell and Moyers, *The Power of Myth*, 1.

65 Jason G. Goldman, "What Do Animals Dream About?," BBC, last modified April 25, 2014, http://www.bbc.com/future/story/20140425-what-do-animals-dream-about.

66 Michel Jouvet, *The Paradox of Sleep: The Story of Dreaming* (Cambridge, MA: MIT Press, 1999); Goldman, "What Do Animals Dream About?"

67   Kenway Louie and Matthew A. Wilson, "Temporally Structured Replay of Awake Hippocampal Ensemble Activity during Rapid Eye Movement Sleep," *Neuron* 29, no. 1 (January 2001): 145–156, doi:10.1016/s0896-6273(01)00186-6.

68   Amish S. Dave and Daniel Margoliash, "Song Replay During Sleep and Computational Rules for Sensorimotor Vocal Learning," *Science* 290, no. 5492 (2000): 812–816.

69   Tim Collins, "Birds Sing in Their Sleep: Scientists Discover Zebra Finches Dream They Are Tweeting and Move Their Vocal Muscles While They Slumber," *Daily Mail*, February 12, 2018, https://www.dailymail.co.uk/science-tech/article-5380969/Scientists-discover-zebra-finches-sing-dream.html.

70   Rodrigo Q. Quiroga, *The Forgetting Machine* (Dallas, TX: BenBella Books, 2017), 14, n. 11.

71   Timothy D. Wilson, "Know Thyself," *Perspectives on Psychological Science* 4, no. 4 (July 2009): 387, doi:10.1111/j.1745-6924.2009.01143.x.

72   Karl S. Lashley, "In Search of the Engram," *Symposium of the Society for Experimental Biology* 4 (1950): 454–482.

73   Moheb Costandi, *Neuroplasticity* (Cambridge, MA: MIT Press, 2016), 55.

74   John Medina, *Brain Rules: 12 Principles for Surviving and Thriving at Work, Home, and School* (Seattle, WA: Pear Press, 2014), 131.

75   Wilson, *Strangers to Ourselves*, 24.

76   Quiroga, *Forgetting Machine*, 120.

77   Anna Gosline, "Why your brain has a 'Jennifer Aniston cell,'" New-Scientist, last modified June 22, 2005, https://www.newscientist.com/article/dn7567-why-your-brain-has-a-jennifer-aniston-cell/; Quiroga, *Forgetting Machine*, 120 et seq.

78   Antonio Damasio, *Self Comes to Mind: Constructing the Conscious Brain* (New York, NY: Vintage Books, 2012), 142.

79   Medina, *Brain Rules*, 146.

80   See, e.g., Brian Boyd, *On the Origin of Stories: Evolution, Cognition, and Fiction* (Cambridge, MA: Belknap Press of Harvard University Press, 2010), 152 et seq.

81   Medina, *Brain Rules*, 150.

82   Ibid., 155.

83   Ibid., 127.

84   Quiroga, *Forgetting Machine*, 120.

85   Norman Doidge, *The Brain that Changes Itself: Stories of Personal Triumph from the Frontiers of Brain Science* (New York, NY: Penguin, 2007), 51–52.

86   Michael M. Merzenich et al., "Somatosensory cortical map changes following digit amputation in adult monkeys," *The Journal of Comparative Neurology* 224, no. 4 (1984): 591–605, doi:10.1002/cne.9012240408.

87   Doidge, *Brain that Changes Itself*, 20 et seq.; Norman Doidge, *The Brain's Way of Healing: Remarkable Discoveries and Recoveries from the Frontiers of Neuroplasticity* (London, England: Penguin, 2015), 240 et seq.

88   Donald O. Hebb, *The Organization of Behavior: A Neuropsychological Theory* (Hoboken: John Wiley & Sons, 1949).

89   Doidge, *Brain that Changes Itself*, 240.

90   See, e.g., Boyd, *On the Origin of Stories*, 152 et seq. See also Jeffrey A. Kleim and Theresa A. Jones, "Principles of Experience-Dependent Neural Pasticity: Implications for Rehabilitation after Brain Damage," *Journal of Speech, Language, and Hearing Research* 51, no. 1 (February 2008): s225–s229, doi:10.1044/1092-4388(2008/018).

91   Merzenich, *Soft-Wired*, 53 et seq.

92   Ibid., 203.

93   Ye Yuan, Judy Major-Girardin, and Steven Brown, "Storytelling is intrinsically mentalistic: A functional magnetic resonance imaging study of narrative production across modalities," *Journal of Cognitive Neuroscience* 30, no. 9 (September 2018): 1298–1314, doi:10.1162/jocn_a_01294. 1298–1314.

94   Adam London, "How Skip Bayless Thinks Tom Brady Will React To Antonio Brown's Aaron Rodgers Remark," NESN, last modified August 20, 2018, https://nesn.com/2018/08/how-skip-bayless-thinks-tom-brady-will-react-to-antonio-browns-aaron-rodgers-remark/.

95   Robin I. M. Dunbar, "Why Are Good Writers So Rare? An Evolutionary Perspective on Literature," *Journal of Cultural and Evolutionary Psychology* 3, no. 1 (March 2005): 7–21, doi:10.1556/jcep.3.2005.1.1.

96   R. I. M. Dunbar, "Gossip in Evolutionary Perspective," *Review*

of General Psychology 8, no. 2 (June 2004): 108, doi:10.1037/1089-2680.8.2.100.

97   Dunbar, "Why Are Good Writers So Rare?," 7.

98   Mohammad Dastjerdi et al., "Differential electrophysiological response during rest, self-referential, and non-self-referential tasks in human postero-medial cortex," *Proceedings of the National Academy of Sciences* 108, no. 7 (February 2011): 3023–3028, doi:10.1073/pnas.1017098108.

99   Louis Cozolino, *The Neuroscience of Psychotherapy: Healing the Social Brain* (New York: W. W. Norton & Co, 2017), 156–162.

100   Ibid., 158.

101   Keith Oatley, Robin Dunbar, and Felix Budelman, "Imagining Possible Worlds," *Review of General Psychology* 22, no. 2 (June 2018): 122, doi:10.1037/gpr0000149122.

102   Diana I. Tamir et al., "Reading fiction and reading minds: the role of simulation in the default network," *Social Cognitive and Affective Neuroscience* 11, no. 2 (February 2016): 221, doi:10.1093/scan/nsv114.

103   Simone Kühn et al., "The Importance of the Default Mode Network in Creativity—A Structural MRI Study," *The Journal of Creative Behavior* 48, no. 2 (December 2013): 152–163, doi:10.1002/jocb.45; Roger E. Beaty et al., "Creativity and the Default Network: A Functional Connectivity Analysis of the Creative Brain at Rest," *Neuropsychologia* 64 (September 2014): 92–98, doi:10.1016/j.neuropsychologia.2014.09.019.

104   Kühn, et al., "The Importance of the Default Mode Network in Creativity," 152–163.

105   See, e.g., Beaty et al., "Creativity and the Default Network," 92–98.

106   V. S. Ramachandran, *The Tell-Tale Brain: A Neuroscientist's Quest for What Makes Us Human* (New York, NY: W. W. Norton & Company, 2012), 117 et seq.

107   Marco Iacoboni, *Mirroring People: The Science of Empathy and How We Connect with Others* (London, England: Picador, 2009), 258.

108   Uri Hasson et al., "Neurocinematics: The Neuroscience of Film," *Projections* 2, no. 1 (Summer 2008): 1 et seq., doi:10.3167/proj.2008.020102.

109   Future of Storytelling, "Empathy, neurochemistry, and the dramatic arc: Paul Zak at the Future of StoryTelling 2012," *YouTube*, October 3, 2012,

accessed July 2, 2019, https://www.youtube.com/watch?v=q1a7tiA1Qzo; Paul J. Zak, "How Stories Change the Brain," *Greater Good Magazine*, December 17, 2013, accessed July 2, 2019, https://greatergood.berkeley.edu/article/item/how_stories_change_brain.

110   Cozolino, *Neuroscience of Psychotherapy*, 19.

111   "Dagger of the Mind," *Star Trek*, directed by Vincent McEveety. NBC, November 3, 1966.

112   Greg J. Stephens, Lauren J. Silbert, and Uri Hasson, "Speaker-Listener Neural Coupling Underlies Successful Communication," *Proceedings of the National Academy of Sciences* 107, no. 32 (August 2010): 14428, doi:10.1073/pnas.1008662107.

113   Mai Nguyen, Tamara Vanderwal, and Uri Hasson, "Shared understanding of narratives is correlated with shared neural responses," *NeuroImage* 184, no. 1 (January 2019): 171–180, doi:10.1016/j.neuroimage.2018.09.010. Emphasis added.

114   Miguel Pais-Vieira et al., "A Brain-to-Brain Interface for Real-Time Sharing of Sensorimotor Information," *Scientific Reports* 3, no. 1 (February 2013): 1319, doi:10.1038/srep01319.

115   Charles Q. Choi, "Real-Life Mind Meld? Scientists Link Animal Brains," Live Science, last modified July 9, 2015, http://livescience.com/51496-animal-brains-linked-into-networks.html.

116   "Monkeys' Brains Synchronize As They Collaborate To Perform A Motor Task," Duke Neurobiology, last modified March 29, 2018, https://www.neuro.duke.edu/research/research-news/monkeys%E2%80%99-brains-synchronize-they-collaborate-perform-motor-task.

117   Mark P. Mattson, "Superior Pattern Processing is the Essence of the Evolved Human Brain," *Frontiers in Neuroscience* 8, no. 8 (2014), doi:10.3389/fnins.2014.

118   Ibid.

119   Boyd, *On the Origin of Stories*, 154–155.

120   Cozolino, *Neuroscience of Psychotherapy*, 19.

121   Fritz Heider and Marianne Simmel, "An Experimental Study of Apparent Behavior," *The American Journal of Psychology* 57, no. 2 (April 1944): 243–249, doi: 10.2307/1416950.

122   Michael S. Gazzaniga, *Tales from Both Sides of the Brain: A Life in Neuroscience* (New York, NY: HarperCollins, 2015), chapter 2, et seq.

123   Michael S. Gazzaniga, *Who's in Charge?: Free Will and the Science of the Brain* (New York, NY: Ecco, 2012). 86.

124   Gazzaniga, *Tales from Both Sides of the Brain*, 153. Emphasis added.

125   Gottschall, *Storytelling Animal*, 102.

126   Gazzaniga, *Who's in Charge?*, 86–87.

127   Gregory S. Berns et al., "Short- and Long-Term Effects of a Novel on Connectivity in the Brain," *Brain Connectivity* 3, no. 6 (December 2013): 590–600, doi:10.1089/brain.2013.0166.

128   Tamir et al., "Reading fiction and reading minds," 215.

129   Marcus Cheetham, Jürgen Hänggi, and Lutz Jancke, "Identifying with fictive characters: structural brain correlates of the personality trait 'fantasy,'" *Social Cognitive and Affective Neuroscience* 9, no. 11 (November 2014): 1841, doi:10.1093/scan/nst179.

130   Keith Oatley, "The Psychology of Fiction," in *Cognitive Literary Studies: Current Themes and New Directions*, ed. Isabel Jaén and Julien J. Simon (Austin: University of Texas Press, 2012), 241.

131   Ibid.

132   Oatley, Dunbar, and Budelman, "Imagining Possible Worlds," 123.

133   Melanie C. Green and Timothy C. Brock, "The Role of Transportation in the Persuasiveness of Public Narratives," *Journal of Personality and Social Psychology* 79, no. 5 (December 2000): 701–721, doi:10.1037//0022-3514.79.5.701.

134   Ibid., 701, citing Melanie C. Green and Timothy C. Brock, "In the Mind's Eye: Transportation-Imagery Model of Narrative Persuasion," in *Narrative Impact: Social and Cognitive Foundations*, ed. Melanie C. Green, Jeffrey J. Strange, and Timothy C. Brock (Hillsdale, NJ: Erlbaum, in press), n.p.

135   P. Matthijs Bal and Martijn Veltkamp, "How Does Fiction Reading Influence Empathy? An Experimental Investigation on the Role of Emotional Transportation," *PLoS ONE* 8, no. 1 (January 2013): 3, doi:10.1371/journal.pone.0055341, citing Green and Brock, "The Role of Transportation in the Persuasiveness of Public Narratives," 701.

136   Bal and Veltkamp, "How Does Fiction Reading Influence Empathy?,"

3, citing Rick Busselle and Helena Bilandzic, "Fictionality and Perceived Realism in Experiencing Stories: A Model of Narrative Comprehension and Engagement," *Communication Theory* 18, no. 2 (May 2008): 255–280.

137   Bal and Veltkamp, "How Does Fiction Reading Influence Empathy?," 3, citing Joshua Goodstein and Deena S. Weisberg, "What Belongs in a Fictional World?," *Journal of Cognition and Culture* 9, no. 1–2 (March 2009): 69–78, doi:10.1163/156853709x414647.

138   Paul J. Zak and Stephen Knack, "Trust and Growth," *The Economic Journal* 111, no. 470 (March 2001): 295–321, doi:10.1111/1468-0297.00609.

139   Nguyen, Vanderwal, and Hasson, "Shared understanding of narratives is correlated with shared neural responses," 168.

BIBLIOGRAPHY

Aamodt, Sandra, and Sam Wang. *Welcome to Your Brain: Why You Lose Your Car Keys but Never Forget How to Drive and Other Puzzles of Everyday Life.* New York, NY: MJF Books, 2010.

Abraham, Anna, and D. Y. Von Cramon. "Reality = relevance? Insights from spontaneous modulations of the brain's default network when telling apart reality from fiction." *PLoS ONE* 4, no. 3 (2009), e4741. doi:10.1371/journal.pone.0004741.

Adams, Kathleen. *Expressive Writing: Foundations of Practice.* Lanham, MD: Rowman & Littlefield Education, 2013.

Aldama, Frederick Luis. "The Science of Storytelling: Perspectives from Cognitive Science, Neuroscience, and the Humanities." *Projections* 9, no. 1 (June 2015), 80–95. doi:10.3167/proj.2015.090106.

Amthor, Frank. *Neuroscience for Dummies*, 2nd ed. Hoboken, NJ: John Wiley & Sons, 2016.

Arden, John B. *Rewire Your Brain: Think Your Way to a Better Life.* Hoboken, NJ: John Wiley & Sons, 2010.

"The Arts and Civic Engagement: Involved in Arts, Involved in Life." National Endowment for the Arts. Last modified 2006. https://www.arts.gov/sites/default/files/CivicEngagement.pdf.

Baboulene, David. *The Story Book*. (n.p.): Dreamengine Media, 2010.

Baikie, Karen A., and Kay Wilhelm. "Emotional and physical health benefits of expressive writing." *Advances in Psychiatric Treatment* 11, no. 5 (September 2005), 338–346. doi:10.1192/apt.11.5.338.

Bal, P. Matthijs, and Martijn Veltkamp. "How Does Fiction Reading Influence Empathy? An Experimental Investigation on the Role of Emotional Transportation." *PLoS ONE* 8, no. 1 (January 2013), e55341. doi:10.1371/journal.pone.0055341.

Bavishi, Avni, Martin D. Slade, and Becca R. Levy. "A Chapter a Day: Association of Book Reading with Longevity." *Social Science & Medicine* 164 (2016), 44–48. doi:10.1016/j.socscimed.2016.07.014.

Beaty, Roger E., Mathias Benedek, Paul J. Silvia, and Daniel L. Schacter. "Creative Cognition and Brain Network Dynamics." *Trends in Cognitive Sciences* 20, no. 2 (February 2016), 87–95. doi:10.1016/j.tics.2015.10.004.

Beaty, Roger E., Mathias Benedek, Robin W. Wilkins, Emanuel Jauk, Andreas Fink, Paul J. Silvia, and Aljoscha C. Neubauer. "Creativity and the Default Network: A Functional Connectivity Analysis of the Creative Brain at Rest." *Neuropsychologia* 64 (September 2014), 92–98. doi:10.1016/j.neuropsychologia.2014.09.019.

Beaty, Roger E., Yoed N. Kenett, Alexander P. Christensen, Monica D. Rosenberg, Mathias Benedek, Qunlin Chen, Andreas Fink, et al. "Robust Prediction of Individual Creative Ability from Brain Functional Connectivity." *Proceedings of the National Academy of Sciences* 115, no. 5 (January 2018), 1087–1092. doi:10.1073/pnas.1713532115.

Bell, James S. *The Art of War for Writers: Fiction Writing Strategies, Tactics, and Exercises*. Cincinnati, OH: Writer's Digest, 2009.

Ben-Shahar, Tal. *Happier: Learn the Secrets to Daily Joy and Lasting Fulfillment*. New York, NY: McGraw Hill Professional, 2007.

Bergland, Christopher. "Music, Fiction, and the Neuroscience of Active Forgetting." *Psychology Today* (blog). December 4, 2018. Accessed July 2, 2019. https://www.psychologytoday.com/intl/blog/the-athletes-way/201812/music-fiction-and-the-neuroscience-active-forgetting.

Berns, Gregory S., Kristina Blaine, Michael J. Prietula, and Brandon E. Pye.

"Short- and Long-Term Effects of a Novel on Connectivity in the Brain." *Brain Connectivity* 3, no. 6 (December 2013), 590–600. doi:10.1089/brain.2013.0166.

Bettelheim, Bruno. *The Uses of Enchantment: The Meaning and Importance of Fairy Tales.* New York, NY: Vintage, 2010.

Bickle, John, and Sean Keating. "Storytelling 2.0: When Old Narratives Meet New Brains." *New Scientist*, November 10, 2010. Accessed July 2, 2019. https://www.newscientist.com/article/mg20827866-200-storytelling-2-0-when-new-narratives-meet-old-brains/.

Boyd, Brian. *On the Origin of Stories: Evolution, Cognition, and Fiction.* Cambridge, MA: Belknap Press of Harvard University Press, 2010.

Boyd, Brian. "The Evolution of Stories: From Mimesis to Language, from Fact to Fiction." *Wiley Interdisciplinary Reviews: Cognitive Science* 9, no. 1 (2017). doi:10.1002/wcs.1444.

Boyd, Brian, Joseph Carroll, and Jonathan Gottschall, editors. *Evolution, Literature, and Film: A Reader.* New York, NY: Columbia University Press, 2010.

Bradbury, Ray. *Zen in the Art of Writing.* Santa Barbara, CA: Joshua Odell Editions, 2013.

Brandt, Anthony, and David Eagleman. *The Runaway Species: How Human Creativity Remakes the World.* New York, NY: Catapult, 2017.

Bronzite, Dan. "The Hero's Journey - Mythic Structure of Joseph Campbell's Monomyth." Movie Outline. Accessed July 2, 2019. http://www.movieoutline.com/articles/the-hero-journey-mythic-structure-of-joseph-campbell-monomyth.html.

Buckner, Randy L. "The Serendipitous Discovery of the Brain's Default Network." *NeuroImage* 62 (October 2011), 1137–1145. doi:10.1016/j.neuroimage.2011.10.035.

Burnett, Dean. *Happy Brain: Where Happiness Comes From, and Why.* New York, NY: W.W. Norton & Company, 2018.

Busselle, Rick, and Helena Bilandzic. "Fictionality and Perceived Realism in Experiencing Stories: A Model of Narrative Comprehension and Engagement." *Communication Theory* 18, no. 2 (May 2008), 255–280. doi:10.1111/j.1468-2885.2008.00322.x.

Cameron, Julia. *The Artist's Way: A Spiritual Path to Higher Creativity*. New York, NY: Jeremy M. Tarcher/Perigree, 2002.

Cameron, Julia. *The Right to Write: An Invitation and Initiation into the Writing Life*. New York, NY: Tarcher Putnam, 1998.

Campbell, Joseph. *A Joseph Campbell Companion: Reflections on the Art of Living*. New York, NY: HarperCollins, 1991.

Campbell, Joseph. *The Hero with a Thousand Faces*, 2nd ed. Princeton, NJ: Princeton University Press, 1968.

Campbell, Joseph. *The Hero with a Thousand Faces*. Princeton, NJ: Bollingen Foundation, 2004.

Campbell, Joseph. *Thou Art That: Transforming Religious Metaphor*. Novato, CA: New World Library, 2001.

Campbell, Joseph, and Bill Moyers. *The Power of Myth*. New York, NY: Anchor, 1991.

Carlton, Lindsay. "The secrets behind the most creative minds of all time." Fox News. Last modified January 25, 2016. https://www.foxnews.com/health/the-secrets-behind-the-most-creative-minds-of-all-time.

Carroll, Joseph. "Why We Need a Journal with the Title Evolutionary Studies in Imaginative Culture." *Evolutionary Studies in Imaginative Culture* 1, no. 1 (Spring 2017), vii–xii. doi:10.26613/esic.1.1.1.

Cheetham, Marcus, Jürgen Hänggi, and Lutz Jancke. "Identifying with Fictive Characters: Structural Brain Correlates of the Personality Trait 'Fantasy'." *Social Cognitive and Affective Neuroscience* 9, no. 11 (November 2014), 1836–1844. doi:10.1093/scan/nst179.

Choi, Charles Q. "Real-Life Mind Meld? Scientists Link Animal Brains." Live Science. Last modified July 9, 2015. http://livescience.com/51496-animal-brains-linked-into-networks.html.

Collins, Tim. "Birds Sing in Their Sleep: Scientists Discover Zebra Finches Dream They Are Tweeting and Move Their Vocal Muscles While They Slumber." *Daily Mail*, February 12, 2018. https://www.dailymail.co.uk/sciencetech/article-5380969/Scientists-discover-zebra-finches-sing-dream.html.

Conner, Janet. *Writing Down Your Soul: How to Activate and Listen to the Extraordinary Voice Within*. San Francisco, CA: Conari Press, 2008.

Cooney, Gus, Daniel T. Gilbert, and Timothy D. Wilson. "The Novelty Penalty: Why Do People Like Talking About New Experiences but Hearing About Old Ones?" *Psychological Science* 28, no. 3 (March 2017), 380–394. doi:10.1177/0956797616685870.

Costandi, Mo. "Spaghetti western reveals differences between human and monkey brains." *The Guardian* (US edition), February 5, 2012. https://www.theguardian.com/science/neurophilosophy/2012/feb/05/1.

Costandi, Moheb. *Neuroplasticity*. Cambridge, MA: MIT Press, 2016.

Cozolino, Louis. *The Neuroscience of Human Relationships: Attachment and the Developing Social Brain*, 2nd ed. New York, NY: W. W. Norton & Company, 2014.

Cozolino, Louis. *The Neuroscience of Psychotherapy: Healing the Social Brain*, 3rd ed. New York: W.W. Norton & Co, 2017.

Cron, Lisa. *Story Genius: How to Use Brain Science to Go Beyond Outlining and Write a Riveting Novel (Before You Waste Three Years Writing 327 Pages That Go Nowhere)*. Berkeley, CA: Ten Speed Press, 2016.

Cron, Lisa. *Wired for Story: The Writer's Guide to Using Brain Science to Hook Readers from the Very First Sentence*. Berkeley, CA: Ten Speed Press, 2012.

Csikszentmihalyi, Mihaly. *Finding Flow: The Psychology of Engagement with Everyday Life*. New York, NY: Basic Books, 1997.

Csikszentmihalyi, Mihaly. *Flow: The Psychology of Optimal Experience*. New York, NY: HarperCollins, 2008.

Csikszentmihalyi, Mihaly. *The Evolving Self: A Psychology for the Third Millennium*. New York, NY: HarperCollins, 1993.

Daftardar, Ishan. "How Are Memories Stored And Retrieved?" Science ABC. Last modified 2016. http://sciabc.us/vJULK.

"Dagger of the Mind." *Star Trek*. Directed by Vincent McEveety. NBC, November 3, 1966.

Damasio, Antonio. *Self Comes to Mind: Constructing the Conscious Brain*. New York, NY: Vintage Books, 2012.

Damasio, Antonio. *The Strange Order of Things*. New York, NY: Pantheon, 2018.

Dastjerdi, Mohammad, Brett L. Foster, Sharmin Nasrullah, Andreas M. Rauschecker, Robert F. Dougherty, Jennifer D. Townsend, Catie Chang, and

Michael D. Greicius. "Differential electrophysiological response during rest, self-referential, and non-self-referential tasks in human posteromedial cortex." *Proceedings of the National Academy of Sciences* 108, no. 7 (2011), 3023–3028. doi:10.1073/pnas.1017098108.

Dave, Amish S., and Daniel Margoliash. "Song Replay During Sleep and Computational Rules for Sensorimotor Vocal Learning." *Science* 290, no. 5492 (2000), 812–816.

DeSalvo, Louise A. *Writing as a Way of Healing: How Telling Our Stories Transforms Our Lives*. Boston, MA: Beacon Press, 2000.

DiMenichi, Brynne C., Karolina M. Lempert, Christina Bejjani, and Elizabeth Tricomi. "Writing About Past Failures Attenuates Cortisol Responses and Sustained Attention Deficits Following Psychosocial Stress." *Frontiers in Behavioral Neuroscience* 12 (2018). doi:10.3389/fnbeh.2018.00045.

Djikic, Maja, and Keith Oatley. "On the Fragility of the Artist: Art's Precarious Triad." In *Creativity and Mental Illness*, edited by James C. Kaufman, 281–294. Cambridge, England: Cambridge University Press, 2014.

Djikic, Maja, and Keith Oatley. "The art in fiction: From indirect communication to changes of the self." *Psychology of Aesthetics, Creativity, and the Arts* 8, no. 4 (2014), 498–505. doi:10.1037/a0037999.

Djikic, Maja, Keith Oatley, and Mihnea C. Moldoveanu. "Reading other minds: Effects of literature on empathy." *Scientific Study of Literature* 3, no. 1 (January 2013), 28–47. doi:10.1075/ssol.3.1.06dji.

Djikic, Maja, Keith Oatley, Sara Zoeterman, and Jordan B. Peterson. "On Being Moved by Art: How Reading Fiction Transforms the Self." *Creativity Research Journal* 21, no. 1 (2009), 24–29. doi:10.1080/10400410802633392.

Doidge, Norman. *The Brain that Changes Itself: Stories of Personal Triumph from the Frontiers of Brain Science*. New York, NY: Penguin, 2007.

Doidge, Norman. *The Brain's Way of Healing: Remarkable Discoveries and Recoveries from the Frontiers of Neuroplasticity*. London, England: Penguin, 2015.

Dor, Daniel. *The Instruction of Imagination: Language as a Social Communication Technology*. New York: Oxford University Press, 2015.

Dudukovic, Nicole M., Elizabeth J. Marsh, and Barbara Tversky. "Telling a story or telling it straight: the effects of entertaining versus accurate retellings on memory." *Applied Cognitive Psychology* 18, no. 2 (March 2004), 125–143. doi:10.1002/acp.953.

Dunbar, R. I. M. "Gossip in Evolutionary Perspective." *Review of General Psychology* 8, no. 2 (June 2004), 100–110. doi:10.1037/1089-2680.8.2.100.

Dunbar, R. I. M. "The Anatomy of Friendship." *Trends in Cognitive Sciences* 22, no. 1 (January 2018), 32–51. doi:10.1016/j.tics.2017.10.004.

Dunbar, Robin I. M. *Human Evolution: Our Brains and Behavior*. New York, NY: Oxford University Press, 2016.

Dunbar, Robin I. M. "The Social Brain Hypothesis and Human Evolution." *Oxford Research Encyclopedia of Psychology*, March 2016. doi:10.1093/acrefore/9780190236557.013.44.

Dunbar, Robin I. M. "Why Are Good Writers So Rare? An Evolutionary Perspective on Literature." *Journal of Cultural and Evolutionary Psychology* 3, no. 1 (March 2005), 7–21. doi:10.1556/jcep.3.2005.1.1.

Dunbar, Robin, Louise Barrett, and John Lycett. *Evolutionary Psychology: A Beginner's Guide*. London, England: Oneworld Publications, 2007.

Dunn, Elizabeth W., Daniel T. Gilbert, and Timothy D. Wilson. "If money doesn't make you happy, then you probably aren't spending it right." *Journal of Consumer Psychology* 21, no. 2 (April 2011), 115–125. doi:10.1016/j.jcps.2011.02.002.

Eagleman, David. *The Brain: The Story of You*. Edinburgh, Scotland: Canongate, 2015.

Eck, Allison. "The "Jennifer Aniston" Neuron Could Help Scientists Decode Memory Formation." Last modified July 6, 2015. https://www.pbs.org/wgbh/nova/article/the-jennifer-aniston-neuron-could-help-scientists-decode-memory-formation/.

Emory Health Sciences. "A novel look at how stories may change the brain." ScienceDaily. Last modified January 3, 2014. http://www.sciencedaily.com/releases/2014/01/140103204428.htm.

Epstein, Mark. *The Trauma of Everyday Life*. New York, NY: The Penguin Press, 2013.

Ethos3. "The neuroscience of storytelling for presentations." Infographic. February 19, 2015. https://www.slideshare.net/ethos3/the-neuroscience-of-storytelling-for-presentations.

Fellowes, Mark, and Nicholas Battey, editors. *30-Second Evolution: The 50 Most Significant Ideas and Events, Each Explained in Half a Minute*. New York, NY: Metro Books, 2018.

Field, Syd. *Screenplay: The Foundations of Screenwriting*. New York, NY: Delta Trade Paperbacks, 2005.

Frankl, Viktor E. *Man's Search for Meaning*, 3rd ed. New York, NY: Simon & Schuster, 1984.

Frattaroli, Joanne. "Experimental disclosure and its moderators: A meta-analysis." *Psychological Bulletin* 132, no. 6 (2006), 823–865. doi:10.1037/0033-2909.132.6.823.

Frazier, Jan. *When Fear Falls Away: The Story of a Sudden Awakening*. San Francisco, CA: Red Wheel/Weiser Books, 2007.

Freeman, Catherine. "What is Mentalizing? An Overview." *British Journal of Psychotherapy* 32, no. 2 (May 2016), 189–201. doi:10.1111/bjp.12220.

Frith, Chris D., and Uta Frith. "The Neural Basis of Mentalizing." *Neuron* 50, no. 4 (2006), 531–534. doi:10.1016/j.neuron.2006.05.001.

Fuentes, Agustin. *The Creative Spark: How Imagination Made Humans Exceptional*. London, England: Penguin, 2017.

Future of StoryTelling. "Empathy, neurochemistry, and the dramatic arc: Paul Zak at the Future of StoryTelling 2012." *YouTube*. Video file. October 3, 2012. Accessed July 2, 2019. https://www.youtube.com/watch?v=q1a7tiA1Qzo.

Gardner, John. *The Art of Fiction: Notes on Craft for Young Writers*. New York, NY: Vintage, 1991.

Gazzaniga, Michael S. *Tales from Both Sides of the Brain: A Life in Neuroscience*. New York, NY: HarperCollins, 2015.

Gazzaniga, Michael S. *The Consciousness Instinct: Unraveling the Mystery of How the Brain Makes the Mind*. New York, NY: Farrar, Straus and Giroux, 2018.

Gazzaniga, Michael S. *Who's in Charge?: Free Will and the Science of the Brain*. New York, NY: Ecco, 2012.

Goldberg, Natalie. *The True Secret of Writing: Connecting Life with Language.* New York: Atria Books, 2013.

Goldberg, Natalie. *Wild Mind: Living the Writer's Life.* New York: Bantam, 1990.

Goldberg, Natalie. *Writing Down the Bones: Freeing the Writer Within.* Boston, MA: Shambhala Press, 2006.

Goldman, Jason G. "What do animals dream about?" BBC. Last modified April 25, 2014. http://www.bbc.com/future/story/20140425-what-do-animals-dream-about.

Goodstein, Joshua, and Deena Skolnick Weisberg. "What Belongs in a Fictional World?" *Journal of Cognition and Culture* 9, no. 1-2 (January 2009), 69–78. doi:10.1163/156853709x414647.

Gopnik, Adam. "Can Science Explain Why We Tell Stories?" *New Yorker*, May 18, 2012. https://www.newyorker.com/books/page-turner/can-science-explain-why-we-tell-stories.

Gornick, Vivian. *The Situation and the Story: The Art of Personal Narrative.* New York, NY: Farrar, Straus and Giroux, 2002.

Gortner, Eva-Maria, Stephanie S. Rude, and James W. Pennebaker. "Benefits of Expressive Writing in Lowering Rumination and Depressive Symptoms." *Behavior Therapy* 37, no. 3 (September 2006), 292–303. doi:10.1016/j.beth.2006.01.004.

Gosline, Anna. "Why your brain has a 'Jennifer Aniston cell'." NewScientist. Last modified June 22, 2005. https://www.newscientist.com/article/dn7567-why-your-brain-has-a-jennifer-aniston-cell/.

Gots, Jason. "Your Storytelling Brain." Big Think. Last modified January 13, 2012. https://bigthink.com/overthinking-everything-with-jason-gots/your-storytelling-brain.

Gotschall, Jonathan. "The Holodeck Is Real." *Psychology Today*, February 20, 2013. https://www.psychologytoday.com/us/blog/the-storytelling-animal/201302/the-holodeck-is-real.

Gottschall, J. "Why Storytelling Is The Ultimate Weapon." *Fast Company*, May 2, 2012. https://www.fastcompany.com/1680581/why-storytelling-is-the-ultimate-weapon.

Gottschall, Jonathan. *The Storytelling Animal: How Stories Make Us Human.*

Boston, MA: Houghton Mifflin Harcourt, 2012.

Gottschall, Jonathan. "Infecting An Audience: Why Great Stories Spread." *Fast Company*, October 20, 2013. https://www.fastcompany.com/3020046/ infecting-an-audience-why-great-stories-spreadInfecting An Audience: Why Great Stories Spread.

Gottschall, Jonathan, Rachel Berkey, Mitchell Cawson, Carly Drown, Matthew Fleischner, Melissa Glotzbecker, Kimberly Kernan, and Tyler Magnan. "Patterns of characterization in folktales across geographic regions and levels of cultural complexity." *Human Nature* 14, no. 4 (December 2003), 365–382. doi:10.1007/s12110-003-1011-3.

Gowin, Joshua. "Why Sharing Stories Brings People Together." *Psychology Today* (blog). June 6, 2011. https://www.psychologytoday.com/us/blog/you-il-luminated/201106/why-sharing-stories-brings-people-together.

Graziano, Michael S. A. *Consciousness and the Social Brain*. New York, NY: Oxford University Press, 2013.

Green, Melanie C., and Timothy C. Brock. "In the Mind's Eye: Transportation-Imagery Model of Narrative Persuasion." In *Narrative Impact: Social and Cognitive Foundations*, edited by Melanie C. Green, Jeffrey J. Strange, and Timothy C. Brock, 315–342. Hillsdale, NJ: Erlbaum, 2002.

Green, Melanie C., and Timothy C. Brock. "The Role of Transportation in the Persuasiveness of Public Narratives." *Journal of Personality and Social Psychology* 79, no. 5 (December 2000), 701–721. doi:10.1037//0022-3514.79.5.701.

Grenville-Cleave, Bridget. *Positive Psychology: A Practical Guide*. New York, NY: MJF Books, 2012.

Grover, Nakul. "24 Joseph Campbell Quotes To Inspire Your Life." Positive Life Project. Last modified December 25, 2018. https://positivelifeproject. com/joseph-campbell/.

Gutirrez, Emma B. "The Hedonic Treadmill — Are We Forever Chasing Rainbows?" Medium. Last modified February 12, 2018. https://medium. com/@emmabgutirrez/the-hedonic-treadmill-are-we-forever-chas-ing-rainbows-bb623ff148cd.

Haidt, Jonathan. *The Happiness Hypothesis: Finding Modern Truth in Ancient*

Wisdom. New York, NY: Basic Books (AZ), 2006.

Hanson, Rick. *Buddha's Brain: The Practical Neuroscience of Happiness, Love, and Wisdom*. Oakland, CA: New Harbinger Publications, 2009.

Hanson, Rick. *Hardwiring Happiness*. New York, NY: Harmony Books, 2013.

Harris, Dan. *10% Happier: How I Tamed the Voice in My Head, Reduced Stress Without Losing My Edge, and Found Self-Help That Actually Works–A True Story*. New York, NY: HarperCollins, 2014.

Harris, Sam. *Waking Up: A Guide to Spirituality Without Religion*. New York, NY: Simon & Schuster, 2014.

Hassabis, Demis, and Eleanor A. Maguire. "The construction system of the brain." *Philosophical Transactions of the Royal Society B: Biological Sciences* 364, no. 1521 (2009), 1263–1271. doi:10.1098/rstb.2008.0296.

Hasson, Uri. "I Can Make Your Brain Look Like Mine." *Harvard Business Review*, December 2010. https://hbr.org/2010/12/defend-your-research-i-can-make-your-brain-look-like-mine.

Hasson, Uri. "This is your brain on communication." *TED*. Video file. February 2016. https://www.ted.com/talks/uri_hasson_this_is_your_brain_on_communication.

Hasson, Uri, Asif A. Ghazanfar, Bruno Galantucci, Simon Garrod, and Christian Keysers. "Brain-to-brain coupling: A mechanism for creating and sharing a social world." *Trends in Cognitive Sciences* 16, no. 2 (2012), 114–121. doi:10.1016/j.tics.2011.12.007.

Hasson, Uri, Ohad Landesman, Barbara Knappmeyer, Ignacio Vallines, Nava Rubin, and David J. Heeger. "Neurocinematics: The Neuroscience of Film." *Projections* 2, no. 1 (Summer 2008), 1–26. doi:10.3167/proj.2008.020102.

Hasson, Uri, Yuval Nir, Ifat Levy, Galit Fuhrmann, and Rafael Malach. "Intersubject Synchronization of Cortical Activity During Natural Vision." *Science* 303, no. 5664 (2004), 1634–1640. doi:10.1126/science.1089506.

Hebb, Donald O. *The Organization of Behavior: A Neuropsychological Theory*. Hoboken, NJ: John Wiley & Sons, 1949.

Heider, Fritz, and Marianne Simmel. "An Experimental Study of Apparent Behavior." *The American Journal of Psychology* 57, no. 2 (April 1944),

243–249. doi: 10.2307/1416950.

Herman, Judith L. *Trauma and Recovery: The Aftermath of Violence—From Domestic Abuse to Political Terror*. New York, NY: Basic Books, 2015.

Herrera, Fernanda, Jeremy Bailenson, Erika Weisz, Elise Ogle, and Jamil Zaki. "Building long-term empathy: A large-scale comparison of traditional and virtual reality perspective-taking." *PLoS ONE* 13, no. 10 (2018), e0204494. doi:10.1371/journal.pone.0204494.

Hickok, Gregory. *The Myth of Mirror Neurons: The Real Neuroscience of Communication and Cognition*. New York, NY: W. W. Norton & Company, 2014.

Hippel, William von. *The Social Leap: The New Evolutionary Science of Who We Are, Where We Come From, and What Makes Us Happy*. New York, NY: HarperCollins, 2018.

Hogenboom, Melissa. "Study confirms social brain theory." BBC. Last modified June 26, 2013. https://www.bbc.com/news/science-environment-23045905.

Huganir, Richard. "How the brain creates memories." LearnNow. n.d. http://learnnow.org/departments/brain-101/how-the-brain-creates-memories.

Iacoboni, Marco. *Mirroring People: The Science of Empathy and How We Connect with Others*. London, England: Picador, 2009.

Immordino-Yang, Mary Helen, Joanna A. Christodoulou, and Vanessa Singh. "Rest Is Not Idleness: Implications of the Brain's Default Mode for Human Development and Education." *Perspectives on Psychological Science* 7, no. 4 (2012), 352–364. doi:10.1177/1745691612447308.

Johnson, Dan R., Brandie L. Huffman, and Danny M. Jasper. "Changing Race Boundary Perception by Reading Narrative Fiction." *Basic and Applied Social Psychology* 36, no. 1 (2014), 83–90. doi:10.1080/01973533.2013.856791.

"Joseph Campbell Quotes." Humoropedia. Last modified March 13, 2015. https://humoropedia.com/joseph-campbell-quotes/.

Jouvet, Michel. *The Paradox of Sleep: The Story of Dreaming*. Cambridge, MA: MIT Press, 1999.

Kahneman, Daniel. *Thinking, Fast and Slow*. New York, NY: Farrar, Straus and Giroux, 2011.

Kaufman, Scott Barry, and James C. Kaufman, editors. *The Psychology of Creative Writing*. Cambridgeshire, England: Cambridge University Press, 2009.

Kaufman, Scott Barry, and Carolyn Gregoire. *Wired to Create: Unraveling the Mysteries of the Creative Mind*. New York, NY: Penguin, 2015.

Keysers, Christian, Bruno Wicker, Valeria Gazzola, Jean-Luc Anton, Leonardo Fogassi, and Vittorio Gallese. "A Touching Sight." *Neuron* 42, no. 2 (2004), 335–346. doi:10.1016/s0896-6273(04)00156-4.

Killingsworth, Matthew A., and Daniel T. Gilbert. "A Wandering Mind Is an Unhappy Mind." *Science* 330, no. 6006 (November 2010), 932. doi:10.1126/science.1192439.

King, Stephen. *On Writing: A Memoir of the Craft*. New York, NY: Simon & Schuster, 2002.

Kleim, Jeffrey A., and Theresa A. Jones. "Principles of Experience-Dependent Neural Pasticity: Implications for Rehabilitation after Brain Damage." *Journal of Speech, Language, and Hearing Research* 51, no. 1 (February 2008), s225–s229. doi:10.1044/1092-4388(2008/018).

Klein, Kitty, and Adriel Boals. "Expressive writing can increase working memory capacity." *Journal of Experimental Psychology: General* 130, no. 3 (September 2001), 520–533. doi:10.1037/0096-3445.130.3.520.

Knight, Nika. "Brian Boyd: Life as We Write It." *Guernica*, November 16, 2015. https://www.guernicamag.com/life-as-we-write-it/.

Koch, Christof. "How Neuroscientists Observe Brains Watching Movies." *Scientific American*, January 1, 2012. https://www.scientificamerican.com/article/movies-in-the-cortical-theater/.

Konishi, Mahiko, Donald George McLaren, Haakon Engen, and Jonathan Smallwood. "Shaped by the Past: The Default Mode Network Supports Cognition that Is Independent of Immediate Perceptual Input." *PLoS One* 10, no. 6 (2015), e0132209. doi:10.1371/journal.pone.0132209.

Kukushkin, Nikolay Vadimovich, and Thomas James Carew. "Memory Takes Time." *Neuron* 95, no. 2 (2017), 259–279. doi:10.1016/j.neuron.2017.05.029.

Kurzweil, Ray. *How to Create a Mind: The Secret of Human Thought Revealed*. New York: Viking, 2014.

Kühn, Simone, Simone M. Ritter, Barbara C. Müller, Rick B. Van Baaren, Marcel Brass, and Ap Dijksterhuis. "The Importance of the Default Mode Network in Creativity—A Structural MRI Study." *The Journal of Creative Behavior* 48, no. 2 (June 2014), 152–163. doi:10.1002/jocb.45.

Lamar, Cyriaque. "The 22 rules of storytelling, according to Pixar." Gizmodo. (Originally shared in 2011 as a series of tweets by Emma Coats, @lawnrocket). Last modified June 8, 2012. https://io9.gizmodo.com/the-22-rules-of-storytelling-according-to-pixar-5916970.

Lanouette, Jennine. "A History of Three-Act Structure." 1999. Screentakes. Last modified December 24, 2012. https://www.screentakes.com/an-evolutionary-study-of-the-three-act-structure-model-in-drama/.

Larsen, Stephen, and Robin Larsen. *Joseph Campbell: A Fire in the Mind: The Authorized Biography*. New York, NY: Doubleday, 1991.

Lashley, Karl S. "In Search of the Engram." *Symposium of the Society for Experimental Biology* 4 (1950), 454–482.

"Left-Brain-Right-Brain-Chart." Infographic. 2008. http://2.bp.blogspot.com/-v8nOV8ryfZ8/UJPG4O7-NhI/AAAAAAAAMdQ/0YusziSqc-GM/s1600/Left-Brain-Right-Brain-Chart.jpg.

Lewis, Penelope A., Amy Birch, Alexander Hall, and Robin I. Dunbar. "Higher order intentionality tasks are cognitively more demanding." *Social Cognitive and Affective Neuroscience* 12, no. 7 (2017), 1063–1071. doi:10.1093/scan/nsx034.

Lieberman, Matthew D. *Social: Why Our Brains Are Wired to Connect*. Danvers, MA: Crown, 2013.

London, Adam. "How Skip Bayless Thinks Tom Brady Will React To Antonio Brown's Aaron Rodgers Remark." NESN. Last modified August 20, 2018. https://nesn.com/2018/08/how-skip-bayless-thinks-tom-brady-will-react-to-antonio-browns-aaron-rodgers-remark/.

Lotze, Martin, Katharina Erhard, Nicola Neumann, Simon B. Eickhoff, and Robert Langner. "Neural correlates of verbal creativity: differences in resting-state functional connectivity associated with expertise in creative writing." *Frontiers in Human Neuroscience* 8 (2014). doi:10.3389/fnhum.2014.00516.

Louie, Kenway, and Matthew A. Wilson. "Temporally Structured Replay of Awake Hippocampal Ensemble Activity during Rapid Eye Movement

Sleep." *Neuron* 29, no. 1 (January 2001), 145–156. doi:10.1016/s0896-6273(01)00186-6.

Mamet, David. *Bambi vs. Godzilla: On the Nature, Purpose, and Practice of the Movie Business*. New York, NY: Vintage Books, 2008.

Mamet, David. *Three Uses of the Knife: On the Nature and Purpose of Drama*. New York, NY: Vintage Books, 2000.

Mar, Raymond A. "The Neural Bases of Social Cognition and Story Comprehension." *Annual Review of Psychology* 62, no. 1 (2011), 103–134. doi:10.1146/annurev-psych-120709-145406.

Mar, Raymond A., Malia F. Mason, and Aubrey Litvack. "How daydreaming relates to life satisfaction, loneliness, and social support: The importance of gender and daydream content." *Consciousness and Cognition* 21, no. 1 (2012), 401–407. doi:10.1016/j.concog.2011.08.001.

Mar, Raymond A., and Keith Oatley. "The Function of Fiction is the Abstraction and Simulation of Social Experience." *Perspectives on Psychological Science* 3, no. 3 (May 2008), 173–192. doi:10.1111/j.1745-6924.2008.00073.x.

Maran, Meredith. *Why We Write: 20 Acclaimed Authors on How and Why They Do What They Do*. London, England: Penguin, 2013.

Marsh, Elizabeth J., and Lisa K. Fazio. "Learning errors from fiction: Difficulties in reducing reliance on fictional stories." *Memory & Cognition* 34, no. 5 (July 2006), 1140–1149. doi:10.3758/bf03193260.

Maslej, Marta M., Marina Rain, Katrina Fong, Keith Oatley, and Raymond A. Mar. "The Hierarchical Personality Structure of Aspiring Creative Writers." *Creativity Research Journal* 26, no. 2 (2014), 192–202. doi:10.1080/10400419.2014.901086.

Mastin, Luke. "The Human Memory." Scribd. Last modified 2010. https://www.scribd.com/document/311171723/The-Human-Memory-Luke-Mastin-2010.

Mattson, Mark P. "Superior pattern processing is the essence of the evolved human brain." *Frontiers in Neuroscience* 8, no. 8 (2014). doi:10.3389/fnins.2014.00265.

Max Planck Institute for Human Development. "Brain on Autopilot." Max Planck Neuroscience. Last modified November 11, 2016. http://max-planck.nautil.us/article/344/brain-on-autopilot.

McBride, Glen. "Storytelling, behavior planning, and language evolution in context." *Frontiers in Psychology* 5 (2014). doi:10.3389/fpsyg.2014.01131.

McDonnell, Jane Taylor. *Living to Tell the Tale: A Guide to Writing Memoir*. New York, NY: Penguin Books, 1998.

McKee, Robert. *Story: Style, Structure, Substance, and the Principles of Screenwriting*, 1st ed. New York, NY: ReganBooks, 1997.

McKie, Robin. "Humans hunted for meat 2 million years ago." The Guardian. Last modified February 14, 2018. http://www.theguardian.com/science/2012/sep/23/human-hunting-evolution-2million-years.

Medina, John. *Brain Rules: 12 Principles for Surviving and Thriving at Work, Home, and School*. Seattle, WA: Pear Press, 2014.

Mehl-Madrona, Lewis. *Healing the Mind through the Power of Story: The Promise of Narrative Psychiatry*. Rochester, VT: Bear & Company, 2010.

Memarian, Negar, Jared B. Torre, Kate E. Haltom, Annette L. Stanton, and Matthew D. Lieberman. "Neural activity during affect labeling predicts expressive writing effects on well-being: GLM and SVM approaches." *Social Cognitive and Affective Neuroscience* 12, no. 9 (September 2017), 1437–1447. doi:10.1093/scan/nsx084.

Merzenich, Michael. *Soft-Wired: How the New Science of Brain Plasticity Can Change Your Life*, 2nd ed. San Francisco, CA: Parnassus Publishing, 2013.

Merzenich, Michael M., Randall J. Nelson, Michael P. Stryker, Max S. Cynader, Axel Schoppmann, and John M. Zook. "Somatosensory cortical map changes following digit amputation in adult monkeys." *The Journal of Comparative Neurology* 224, no. 4 (1984), 591–605. doi:10.1002/cne.902240408.

Miall, David S., and Don Kuiken. "A feeling for fiction: becoming what we behold." *Poetics* 30, no. 4 (August 2002), 221–241. doi:10.1016/s0304-422x(02)00011-6.

Molnar-Szakacs, Istvan, and Lucina Q. Uddin. "Self-processing and the default mode network: interactions with the mirror neuron system." *Frontiers in Human Neuroscience* 7 (2013). doi:10.3389/fnhum.2013.00571.

"Monkeys' Brains Synchronize As They Collaborate To Perform A Motor Task."

Duke Neurobiology. Last modified March 29, 2018. https://www.neu-ro.duke.edu/research/research-news/monkeys%E2%80%99-brains-syn-chronize-they-collaborate-perform-motor-task.

Morgan, J. P. "Follow Your Bliss: A Collection of Joseph Campbell Quotes." J. P. Morgan Creating. Last modified September 26, 2012. http://jpmorgan-jr.com/follow-your-bliss-a-collection-of-joseph-campbell-quotes/.

Murdock, Maureen. *The Heroine's Journey*. Boulder, CO: Shambhala Publications, 1990.

Nauert, Rick. "Cognitive Science Helps to Unravel the Power of Storytelling." PsychCentral. Last modified November 10, 2018. https://psychcentral.com/news/2018/11/10/cognitive-science-helps-to-unravel-the-pow-er-of-storytelling/138694.html.

Nguyen, Mai, Tamara Vanderwal, and Uri Hasson. "Shared understanding of narratives is correlated with shared neural responses." *NeuroImage* 184, no. 1 (2019), 161–170. doi:10.1016/j.neuroimage.2018.09.010.

Nicholls, Sophie. "Beyond Expressive Writing: Evolving Models of Developmental Creative Writing." *Journal of Health Psychology* 14, no. 2 (March 2009), 171–180. doi:10.1177/1359105308100201.

Niles, Andrea N., Kate E. Haltom, Catherine M. Mulvenna, Matthew D. Lieberman, and Annette L. Stanton. "Randomized controlled trial of expressive writing for psychological and physical health: the moderating role of emotional expressivity." *Anxiety, Stress & Coping* 27, no. 1 (2013), 1–17. doi:10.1080/10615806.2013.802308.

Oates, Joyce Carol. *The Faith of a Writer: Life, Craft, Art*. New York: HarperCollins, 2003.

Oatley, K. *Such Stuff as Dreams: The Psychology of Fiction*. Hoboken, NJ: John Wiley & Sons, 2011.

Oatley, K., and M. Djikic. "The Creativity of Literary Writing." In *The Cambridge Handbook of Creativity across Domains*, edited by James C. Kaufman, Vlad P. Glăveanu, and John Baer, 63–79. New York, NY: Cambridge University Press, 2017. https://doi.org/10.1017/9781316274385.005.

Oatley, Keith. *The Passionate Muse: Exploring Emotion in Stories*. New York, NY: Oxford University Press, 2012.

Oatley, Keith. "Fiction: Simulation of Social Worlds." *Trends in Cognitive Sciences* 20, no. 8 (August 2016), 618–628. doi:10.1016/j.tics.2016.06.002.

Oatley, Keith. "The cognitive science of fiction." *Wiley Interdisciplinary Reviews: Cognitive Science* 3, no. 4 (2012), 425–430. doi:10.1002/wcs.1185.

Oatley, Keith, and Maja Djikic. "Psychology of narrative art." *Review of General Psychology* 22, no. 2 (June 2018), 161–168. doi:10.1037/gpr0000113.

Oatley, Keith, and Maja Djikic. "How Reading Transforms Us." *New York Times*, December 19, 2014. https://www.nytimes.com/2014/12/21/opinion/sunday/how-writing-transforms-us.html.

Oatley, Keith, Robin Dunbar, and Felix Budelman. "Imagining possible worlds." *Review of General Psychology* 22, no. 2 (June 2018), 121–124. doi:10.1037/gpr0000149.

Oatley, Keith, Raymond A. Mar, and Maja Djikic. "The Psychology of Fiction." In *Cognitive Literary Studies: Current Themes and New Directions*, edited by Isabel Jaén and Julien J. Simon, 235–249. Austin: University of Texas Press, 2012.

Oatley, Keith, and Raymond A. Mar. "Evolutionary Pre-Adaptation and the Idea of Character in Fiction." *Journal of Cultural and Evolutionary Psychology* 3, no. 2 (2005), 179–194. doi:10.1556/jcep.3.2005.2.5.

Osbon, Diane K., editor. *Reflections on the Art of Living: A Joseph Campbell Companion.* New York, NY: HarperCollins, 1991.

Paez, Danny. "New Study Shows That Virtual Reality Creates More Empathy Than News Reports." Inverse. Last modified October 17, 2018. https://www.inverse.com/article/49957-virtual-reality-influence-opinions-empathy.

Pagel, Mark. *Wired for Culture: Origins of the Human Social Mind.* New York, NY: W. W. Norton & Company, 2012.

Pais-Vieira, Miguel, Gabriela Chiuffa, Mikhail Lebedev, Amol Yadav, and Miguel A. L. Nicolelis. "Building an organic computing device with multiple interconnected brains." *Scientific Reports* 5, no. 1 (2015). doi:10.1038/srep11869.

Pais-Vieira, Miguel, Mikhail Lebedev, Carolina Kunicki, Jing Wang, and Miguel A. L. Nicolelis. "A Brain-to-Brain Interface for Real-Time Sharing of Sensorimotor Information." *Scientific Reports* 3, no. 1 (2013).

doi:10.1038/srep01319.

Palmer, Helen. *The Enneagram in Love and Work: Understanding Your Intimate and Business Relationships*. New York, NY: HarperCollins, 1995.

Pearson, Carol S. *The Hero Within: Six Archetypes We Live By. Revised & expanded ed*, 3rd ed. San Francisco, CA: HarperSanFrancisco, 2013.

Pennebaker, James W. "Writing your wrongs." *American Health* 10 (January/ February 1991), 64–67.

Pennebaker, James W., and Sandra K. Beall. "Confronting a traumatic event: Toward an understanding of inhibition and disease." *Journal of Abnormal Psychology* 95, no. 3 (August 1986), 274–281. doi:10.1037//0021-843x.95.3.274.

Pennebaker, James W., and John F. Evans. *Expressive Writing: Words that Heal*. Enumclaw, WA: Idyll Arbor, 2014.

Pennebaker, James W., and Joshua M. Smyth. *Opening Up by Writing It Down: How Expressive Writing Improves Health and Eases Emotional Pain*, 3rd ed. New York, NY: The Guilford Press, 2016.

Popova, Maria. "How to Find Your Bliss: Joseph Campbell on What It Takes to Have a Fulfilling Life." *Brain Pickings*, April 9, 2015. https://www.brainpickings.org/2015/04/09/find-your-bliss-joseph-campbell-power-of-myth/.

Popova, Maria. "Neil Gaiman's 8 Rules of Writing." Brain Pickings. Last modified September 18, 2015. https://www.brainpickings.org/2012/09/28/neil-gaiman-8-rules-of-writing/.

Quick Reads, and Josie Billington. "Reading Between the Lines: the Benefits of Reading for Pleasure." Last modified 2015. http://letterpressproject.co.uk/media/file/The_Benefits_of_Reading_for_Pleasure.pdf.

Quiroga, Rodrigo Q. *The Forgetting Machine*. Dallas, TX: BenBella Books, 2017.

"Quotation #5053 from Cole's Quotables." The Quotations Page. n.d. http://www.quotationspage.com/quote/5053.html.

Ramachandran, V. S. *The Tell-Tale Brain: A Neuroscientist's Quest for What Makes Us Human*. New York, NY: W. W. Norton & Company, 2012.

"Review of Mirroring People: The Science of Empathy and How We Connect with Others." *Partner Abuse* 4, no. 2 (2013), 287–292.

doi:10.1891/1946-6560.4.2.287.

Robley, Chris. "Kurt Vonnegut's 8 rules for writing a short story." BookBaby Blog. Last modified November 20, 2013. https://blog.bookbaby.com/2013/11/kurt-vonneguts-8-rules-for-writing-a-short-story/.

Robson, David. "Heroes and villains." *The Psychologist*, August 2016. https://thepsychologist.bps.org.uk/heroes-and-villains.

Robson, David. "Our fiction addiction: Why humans need stories." BBC. Last modified May 3, 2018. http://www.bbc.com/culture/story/20180503-our-fiction-addiction-why-humans-need-stories.

Rodriguez, Giovanni. "This Is Your Brain On Storytelling: The Chemistry Of Modern Communication." *Forbes*, July 21, 2017. https://www.forbes.com/sites/giovannirodriguez/2017/07/21/this-is-your-brain-on-storytelling-the-chemistry-of-modern-communication/#1207c998c865.

Sapolsky, Robert. "This is your brain on metaphors." *Opinionator* (blog). November 14, 2010. https://opinionator.blogs.nytimes.com/author/robert-sapolsky/.

Seger, Linda. *Making a Good Script Great*. Hollywood, CA: Samuel French, 1987.

Seger, Linda. *Making a Good Writer Great: A Creativity Workbook for Screenwriters*. Los Angeles, CA: Silman James Press, 1999.

Seiter, Courtney. "Reading a good story is good for mind, body, career." *Chicago Tribune*, November 5, 2015. https://www.chicagotribune.com/bluesky/hub/ct-buffer-read-to-clear-your-mind-bsi-hub-20151030-story.html.

Seligman, Martin E. P. *Authentic Happiness: Using the New Positive Psychology to Realize Your Potential for Lasting Fulfillment*. New York, NY: Simon & Schuster, 2002.

Seligman, Martin E. P. *Flourish: A Visionary New Understanding of Happiness and Well-being*. New York, NY: Simon & Schuster, 2012.

Seligman, Martin E. P. *Learned Optimism: How to Change Your Mind and Your Life*. New York, NY: Vintage Books, 2006.

Seligman, Martin E. P. *What you can change . . . and what you can't: The complete guide to successful self-improvement*. New York, NY: Vintage Books, 2007.

Seligman, Martin E. P. "Happiness Is Not Enough." Authentic Happiness. Last

modified April 2011. https://www.authentichappiness.sas.upenn.edu/
newsletters/flourishnewsletters/newtheory.

Seligman, Martin E. P. "The Original Theory: Authentic Happiness." Authentic
Happiness. Last modified April 2011. https://www.authentichappiness.
sas.upenn.edu/learn/wellbeing.

Seligman, Martin E. P., and John Tierney. "We Aren't Built to Live in the
Moment." *New York Times*, May 19, 2017. https://www.nytimes.
com/2017/05/19/opinion/sunday/why-the-future-is-always-on-your-
mind.html.

Seung, Sebastian. *Connectome: How the Brain's Wiring Makes Us Who We Are.*
New York: Houghton Mifflin Harcourt, 2013.

Shah, Carolin, Katharina Erhard, Hanns-Josef Ortheil, Evangelia Kaza, Christof
Kessler, and Martin Lotze. "Neural correlates of creative writing: An
fMRI study." *Human Brain Mapping* 34, no. 5 (May 2013), 1088–
1101. doi:10.1002/hbm.21493.

Simpson, Jon. "Finding Brand Success In The Digital World." Forbes Agency
Council. Last modified August 25, 2017. https://www.forbes.com/sites/
forbesagencycouncil/2017/08/25/finding-brand-success-in-the-digital-
world/#3923c536626e.

Singleton, Omar, Britta K. Hölzel, Mark Vangel, Narayan Brach, James Carmo-
dy, and Sara W. Lazar. "Change in brainstem gray matter concentration
following a mindfulness-based intervention is correlated with improvement in psychological well-being." *Frontiers in Human Neuroscience* 8
(2014). doi:10.3389/fnhum.2014.00033.

Slater, Michael D., Benjamin K. Johnson, Jonathan Cohen, Maria Leonora G.
Comello, and David R. Ewoldsen. "Temporarily Expanding the Boundaries of the Self: Motivations for Entering the Story World and Implications for Narrative Effects." *Journal of Communication* 64, no. 3 (June
2014), 439–455. doi:10.1111/jcom.12100.

Smith, Emily E. *The Power of Meaning: Finding Fulfillment in a World Obsessed
with Happiness.* New York: Broadway Books, 2017. Kindle edition.

Snyder, Blake. *Save the Cat!: The Last Book on Screenwriting You'll Ever Need.*
Studio City, CA: Michael Wiese Productions, 2005.

Somphanith, Souri. "Wrapped up in a Book: The Role of Emotional Engage-

ment in Reading." *EveryONE* (blog). February 21, 2013. https://blogs.
plos.org/everyone/2013/02/21/wrapped-up-in-a-book-the-role-of-emo-
tional-engagement-in-reading/.

Specktor, Brandon. "Here's Why Your Brain Needs You to Read Every Single
Day." *Reader's Digest*, n.d. https://www.rd.com/culture/benefits-of-read-
ing/.

Spreng, R. Nathan, and Cheryl L. Grady. "Patterns of Brain Activity Support-
ing Autobiographical Memory, Prospection, and Theory of Mind, and
Their Relationship to the Default Mode Network." *Journal of Cognitive Neuroscience* 22, no. 6 (June 2010), 1112–1123. doi:10.1162/
jocn.2009.21282.

Spreng, R. Nathan, Raymond A. Mar, and Alice S. N. Kim. "The Common
Neural Basis of Autobiographical Memory, Prospection, Navigation,
Theory of Mind, and the Default Mode: A Quantitative Meta-analysis."
Journal of Cognitive Neuroscience 21, no. 3 (March 2009), 489-510.
doi:10.1162/jocn.2008.21029.

Spunt, Robert P., Meghan L. Meyer, and Matthew D. Lieberman. "The Default Mode of Human Brain Function Primes the Intentional Stance."
Journal of Cognitive Neuroscience 27, no. 6 (June 2015), 1116–1124.
doi:10.1162/jocn_a_00785.

Stephens, Greg J., Lauren J. Silbert, and Uri Hasson. "Speaker–listener neural coupling underlies successful communication." *Proceedings of the
National Academy of Sciences* 107, no. 32 (2010), 14425–14430.
doi:10.1073/pnas.1008662107.

Sternberg, Marissa. "The science of storytelling." *One Spot.* Infographic. 2017.
https://www.onespot.com/blog/infographic-the-science-of-storytelling/.

Stockton, Nick. "Your Brain Doesn't Contain Memories. It Is Memories."
Wired, July 19, 2017. https://www.wired.com/story/your-brain-is-mem-
ories/.

Story, Louise. "Anywhere the Eye Can See, It's Likely to See an Ad." *New York
Times*, February 15, 2007. https://www.nytimes.com/2007/01/15/busi-
ness/media/15everywhere.html.

Stuckey, Heather L., and Jeremy Nobel. "The Connection Between Art,
Healing, and Public Health: A Review of Current Literature." *Amer-*

ican Journal of Public Health 100, no. 2 (February 2010), 254–263. doi:10.2105/ajph.2008.156497.

Takeuchi, Hikaru, Yasuyuki Taki, Hiroshi Hashizume, Yuko Sassa, Tomomi Nagase, Rui Nouchi, and Ryuta Kawashima. "Failing to deactivate: The association between brain activity during a working memory task and creativity." *NeuroImage* 55, no. 2 (2011), 681–687. doi:10.1016/j. neuroimage.2010.11.052.

Tamas, Sophie. "Writing Trauma: Collisions at the Corner of Art and Scholarship." *Theatre Topics* 22, no. 1 (March 2012), 39–48. doi:10.1353/ tt.2012.0009.

Tamir, Diana I., Andrew B. Bricker, David Dodell-Feder, and Jason P. Mitchell. "Reading fiction and reading minds: the role of simulation in the default network." *Social Cognitive and Affective Neuroscience* 11, no. 2 (February 2016), 215–224. doi:10.1093/scan/nsv114.

Tayag, Yasmin. "Vulcan mind melding is totally real." Inverse. Last modified July 9, 2015. https://www.inverse.com/article/4425-vulcan-mind-melding-is-totally-real.

Teicher, Martin H., Susan L. Andersen, Ann Polcari, Carl M. Anderson, Carryl P. Navalta, and Dennis M. Kim. "The neurobiological consequences of early stress and childhood maltreatment." *Neuroscience and Behavioral Reviews* 27, no. 1-2 (2003), 33–44. doi:10.1016/S0149-7634(03)00007-1.

Thompson, Brittany N. "Theory of Mind: Understanding Others in a Social World." *Psychology Today* (blog). July 3, 2017. https://www.psychology-today.com/us/blog/socioemotional-success/201707/theory-mind-understanding-others-in-social-world.

Tooby, John, and Leda Cosmides. "Does Beauty Build Adapted Minds? Toward an Evolutionary Theory of Aesthetics, Fiction, and the Arts." *SubStance* 30, no. 1 (2001), 6–27. doi:10.1353/sub.2001.0017.

Torres, Mike. "Neuroplasticity: Your Brain's Amazing Ability to Form New Habits." Refocuser. Last modified May 27, 2009. http://www. refocuser.com/2009/05/neuroplasticity-your-brains-amazing-ability-to-form-new-habits/.

Van Harmelen, Anne-Laura, Marie-José Van Tol, Nic J. A. Van der Wee, Dick J.

Veltman, André Aleman, Philip Spinhoven, Mark A. Van Buchem, Frans G. Zitman, Brenda W. J. H. Penninx, and Bernet M. Zelinga. "Reduced Medial Prefrontal Cortex Volume in Adults Reporting Childhood Emotional Maltreatment." *Biological Psychiatry* 68, no. 9 (2010), 832–838. doi:10.1016/j.biopsych.2010.06.011.

Vanderbes, Jennifer. "The Evolutionary Case for Great Fiction." *The Atlantic*, September 5, 2013. https://www.theatlantic.com/entertainment/archive/2013/09/the-evolutionary-case-for-great-fiction/279311/.

Vessel, Edward A., G. Gabrielle Starr, and Nava Rubin. "Art reaches within: aesthetic experience, the self and the default mode network." *Frontiers in Neuroscience* 7 (2013). doi:10.3389/fnins.2013.00258.

Vogler, Christopher. *The Writer's Journey: Mythic Structure for Writers*, 3rd ed. Studio City, CA: Michael Wiese Productions, 2007.

Weldon, Michele. "Your Brain on Story: Why Narratives Win Our Hearts and Minds." *The Pacific Standard*, April 22, 2014. https://psmag.com/social-justice/pulitzer-prizes-journalism-reporting-your-brain-on-story-why-narratives-win-our-hearts-and-minds-79824#The%20Pacific%20Standard.

"Why Storytelling Works: The Science." *Ariel* (blog). October 1, 2014. https://info.arielgroup.com/blog/storytelling-works-science/.

Widrich, Leo. "The Science of Storytelling: Why Telling a Story is the Most Powerful Way to Activate Our Brains." *Lifehacker*, December 5, 2012. https://lifehacker.com/the-science-of-storytelling-why-telling-a-story-is-the-5965703.

Wilfong, Cheryl. *The Meditative Gardener: Cultivating Mindfulness of Body, Feelings, and Mind*. Putney, VT: Heart Path Press, 2010.

Wilson, Timothy D. *Redirect: Changing the Stories We Live By*. New York, NY: Back Bay Books, 2015.

Wilson, Timothy D. *Strangers to Ourselves: Discovering the Adaptive Unconscious*. Cambridge, MA: Harvard University Press, 2004.

Wilson, Timothy D. "Know Thyself." *Perspectives on Psychological Science* 4, no. 4 (2009), 384–389. doi:10.1111/j.1745-6924.2009.01143.x.

Wilson, Timothy D., and Elizabeth W. Dunn. "Self-Knowledge: Its Limits, Value, and Potential for Improvement." *Annual Review of Psychology* 55, no.

1 (2004), 493–518. doi:10.1146/annurev.psych.55.090902.141954.

Wong, Kristin. "The Benefits of Talking to Yourself." *New York Times*, June 8, 2017. https://www.nytimes.com/2017/06/08/smarter-living/benefits-of-talking-to-yourself-self-talk.html.

Wood, Janice. "Novel Look at How Stories Can Change The Brain." PsychCentral. Last modified August 8, 2018. https://psychcentral.com/news/2014/01/04/novel-look-at-how-stories-can-change-the-brain/64082.html.

Young, Kay. *Imagining Minds: The Neuro-Aesthetics of Austen, Eliot, and Hardy.* Columbus, OH: The Ohio State University Press, 2010.

Young, Kay, and Jeffrey L. Saver. "The Neurology of Narrative." *SubStance* 30, no. 94/95 (n.d.), 72–84. doi:10.1353/sub.2001.0020.

Yuan, Ye, Judy Major-Girardin, and Steven Brown. "Storytelling Is Intrinsically Mentalistic: A Functional Magnetic Resonance Imaging Study of Narrative Production across Modalities." *Journal of Cognitive Neuroscience* 30, no. 9 (September 2018), 1298–1314. doi:10.1162/jocn_a_01294.

Zak, Paul J. "Why Inspiring Stories Make Us React: The Neuroscience of Narrative." *Cerebrum*, January/February 2015. http://www.dana.org/Cerebrum/2015/Why_Inspiring_Stories_Make_Us_React__The_Neuroscience_of_Narrative/.

Zak, Paul J. "How Stories Change the Brain." *Greater Good Magazine*, December 17, 2013. https://greatergood.berkeley.edu/article/item/how_stories_change_brain.

Zak, Paul J., and Stephen Knack. "Trust and Growth." *The Economic Journal* 111, no. 470 (March 2001), 295–321. doi:10.1111/1468-0297.00609.

Zimmer, Carl. "This Is Your Brain on Writing." *New York Times*, June 20, 2014. https://www.nytimes.com/2014/06/19/science/researching-the-brain-of-writers.html.

Zolli, Andrew, and Ann Marie Healy. *Resilience: Why Things Bounce Back.* New York, NY: Simon & Schuster, 2013.

Zunshine, Lisa. "Why We Read Fiction." *Skeptical Inquirer*, November/December 2006. https://skepticalinquirer.org/2006/11/why_we_read_fiction/.

ABOUT THE AUTHOR

Samantha Shad was a member of the bar in three states and a practicing entertainment attorney in Beverly Hills before she turned her attention to screenwriting. She wrote twenty feature film scripts for the major motion picture studios, including *Class Action* (Twentieth Century Fox), as well as feature length and episodic television for each of the major networks, including the movie *Vanished Without A Trace* (NBC-Universal). She served as the Chair of the Women's Committee of the Writers Guild of America, West, and President and Chair of the Writers Guild of America, West – Directors Guild of America Joint Foundation for Women Filmmakers, among other positions. She has taught advanced writing, media, and law at UCLA, The American Film Institute and Pierce College. She now teaches advanced writing and leads seminars on how to Write to Happiness.

Visit with her at samanthashad.com

CPSIA information can be obtained
at www.ICGtesting.com
Printed in the USA
BVHW080012290120
570798BV00002B/5